Table of Contents

Introduction. xiii

Avid Educational Services. xvi

Other Resources xvii

Symbols and Conventions. xviii

Comments? xix

Copying the Files from the Accompanying DVD-ROM. xx

Lesson 1   **Avid System Overview** 1

System Hardware. 2

Basic Editing Steps 2

Avid Terms and Concepts. 3

Starting the System. 6

Creating and Opening a Project 8

Working in the Project Window 11

Working in Bins 20

Using Online Help 26

Review Questions. 27

Exercise: Get Started 30

Lesson 2   **Basic Editing**. 39

The Editing Interface. 40

Playing Clips 42

Marking the Edit Points in a Clip. 50

Creating a New Sequence 52

Adding Shots 54

Removing Material from a Sequence. 59

Essential Basic Tools 61

Review Questions. 64

Exercise: Basic Editing 67

Lesson 3   **Fine-Tuning** 81
Locating an Audio Edit Cue 82
Trimming. 88
Explaining Single-Roller Trims 90
Performing a Single-Roller Trim. 96
Dual-Roller Trimming 99
Additional Trim Features. 102
Real-Time Effect Playback 104
Adding Dissolves 105
Review Questions 111
Exercise: Trim the Rainforest Sequence. 114
Use Trim Buttons 124

Lesson 4   **Additional Editing Tools**. 125
Viewing and Changing Settings 126
Using the SuperBin 128
Additional Navigation Tools. 131
Mapping User-Selectable Buttons 137
Using Toolsets 142
Subclipping and Storyboarding 145
Review Questions 150
Exercise: Subclips and Storyboards 151

Lesson 5   **Saving Your Work** 165
Saving Bins. 166
Retrieving Bins from the Avid Attic. 168
Ending the Session. 170
Review Questions 172
Exercise: Back Up Your Project 173

Lesson 6   **Editing Dialog** 177
Trimming Dialog 178
Creating Split Edits 181
Maintaining Sync 185
Review Questions 191
Exercise: Edit Dialog 193

Lesson 7   **Working in the Timeline**. 199
Using Locators. 200
Adding and Patching Tracks 203
Configuring the Timeline. 206
Saving a Customized Timeline View 209

£29-99

Editing with Avid Xpress Pro and Avid Xpress DV

Editing with Avid Xpress Pro and Avid Xpress DV

The Avid Educational Series of instructional books is published in association with Peachpit Press.

For information on Avid Educational Series books, contact:
Peachpit Press
1249 Eighth Street
Berkeley, California 94710
510-524-2178 (tel), 510-524-2221 (fax)

Find us on the World Wide Web at: www.peachpit.com.

To report errors, please send a note to errata@peachpit.com.

Peachpit Press is a division of Pearson Education

Footage/Music

Rain Forest footage provided courtesy of Fireside Productions, Atlanta, GA.
ECO Challenge Utah footage provided courtesy of ECO Challenge Lifestyles, Inc. All Rights Reserved.
PrimeTime Math: Emergency! footage provided courtesy of Tom Snyder Productions.
Music is provided courtesy of Nightingale Music Productions. The music is copyright protected and may not be used for anything else without permission from the copyright owner. For a license to use this music in your productions or for additional music, contact Nightingale Music (416) 221-2393, http://www.NightingaleMusic.com.

The footage provided with this book is to be used *only* to complete the exercises contained herein. Rights are *not* granted to use the footage in any commercial or non-commercial production or video.

Avid Xpress Pro and Avid Xpress DV • Software Version 4.2 (Macintosh OS X and Windows XP)

Editing with Avid Xpress Pro and Avid Xpress DV • November 2003

ISBN 0-321-19969-3

9 8 7 6 5 4 3 2 1

Printed and bound in the United States of America

Editing Segments in the Timeline .211

Slipping and Sliding Segments 215

Review Questions. 220

Exercise: Work in the Timeline. 221

Lesson 8   Working with Audio. 231

Introduction 232

Adjusting Level and Pan in the Audio Mix Tool 233

Adjusting Audio Gain with Keyframes 239

Automation Gain Real-Time Recording. 245

Review Questions 248

Exercise: Fine-Tune Audio 250

Lesson 9   Capturing Media. 263

Setting the Capture Options. 264

Choosing the Video Resolution. 269

Setting Audio Levels 274

Capturing Footage 278

Logging and Batch Capturing. 287

Review Questions. 293

Exercise: Capture Video 295

Lesson 10   Preparing Your Bin for Editing. 307

Using Text View 308

Adding a Custom Column to a Bin 310

Sorting and Sifting Clips. 315

Moving Clips Between Bins. 324

Review Questions. 326

Exercise: Organize Your Bins 329

Lesson 11   Creating Titles 333

Getting Started 334

Working with the Title Tool 335

Formatting Text 340

Applying Shadows and Borders. 348

Choosing Colors 351

Saving, Fading, and Revising Titles. 354

Rolling and Crawling Titles. 357

Review Questions. 359

Exercise: Create Titles 361

Lesson 12 **Media Management** 371
Locking Items in the Bin 372
Deleting Clips and Media Files. 373
The Media Tool 377
Identifying Media Relatives 380
Review Questions 382
Exercise: Media Management 383

Lesson 13 **Recording a Digital Cut** 389
Preparing to Record a Digital Cut 390
Creating Insert, Assemble, and Manual Edits 393
Review Questions 400

Index 401

Tables

Motion Control Buttons and Keys	49
Marking Buttons and Keys	51
Edit Buttons and Keyboard Equivalents	60
Dual-Roller Trims	99
Trimming Backward and Forward in a Clip	103
Trim Keys and Buttons	124
Display Options in the Timeline Menu	207
Statistical Column Headings	308
Operations in Text View	312
Commonly Used Special Characters	347

Figures

Avid project hierarchy   3

Selecting or creating a project in the Select Project dialog box   8

Project window with components labelled   11

Clips in a bin   12

Folders in a bin   14

Partial list of settings in the Project window   18

Bin in Text view   21

Bin in Brief view   21

Bin in Frame view   22

Bin in Script view   22

Bin opened from another project   25

Online Help: a great reference tool   26

Pop-up monitor display   40

Composer monitor with components labelled   41

Timeline window with components labelled   42

Source monitor   43

Pop-up monitor with components labelled   44

Source monitor toolbar with components labelled   47

Composer monitor with components labelled   69

Monitoring audio by selecting the Speaker icon   82

Audio waveform displayed as a sample plot   85

J-K-L keys for shuttling power   86

Trim mode interface 89

Handle: the frames in a clip before and after the shot in the
sequence 91

Displaying the outgoing and incoming images in Trim mode 91

Trimming the A side of a transition 93

Result of trimming the A side of a transition 93

Trimming the B side of a transition 95

Result of trimming the B side of a transition 95

Trim buttons 97

Using Trim mode to move a transition point 99

Adding and customizing dissolves in the Quick Transition
dialog box 105

Insufficient handle to make a dissolve 109

Trim mode toolbar with buttons labelled 116

Exiting Trim mode by clicking in the Timecode track 117

Bin settings options 127

SuperBin: to make efficient use of screen real estate 129

Clip Name menu in the Source monitor 132

Clip Name menu in the Record monitor 132

Timecode display options 133

Move tab of the Command palette 137

Play tab of the Command palette 137

Edit tab of the Command palette 138

Trim tab of the Command palette 138

Other tab of the Command palette 138

Customizing the keyboard 141

Linking toolsets to settings 144

Naming subclips in the bin 146

Creating a storyboard of clips in the Timeline 148

Unsaved bin symbol 166

Navigating to the Avid Attic 169

Green light (in Trim mode) for monitoring audio 180

Split edit operation 181

Extend edit to the mark OUT 183

Extend edit to the mark IN 183

Trimming with sync locks on 186

Turning on sync lock   187

Detecting out-of-sync frames using sync breaks   189

Displaying a locator in the Source or Record monitor   201

Displaying locators and comments in the Locator window   201

Locator text displayed in the Source or Record monitor   202

Adding an out-of-sequence track in the Add Track
    dialog box   204

Using the mouse to patch tracks   205

Display options in the Timeline Fast menu   206

Selecting segments in Segment mode   212

Moving segments in Segment mode   212

Changing the contents of a shot with Slip mode   215

Changing the position of a shot with Slide mode   215

Setting up for a slip operation   216

Setting up for a slide operation   218

Moving a segment in Segment mode   226

Audio Mix tool with components labelled   235

Volume level displayed in the Audio Mix tool   236

Pan values displayed in the Audio Mix tool   236

Global options in the Audio Mix Fast menu   237

In/Out options in the Audio Mix Fast menu   239

Dragging a keyframe to adjust level   241

Alt/Option+dragging a keyframe to adjust the audio ramp   242

Using two keyframes to adjust level gradually   243

Using keyframes to adjust level for a portion of the sequence   244

Sequence in the Timeline with pink triangles displayed   245

Automation Gain tool with components labelled   246

Capture tool with components labelled   264

Selecting or adding tape names in the Select Tape dialog box   266

Activating tracks in the Capture tool   267

Choosing resolutions in the Media Creation tool   271

Sample rate options in the Audio Project Settings dialog box   275

Audio tool with digital and analog scales   276

Adjusting audio mix during capture in the
    Passthrough Mix tool   277

Capture tool's deck control options labelled   280

Setting up DV Scene Extraction — 283

Configuration of transcoder, analog deck, and Avid system — 284

Adding DV Capture Offset in the Deck Preferences setting — 286

Log mode of the Capture tool with components labelled — 288

Entering text in a custom column — 310

Saving a bin view — 313

Selecting a bin column that you want to sort — 316

Setting up bin columns for a multiple sort — 317

Setting up the Sift dialog box for a multicriterion inclusive sift — 320

Results of an inclusive sift — 321

Setting up the Sift dialog box for a multicriterion exclusive sift — 322

Results of an exclusive sift — 322

Title tool with components labelled — 335

Title tool toolbar with components labelled — 337

Windows Character Map — 345

Macintosh Key Caps window — 346

Drop and depth shadows illustrated — 348

Title tool color picker with components labelled — 352

Saving the title — 354

Roll and crawl section of the Title tool toolbar — 357

Locked clips in a bin — 372

Options in the Delete dialog box — 375

Offline clips in a bin — 376

Options in the Media Tool Display dialog box — 377

Options in the Delete Media dialog box — 379

Setting up the ExpertRender dialog box — 390

Changing the audio sample rate — 391

Changing between a drop-frame and a non-drop-frame
    sequence — 392

Digital Cut tool with components labelled — 394

Introduction

This book was developed by the award-winning team of Avid course developers and education specialists to provide you with an in-depth overview of the concepts and techniques necessary to create a program on Avid Xpress Pro or Avid Xpress DV.

The book is divided into lessons and exercises. The lessons provide step-by-step procedures for all basic editing operations, including many screen captures and explanatory notes as aids to learning. Exercises provide hands-on practice, with ample time for experimentation with sample material.

You will use the Avid system to input and organize source footage, edit sync and non-sync material, trim sequences, adjust audio, create titles, and output work. The final product will be a finished program.

Instructions for copying the files from the DVD-ROM to your computer are found at the end of the Introduction and in a Read Me file on the DVD itself. If you experience any difficulty installing the DVD-ROM or loading the files from it, contact Avid Educational Services at edservices@avid.com.

Goals

After completing this book, you will be able to:

- Explain Avid system software terms and concepts.

- Independently create a finished program using the Avid system software interface, including menus, dialog boxes, tools, and buttons.

- Identify and execute basic steps to input media into the system, and to output a finished program.

Book Structure

This book's **modular structure** generally follows the workflow of a typical project, with one exception. The typical workflow is capturing media, followed by all phases of editing, and ending with outputting the program. We want you to jump right into editing, and so we moved capturing to a later part of the book.

In the lessons, a combination of conceptual material, step-by-step procedures, and illustrations is used to teach the operation of the Avid system. You will also find sections called **Useful Applications** peppered throughout the lessons. These sections provide you with real-world examples of how you might use a specific tool or technique. **Tips** and **Notes** also provide useful guidance.

Review questions are found at the end of each lesson. If you are unsure of the correct answer to any question, you should review the appropriate material in the lesson before continuing to the exercise or to the next lesson. (At the end of each question we provide a reference to the relevant section in the lesson.)

Exercises typically follow each lesson, and use the media that accompanies the book. Most of the exercises provide you with a choice: you can be guided step-by-step through a sequence of tasks, or you can work through a list of tasks on your own, using the preceding lesson as a reference, if necessary.

At the back of the book you will find a detailed **index** to help you locate specific items.

Who Should Use This Book

This book provides sufficiently detailed instructions on how to operate the Avid system for the beginning user. In addition, it includes a comprehensive feature set that should be useful for the intermediate user.

You might be an experienced or novice editor, graphic designer, or a developer of interactive media. You need not have prior experience with any Avid systems.

Book Prerequisites

This book assumes that you are familiar with the Windows® or Macintosh® computer system software, whichever one you use.

Windows: You should complete an introductory course on Windows XP or have equivalent experience. You should be familiar particularly with the user interface and navigational tools.

Macintosh: You should complete a Macintosh introductory course or have equivalent experience. This should include knowledge of Macintosh computer system software OS X and familiarity with the Macintosh Finder.

Users unfamiliar with the Windows or Macintosh user interface can get up-to-speed by practicing using the interface before going through the book. You should feel comfortable performing the following tasks on your system: selecting multiple files and other objects; navigating through the file hierarchy; opening, closing, and saving files; and using other common commands and menu items (and preferably using some keyboard shortcuts) such as moving and copying files.

Avid Educational Services

Avid Educational Services produces an extensive range of instructor-led courses and self-study books and DVDs developed by an award-winning team of Avid course developers and education specialists. Courses are offered worldwide through a network of Avid Authorized Education Centers and at select universities. Self-study books and DVDs are available at booksellers worldwide and through Avid's online store. A complete list of courses, books and DVDs is provided at the back of this book.

Certification programs are also provided for those wishing to be certified as a support representative or instructor.

Contact Avid Educational Services

For information about Avid courseware, schedules of up-coming classes, locations of Avid Authorized Education Centers, or how to order self-paced books and DVDs, visit the Avid web site, www.avid.com/training. In addition, to find out more about Avid Educational Services offerings from within North America, call 800 867 AVID (2843), or from elsewhere, call 978 275-2071.

Other Resources

Avid Technology, Inc. offers additional resources that you can use to enhance your understanding of the product.

Avid Knowledge Center

The Knowledge Center is a repository for thousands of technical documents, file downloads, and tutorials. It is a great place to visit to help solve a problem or to learn more about Avid products. It can be accessed at support01.avid.com.

Avid Communities

The Avid Communities offer a variety of ways for you to interact, share, and find out more about Avid products and services from fellow users and industry professionals. No matter what your focus, the Avid Communities help you harness the collective power of an entire industry. They can be accessed at www.avid.com/community.

Avid Product Documentation

Documentation for all Avid products can be downloaded from the Avid Knowledge Center. Additionally, the printed versions of the documentation can be ordered directly from Avid. If you live within the United States, call Avid Sales at 800-949-AVID (800-949-2843). If you live outside the United States, contact your local Avid representative.

Symbols and Conventions

Unless noted otherwise, the material in this document applies to the Windows XP and Mac OS X Operating Systems. When the text applies to a specific Operating System, it is marked as follows:

- (Windows) or (Windows only) means the information applies to the Windows XP Operating System.

- (Macintosh) or (Macintosh only) means the information applies to the Mac OS X Operating System.

The majority of screen shots in this book were captured on a Windows system, but the information applies to both Windows and Mac systems. Where differences exist, both Windows and Mac screen shots are shown.

This book uses the following symbols and conventions:

Table 1   Symbols and Conventions

Symbol or Convention	Meaning or Action
Margin Tips and Notes	In the margin you will find tips that help you perform tasks more easily and notes that provide related information and recommendations.
❗ **Important**	Important information is called out in bold face and is preceded by an exclamation point.
⚠ **Warning**	Warnings describe an action that could cause you or the system physical harm. Follow the guidelines in this book or on the unit itself when handling electrical equipment.
▶	This symbol indicates a single-step procedure.
Courier Bold	The use of the Courier Bold font identifies text that you type.
Ctrl+key ⌘+key	Press and hold the first key while you press the second key. These keys are used when performing keyboard shortcuts on Windows and Macintosh systems, respectively.

Table 1 Symbols and Conventions (Continued)

Symbol or Convention	Meaning or Action
Alt+key Option+key	Press and hold the first key while you press the second key. These keys are also used when performing keyboard shortcuts on Windows and Macintosh systems, respectively.
Click	Quickly press and release the left mouse button or the mouse button (Macintosh single button mice).
Double-click	Click the left mouse button or the mouse button (Macintosh single button mice) twice rapidly.
Right-click *or* ⌘+Shift+click (Macintosh only)	Quickly press and release the right mouse button. Used to display the contextual menu for the active window or object. Macintosh systems with single-button mice must hold down the ⌘ and Shift keys when clicking on the mouse button to display the contextual menu.

Comments?

We appreciate any comments or suggestions you may have about this book or any other class, book or DVD produced by Avid Educational Services. Send your feedback to: **edserv@avid.com**.

Copying the Files from the Accompanying DVD-ROM

The DVD-ROM that accompanies this book contains media formatted for the Avid Xpress Pro or DV system. It should not be used on any other Avid system.

This disc does not contain DVD video or audio. (Macintosh only) If the DVD player opens on your Macintosh system, simply close it.

The files on this DVD-ROM are compatible with both the Windows XP and the Macintosh OS X versions of the Avid system.

If you are installing this media on a Windows 2000 system, there are additional steps required beyond simply copying the media to the system. Please see the instructions later in this section.

This DVD contains the following:

- **Avid Projects** — This folder contains the four projects you will use with this book, Rainforest, ECO Challenge, Trauma Room, and Stock Music.

- **OMFI MediaFiles** — This folder contains the media required for the *Editing with Avid Xpress Pro and Avid Xpress DV 4* book. **The space required for the media is 3.2 GB.**

To copy the project files to your system:

Windows:

On the DVD, open the Avid Projects folder. Copy the four folders you find inside (Rainforest, ECO Challenge, Trauma Room, and Stock Music) to the C:/Program Files/Avid/Avid Xpress Pro/Avid Projects. (If the Avid folder is on a drive other than the C: drive, copy to that Avid folder.)

Macintosh:

On the DVD, open the Avid Projects folder. Copy the four folders you find inside (Rainforest, ECO Challenge, Trauma Room, and Stock Music) to the Avid Projects folder on your internal hard drive. (If the Avid folder is on an external drive, copy to that folder.)

To copy the media files to your system:

You have a couple of options for copying the media files.

- **If your drive already has an *OMFI MediaFiles* folder,** you can open the DVD's *OMFI MediaFiles* folder and copy the contents into your existing folder. OR:

- **If your drive does not have an *OMFI MediaFiles* folder,** copy the entire *OMFI MediaFiles* folder from the DVD to your drive.

! **If you need to spread the media files among multiple drives, simply copy a portion of the folder to the *OMFI MediaFiles* folder on one drive, and then copy remaining files to the *OMFI MediaFiles* folder(s) on other drive(s).**

Opening the Project Files

The book describes how to open and use the projects on this disc. However, if you didn't install the Avid software on the C: drive, then the first time you open a project in the Avid application, you will see the following message:

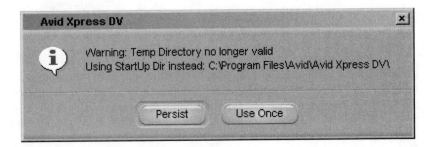

Click Persist, and the Avid system handles the rest. You will not see this message again.

The projects are now ready for you to use!

Lesson 1 **Avid System Overview**

Before editing on the Avid editing system, you must understand some basic terminology and something about how the system works. This lesson introduces you to the Avid system, its basic editing model, and basic Avid terms and concepts. You should also know how to turn on the Windows or Macintosh system, launch the Avid application, and begin working in a project and bins.

Objectives

After you complete this lesson, you will be able to:

- Identify the hardware components of the Avid system
- Explain the basic Avid editing process
- Define project, bin, and clip, and other terms related to file organization
- Start the Windows or Macintosh system
- Launch the Avid application
- Create and open an Avid project
- Work in the Project window
- Work in bins
- Open a bin from another project
- Use online Help

System Hardware

Let's first take a tour of the hardware components that make up the Avid system. Regardless of your particular model, the basic components are the same:

- Central processing unit — a Windows or Macintosh system, with an internal hard disk

- (Optional) Avid Mojo DNA (Digital Nonlinear Accelerator) hardware

- Monitors, for viewing

- Speakers, for listening

- Deck and deck control connections, to input and output your work

- (Optional) External disk drives or Avid Unity system, for storing your captured video and audio

Basic Editing Steps

The basic Avid editing system work model is very simple — there are three steps to perform when converting raw footage to master tape:

1 *Input* the source media onto storage disk(s).

- Capture from tapes

- Import still graphics and animations

2 *Edit* the sequence.

Editing the sequence (program), could be as simple as stringing a dozen video shots together over some narration and a music track, or it could require a series of five-frame edits, with split edits, dissolves, and audio crossfades. Typically, the process includes the following stages:

a Assemble the rough cut.

b Trim the shots.

c Import graphics.

d Add effects.

   e   Add titles.

   f   Adjust the audio

3 *Output* your material.

   •   Lay off a program to tape

   •   Export electronic files, including a QuickTime™ movie, MPEG, or Open Media Framework Interchange (OMFI) file, for use on the web, DVD, or CD-ROM

   •   Generate an Edit Decision List (EDL) that can be used by a conventional linear online system

Avid Terms and Concepts

The terms and concepts presented in this section are used throughout the editing process and are integral to your learning the system.

Project Hierarchy

The Avid project items are organized as a hierarchy.

Avid project hierarchy

Project — The project, at the top of the project hierarchy, is an Avid device for organizing your work. When you create a project, the system creates two items: a file and a folder.

- The Project file contains all the information about your current job.

- The Project folder contains all files of your project, including the Project file. It is stored in the Avid Projects folder.

Bin — A bin is the electronic equivalent of the physical bin in which film is stored for retrieval during editing. The bin is simply a file containing clips and sequences. Bins are stored in the Project folder.

Clip — A clip is stored in a bin and contains information about the source of the material — tape name, start and end timecodes, and so on — and about the way you want it to be captured. (A subclip is a subset of a clip.)

Sequence — A sequence is your edited program. You create a sequence by editing clips together. A sequence is stored in a bin, and holds references to its clips.

Media File/Clip Relationship

A key relationship in the Avid system is the one between media files and clips. Understanding this relationship will help you effectively manage your project and media, and troubleshoot problems that may arise.

Media File — A media file is actual captured video and audio. Media files require substantial storage space, and thus are stored on separate external media drives or on an internal IDE hard drive, within a folder named "OMFI MediaFiles."

Media files should not be stored on the same partition (drive) where the application resides.

Clip — A clip is a pointer to actual media files. The clip does not contain the actual picture and sound data, just references to it.

During the capture process, a media file is created for each track of video and audio in the clip. When you play a clip, the system looks for media files that contain the video and audio. If the media files aren't found, the clip shows the message, Media Offline.

When you play a sequence, the Avid system accesses and plays back the clips that make up the sequence.

Quick Review

Since you should be comfortable with Avid terminology before continuing, please check your understanding by taking this Quick Review.

Please fill in the appropriate term for each definition.

_____ *Pointer to media files*

_____ *Actual video and audio files*

_____ *Edited program*

_____ *Holder for clips and sequences*

_____ *Holder for bins*

Starting the System

It's important to power up the system and all other hardware correctly.

1 Make sure the system is plugged in.

2 Turn on all peripheral hardware such as Avid Mojo box, monitors, and speakers. (Or use a powerstrip.)

3 Turn on all external drives, keeping in mind the following:

- If you're using external drives, wait about 15-20 seconds for them to spin up-to-speed.

- If you're using an Avid Unity MediaNetwork, launch it and log in.

Starting the Avid System (Windows)

To start the Avid system:

1 Turn on the PC.

The computer goes through a self-check, and the Windows startup screen appears.

2 Press Control+Alt+Delete and log on.

The Windows desktop appears.

The system's internal C: drive contains the Avid application, projects, and bins.

The external drives hold the media files.

To launch the Avid application software:

Tip: You can create a shortcut for the Avid application, place it on your desktop, and use it to launch the application.

1 Locate the Avid application icon in C:\Program Files\Avid*Avid application*.

2 Double-click the Avid application icon.

You can also launch via the Start menu by choosing Start>Programs>Avid>*Avid application*.

Starting the Avid System (Macintosh)

To start the Avid system:

1 Turn on the Macintosh system.

2 Listen for the tone indicating that the hardware powered-up normally.

3 Wait for the Finder to appear on the screen.

The storage devices in this example are:

• The OS X drive: the Macintosh internal hard drive that contains the Avid application, projects, and bins

• Media: an external media drive that holds the media files (your system might have more than one media drive)

You can rename the internal and media drives at any time.

Note: The Avid application icon may be on the Dock.

To launch the Avid application:

▶ Click the Avid icon on the dock (the row of buttons at the bottom of the screen).

Creating and Opening a Project

When you launch the Avid application, the Select Project dialog box appears. In this box, you select the project you want to open or create a new one. The Avid application uses your login name, by default, in the User box.

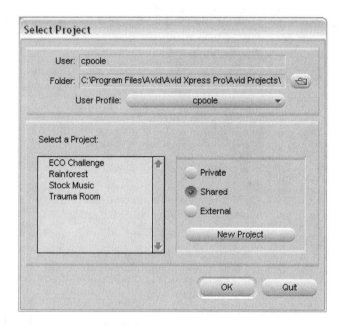

Selecting or creating a project in the Select Project dialog box

Opening an Existing Project

To open an existing project:

1 Select the Shared, Private, or External button.

- Shared if you want other users to have access to your project

- Private if you don't want other users to have access to your project

- External to select a project that is external to the Avid Projects folder

 2 If you selected External, click the Browse button.

The Browse for Folder (Windows) or Project Directory (Macintosh) dialog box opens.

3   Navigate to the folder that contains the project you want.

4   Click OK (Windows) or Choose (Macintosh), and then click OK.

5   Select the Avid Project you want to use.

6   Click OK.

The Project window appears on the monitor.

Creating a New Project

To create a new project:

1   Select New Project.

The New Project dialog box appears.

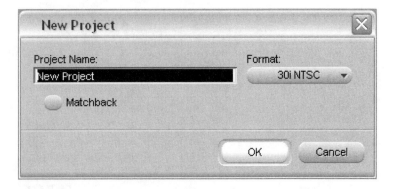

Note: For video-originated footage, which is the focus of this book, choose 30 NTSC (or 30i if your system supports 24p) or 25 PAL (or 25i if your system supports 25p).

2   Type the name of the project, choose the appropriate NTSC or PAL format from the Format pop-up menu, and click OK.

3   Click OK in the Select Project dialog box.

The Project window appears.

When you create a project, the system creates a file that holds all of the information about your project and stores it in a folder that is given the same name. For example, the ECO Challenge project file is stored in a folder called ECO Challenge. The project folder is in turn stored in the Avid Projects folder.

Once you create a project, the project name will appear in the Select Project dialog box, so you can easily select it.

Opening an Existing User or Creating a New User Profile

The default user is your system login. However, you can choose another existing User profile or create a new one.

▶ Click the User Profile pop-up menu, and choose one of the following:

- An existing user.

- Create User Profile. If you choose this option:

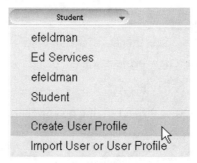

a Type a name in the Create User Profile dialog box and click OK.

The new user appears in the User Profile pop-up menu.

b Modify the User settings as you like. (We cover User settings in a later lesson.)

Working in the Project Window

The Project window shows all the information about your current job, including a list of all the bins that you have ever created in the current project, their size and status (open or closed), folders for organizing bins, and the Trash icon, if you have deleted any bins.

! **The Project window must remain open while you are working in a project.**

Project Window

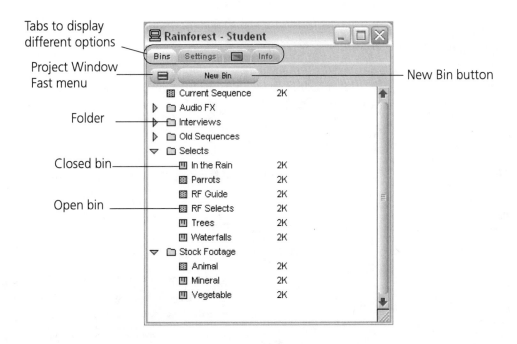

Tabs to display different options

Project Window Fast menu

Folder

Closed bin

Open bin

New Bin button

Project window with components labelled

You can identify the Project window by these characteristics:

- Just below the title bar are buttons and tabs, among them:
    - Bins: repository of all source clips and sequences for a project
    - Settings: used to customize the way you work in the Avid system
    - Effect Palette (designated by an icon): contains all effects
    - Info: information about a project
    - New Bin: used to create new bins
- To the left of a bin name is a Bin icon; the icon differs for a closed and open bin.
- To the right of the bin name is its size.

Opening and Closing a Bin

While you edit, you will need to frequently access clips (and sequences) from bins.

To open an existing bin:

Tip: You can also right-click (Windows) or Shift+⌘-click (Macintosh) the Bin icon and choose Open Selected Bins.

1 Click the Bins button in the Project window to view the list of bins.

2 Double-click the Bin icon next to a bin name.

The bin opens on the monitor.

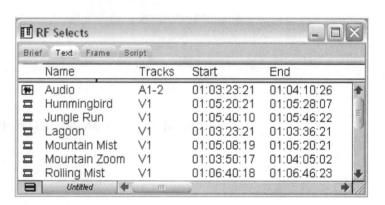

	Name	Tracks	Start	End
	Audio	A1-2	01:03:23:21	01:04:10:26
	Hummingbird	V1	01:05:20:21	01:05:28:07
	Jungle Run	V1	01:05:40:10	01:05:46:22
	Lagoon	V1	01:03:23:21	01:03:36:21
	Mountain Mist	V1	01:05:08:19	01:05:20:21
	Mountain Zoom	V1	01:03:50:17	01:04:05:02
	Rolling Mist	V1	01:06:40:18	01:06:46:23

RF Selects — Brief Text Frame Script — Untitled

Clips in a bin

It's a good idea to close bins that you are not using; you will keep your desktop neat and consume less memory.

To close a bin:

▸ In the Bin window, click the X in the upper-right corner (Windows) or the box in the upper-left corner (Macintosh).

When you close a bin, you also close all open objects within it.

Tip: You can also right-click (Windows) or Shift+⌘+click (Macintosh) the Bin icon and choose Close Selected Bins.

To display an open bin that is hidden from view:

▸ Choose the bin from the Windows menu.

Open bins

Creating a New Bin

It is good practice to create separate bins for source clips and sequences. To have fast and easy access to your clips, it is better to create more bins with fewer objects than to create few bins with many objects.

You might want to organize source footage by storing different types of shots in different bins. For instance, you might store all Scene 1 clips in a Scene 1 bin, or store the clips for separate characters in separate bins.

To create a new bin:

1 Click New Bin in the Project window.

A new, empty bin opens on the Bin monitor. It has the name of your project with the word Bin appended to the name. The new bin is also listed in the Project window. It is highlighted, ready for you to type a new name.

Tip: Always name your bins, and give them meaningful names.

2 To name the bin, type the new name, and press Enter (Windows) or Return (Macintosh).

Activating a Bin

To work in a bin (or any other Avid window), you must activate it.

▶ Click anywhere in the bin and notice that the title bar becomes purple.

Creating Folders in a Project

For organization purposes, you can add folders to a project, and drag and drop bins into folders, or folders into folders. For example, you might want to create a Source Tapes folder, where each bin contains the footage of a different source tape, and a Content folder where the bins are organized by subject.

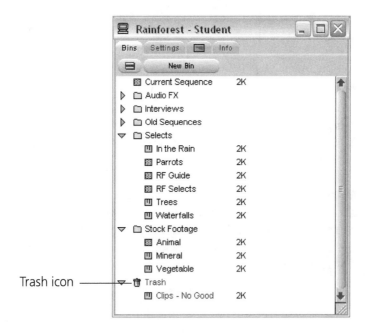

Trash icon

Folders in a bin

Creating a Folder

1 Choose New Folder from the Project Window Fast menu.

A new untitled folder appears.

2 Type a new name, and press Enter (Windows) or Return (Macintosh).

Opening and Closing Folders

1 Click the triangle (pointing to the side) next to a folder to view its contents.

2 Click the triangle (pointing down) again to close the folder.

Moving a Bin into a Folder

▶ Click and drag the Bin icon to the folder triangle. When you release the mouse, the bin appears in the folder.

Deleting a Bin or Folder

1 Click the bin or folder you want to delete to select it.

Tip: You can also right-click (Windows) or Shift+⌘+click (Macintosh) the Bin icon and choose Delete Selected Bins.

2 Press the Backspace key (Windows) or Delete key (Macintosh).

If this is the first item you deleted during the current session, the Trash icon appears at the bottom of the bin, with the deleted item in it.

Trash icon ——————

The deleted item is stored in the Trash until you empty it or move it out of the Trash. (If this is the first item you've deleted during this session, the Trash bin appears in the Project window after you delete.)

Viewing Contents in the Trash

You can move bins and folders out of the Trash. (To view items in the Trash, you must move them out of the Trash first.)

1 If you don't see the Trash contents, click the Trash triangle so that it points down.

2 Click and drag the desired items from the Trash to the Project.

3 Double-click the bin or folder to view it.

Emptying the Trash

1 Choose Project Window Fast menu > Empty Trash.

An alert box appears.

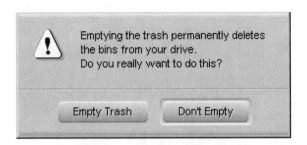

2 Click Empty Trash to delete the bins from the Trash.

The Trash bin disappears from the Project window.

Working with Settings

The Settings button in the Project window opens a list of features that a user can customize, such as the automatic saving frequency.

To view or change settings:

1 Click the Settings button in the Project window.

The Project Settings window opens.

Partial list of settings in the Project window

2 Double-click the name of a setting to open a window that lists the options you can adjust.

Settings are further discussed in Lesson 4.

Locating the Project Window

Unlike bins, which you can close while you work in a project, the Project window must remain open. Sometimes, however, it becomes hidden from view. To locate the Project window, do one of the following:

- Choose Tools > Project or press Control+9 (Windows) or ⌘+9 (Macintosh).

- Click any unobstructed part of the Project window to bring it forward.

Closing the Project Window

To leave the project:

1 Click the close box in the Project window.

   The Select User and Project window dialog box appears.

2 Quit the Avid application or open another project.

Working in Bins

The bin contains the clips, sequences, and subclips you create.

Bin windows open on the Bin monitor. There is technically no limit to the number of bins you can open in a project. To improve bin management, we recommend that you have no more than 100 clips in a bin at any time; however, it is usually better to have far fewer clips in a bin.

Selecting Clips in a Bin

To select clips in a bin, do one of the following:

- To select all the clips in a bin, choose Edit > Select All, or press Control+A (Windows) or ⌘+A (Macintosh).

- To select specific clips in the bin, hold down the Control (Windows) or Shift (Macintosh) key and click the icon for each clip.

- To select a range of clips, click the first clip and Shift+click the last clip in the range (Windows).

Bin Views

You can display the bin in four views — Text view, Brief view, Frame view, and Script view. As you become more experienced on the system, you may find you prefer one view over the others. On the other hand, you will probably find it useful to use different views for different situations.

Text View

Text view lists clips and sequences along with statistical information. Text view gives you fast access to data about your clips as you edit.

Bin in Text view

Brief View

Brief view displays five and only five statistical columns: Name, Start [timecode], Duration [of clip], Tracks [of clip], and Offline [indicates that the clip's associated media is offline].

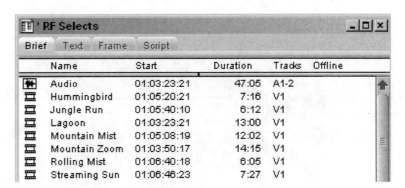

Bin in Brief view

Frame View

Frame view displays the head (first) frame of each clip and sequence in the bin. This view is handy for getting a quick glimpse of the content of each clip. It can also be used to create storyboards.

Bin in Frame view

Script View

Script view combines the features of Text view with Frame view. The frames are displayed vertically on the left side of your screen and there is a box next to each for typing in a portion of the script. Text from word processing programs can be cut and pasted into this box. This view can be used to create annotated storyboards.

Click and type in this box.

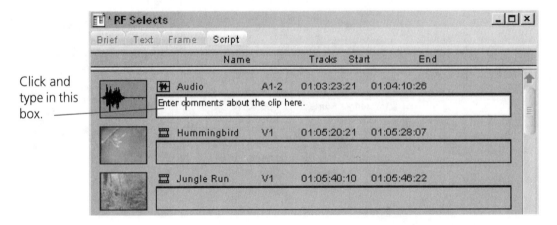

Bin in Script view

Displaying a Bin View

To display Brief, Text, Frame, or Script view, click the appropriate tab in the upper-left corner of the bin.

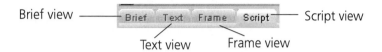

Brief view ——————— Brief   Text   Frame   Script ——— Script view

Text view   Frame view

Frame View Options

You can adjust several Frame view properties to improve the display.

Changing Frame Size

To make your frames smaller or larger:

1 Click the Frame tab in the upper-left corner of the bin to place the bin in Frame view.

2 Choose one of the following:

- To make the frames bigger, choose Edit > Enlarge Frame, or use the keyboard equivalent Control+L (Windows) or ⌘+L (Macintosh).

- To make the frames smaller, choose Edit > Reduce Frame, or use the keyboard equivalent Control+K (Windows) or ⌘+K (Macintosh).

Cleaning Up the Frame View Display

To clean up the Frame view of your bin, try the following options:

▶ Choose Bin > Fill Window.

This arranges the clips so that you can see most, if not all, of them within your current window. The clips are arranged in the bin in the order they are found in Text view.

Some clips may now be off screen.

▶ Choose Bin > Align to Grid.

Changing the Representative Frame

By default, the first frame of the clip or sequence is displayed in Frame view. This may not be the best frame to display. To change the representative frame:

1   Select the clip or sequence (by clicking the clip *frame*).

2   Do any of the following:

Tip: To change the frame of multiple clips all at once, select the clips and then perform the operation. For example, select all clips in a bin and press the 2 key twice to move forward 20 frames.

- Step through the clip using the Step Forward and Backward keys:
  - 1 key: 10 frames back
  - 2 key: 10 frames forward
  - 3 key: 1 frame back
  - 4 key: 1 frame forward

- Play through the clip using the Play (5) key. Press 5 again or the space bar to stop.

- Use the Home (First Frame) key on the keyboard to see the first frame in the clip or sequence, or use the End (Last Frame) key to see the last frame.

Rearranging Clips

In Frame view, it is sometimes useful to rearrange clips in the bin into a storyboard prior to editing them together.

1   Create a clear area in the bin by making all your frames smaller and/or making the bin larger.

2   Select the first clip for your storyboard.

3   Drag the clip to a clear part of the bin.

4   Repeat this procedure for other clips you want in your storyboard until you have them in the order you want.

Printing a Storyboard

Tip: You can also print a list of the text in Text view or the frames and the text in Script view.

If your system is connected to a printer, you can print this storyboard by choosing File > Print Bin.

Bin Fast Menu

The Bin menu is duplicated within the bin as the Bin Fast menu. Whenever we mention Bin menu, you may prefer to use the Bin Fast menu, located in the bottom-left corner of each bin.

Bin Fast menu

Opening a Bin from Another Project

Sometimes you will want access to material from another bin, but you will not want to permanently bring the material into the project. For example, you might have a separate project with bins of stock footage or sound effects, or other commonly used material. You can easily open a bin from another project.

1 With any bin highlighted, choose File > Open Bin.

   The Select a Bin dialog box appears.

2 If you do not see the name of the bin you are looking for, look in other Project folders.

3 When you locate the bin in the dialog box, click on it and click Open.

   The bin opens in your project, and a folder, "*Other Bins*," appears in the Project window in italics. The bin is listed inside this folder, with the originating project in the column to the right of the bin name. Remember you are simply borrowing this bin from the other project.

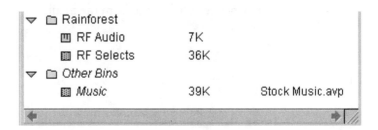

Bin opened from another project

Using Online Help

The Avid application includes an online Help system which you can use to look up specific features and functions.

▶ Choose Help > *Avid system* Help or press F1 (Windows) or the Help button on the keyboard (Macintosh).

Online Help: a great reference tool

To find specific information for a specific feature, such as a button or window:

1 Right-click (Windows) or Shift+ ⌘ +click (Macintosh) on the object to display a contextual menu.

2 Choose What's This from the menu.

Review Questions

1 What are the main hardware components of the Avid system? (See "System Hardware" on page 2.)

2 Fill in the missing step of the Avid system editing model. (See "Basic Editing Steps" on page 2.)

   a Input footage.

   b Edit the sequence.

   c _____

3 Where are the project files stored? (See "Project Hierarchy" on page 3.)

4 Match the following terms with their definitions.

Term	Definition
1. media file	a. an edited program
2. bin	b. repository for bins
3. clip	c. a file containing clips and sequences
4. project	d. captured media
5. sequence	e. pointer to a media file

5 When turning on your system, which should you turn on first, the external drives or the computer? (See "Starting the System" on page 6.)

6 Label the following components in the Project window.

   a   Closed bin

   b   Open bin

   c   Tab to use to reach options you can customize

   d   Fast menu

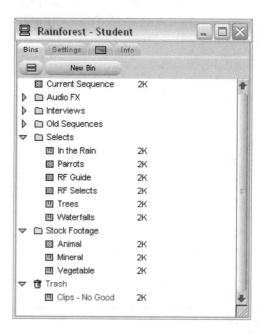

7 What happens if you close the Project window while you are working? (See "Working in the Project Window" on page 11.)

8 Where are the Frame view, Brief view, Text view, and Script view tabs?

   a   Project window

   b   Bin window

   c   Timeline

   d   All of the above

9 Which bin view(s) could you use to check the start timecode of a clip? (See "Working with Settings" on page 18.)

10 What dialog box appears when you close the Project window? (See "Locating the Project Window" on page 19.)

11 What key do you press to advance the representative frame of a clip in the bin by 10 frames? (See "Changing the Representative Frame" on page 24.)

Exercise: Get Started

In this exercise you start to use the Avid system interface, and get ready to work on the Rainforest (RF) sequence. We have already created a project and a bin with audio and video clips for you to use.

Working in Projects...   ... and Bins

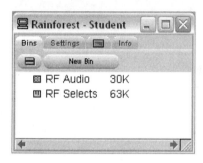
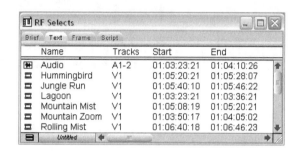

Note: Most exercises in this book provide you with a choice: you can carefully follow the steps of each procedure or work more on your own, by following the instructions in the outlined version at the end of the exercise.

Goals

- Launch the Avid System

- Open a project and bins

- Create new bins

- View clips in a bin

- Open a bin in another project

Start the System and Avid Application

The first step is to start the Avid system hardware and software.

1 Power on your storage disks.

2 Power on all other hardware except the PC or Macintosh. Include decks, audio processing hardware, speakers, and monitors.

Launch the System and the Avid Application (Windows)

1 Press Control+Alt+Delete to log on at the Windows startup screen.

The Windows desktop appears.

The system's C: drive contains the Avid application, projects, and bins.

The external drives hold the media files.

2 If a shortcut of the Avid application appears on the desktop, double-click it and proceed to the next section.

If not:

3 Locate the Avid application icon in C:\Program Files\Avid*Avid application*.

4 Double-click the Avid application icon to launch it.

Launch the System and the Avid Application (Macintosh)

1 Power on the Macintosh system.

The Finder desktop appears.

2 Click the Avid icon on the dock (the row of buttons at the bottom of the screen).

Open the Rainforest Project

A few moments after the application is launched, a dialog box opens on the Bin monitor.

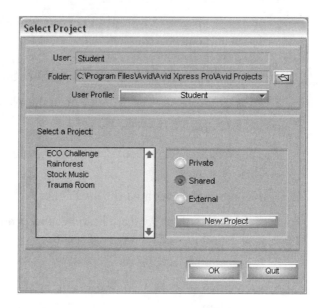

This is the Select Project dialog box where you can open or create projects and users. For this exercise, we'll open an existing project and user profile.

1 If not already highlighted, click the **Rainforest** project.

2 Use your login name as the User.

3 Click OK.

The project opens. The monitor shows the Project window, and the Composer and Timeline windows.

The menu bar now shows a different set of commands — ones specific to the Avid application.

Create a New Bin and Open an Existing Bin

You store clips and sequences in bins, and optionally, you can store bins in folders. Let's create a bin to hold your finished sequences (naming it RF Sequences).

1 Click the New Bin button in the Project window.

The new bin opens and is given the name of your project with the word Bin appended to the name. Let's rename this bin.

2 It is already highlighted in the Project window, so all you need to do is type the new name. Name the bin **RF Sequences** and press Enter (Windows) or Return (Macintosh).

To begin working, you'll also need to open the bin that was created for you containing the captured clips.

3 Double-click the Bin icon to the left of **RF Select**s to open the bin.

! **If you accidentally single-clicked the Bin icon, the icon in the upper-left corner of the bin will look unfamiliar, meaning that you opened the SuperBin. Close the bin, and open it again by double-clicking. We will discuss SuperBins in a later lesson.**

View the Bin

The information in the bin can be viewed in four ways: Text view, Brief view, Frame view, and Script view. We'll switch between the views, and adjust the size of clips in Frame view.

The following illustration shows clips displayed in Text view.

1 To switch to Brief view, click the Brief tab in the upper-left corner of the bin.

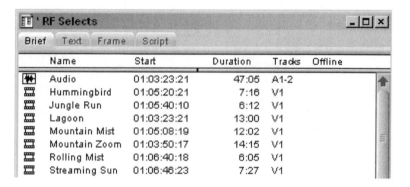

Brief view always displays the same five statistical columns.

2 To switch to Script view, click the Script tab in the upper-left corner of the bin.

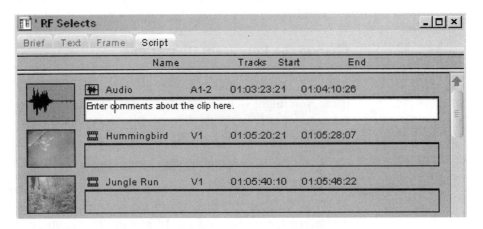

3 To add information about a clip, click in the box to the right of the frame and type some text.

4 To switch to Frame view, click the Frame tab in the upper-left corner of the bin.

5 To make the frames bigger, choose Edit > Enlarge Frame, or use the keyboard equivalent Control+L (Windows) or ⌘+L (Macintosh).

6 To make the frames smaller, choose Edit > Reduce Frame, or use the keyboard equivalent Control+K (Windows) or ⌘+K (Macintosh).

7 Click the Maximize button (Windows) or zoom box (Macintosh) of the Bin window (upper-right corner).

The bin zooms to fill the screen. Some clips may appear off screen.

8 Choose Bin > Fill Window.

This arranges the clips so that you can see most, if not all, of them within your current window.

Change the Representative Frame

Although the clips used in this project are easily identified by their name, you might sometimes find it helpful to use a more representative frame to identify a clip. By default, clips are represented with their first frame. For practice, let's modify one of the clips in the bin.

1 Select the **Hummingbird** clip by clicking on the clip's *frame* (not the name).

2 Press the Step 10-Frames Forward key (the 2 key above the Q key) several times until you see the hummingbird appear in the frame.

3 When you edit, you will often find it useful to rearrange clips in the bin in Frame view (for example, to storyboard clips, which we cover later). For now, simply move the **Hummingbird** clip to the bottom of the bin. (If it doesn't fit there, figure out a way to make it fit.)

4 Close all open bins.

Open the Music Bin (Stock Music Project) from within the Rainforest Project

The objective of this part of the exercise is to familiarize you with the process of opening bins, moving through the file hierarchy, and generally making you feel more comfortable with the structure of projects, bins, and sequences.

The exercise is simple: We have created a project, a bin within that project, and a couple of music clips within that bin. Your task is to find and open the bin, without leaving the Avid Editing project. The only clue you get is the name of the bin: **Music**. Try to do this exercise without help. **If you have difficulty, use the following directions.**

1 With the Project window or any bin highlighted, choose File > Open Bin.

The Select a Bin dialog box appears.

If you do not see the name of the bin you are looking for, continue looking in other project folders, as follows:

2 In the Select a Bin dialog box, press the down arrow and navigate to the Avid Projects folder.

3 Double-click the **Stock Music** folder to see its contents.

You should see the bin, **Music**, in this folder.

4 Double-click the bin to open it.

Remember you are simply borrowing this bin from the Stock Music project.

Additional Exercises

Try any of the following:

1 Create a new project. (How do you get to the New Project dialog box?)

2 Open the new project.

3 Open the RF Selects bin from within the new project, and then repeat for the RF Audio bin.

4 Place the RF Selects bin in Frame view, and change the representative frame of various clips.

5 Close the bins and close the project.

Get Started (Outlined)

Complete this sequence of procedures, referring to Lesson 1, if necessary. All of the procedures in this exercise are stepped out in Lesson 1.

1 Power on the system hardware.

2 Launch the Avid application.

3 Open the **Rainforest** project.

The User, displayed in the dialog box, is your login name.

4 Create a new bin, name it **RF Sequences**.

5 Open the **RF Selects** bin.

6 View the **RF Selects** bin in Text view and Brief view.

7 View the **RF Selects** bin in Script view, and add comments about a clip.

8 View the **RF Selects** bin in Frame view, and do the following:

  a Make sure all clips are visible in the bin.

  b Make any size adjustments to the frames so they are just the right size for viewing.

  c Arrange the clips nicely in the bin and make sure they are all still visible.

  d Change the image displayed in each frame so that it shows a good, representative image.

  e Move a clip to another part of the bin.

9 Close the **RF Selects** and the **RF Sequences** bins.

10 For the final part of the exercise, from within the **Rainforest** project, open the **Music** bin from the **Stock Music** project.

11 If time still remains, see "Additional Exercises" on page 37.

Lesson 2 **Basic Editing**

Now that you know how to navigate around a project and bins, it's time to edit! The basic procedure for editing on an Avid system involves viewing a source clip, marking the portion of the clip you want to edit into the sequence, and then adding the clip to the sequence by splicing or overwriting. You can also remove a clip (or a portion of one) from the sequence by extracting or lifting.

Nonlinear editing means that you can add and remove material from a sequence in any order, at any time. You can start by building a middle section before tackling the beginning of a show, build all the scenes from one shooting location before moving to another, edit scenes as the material comes in from the shoot, and so on. The possibilities are endless, and the sooner you become used to the nonlinear work process the better you will be as an editor.

This lesson covers how to use the Avid system's basic editing functions to create a rough-cut of a sequence.

Objectives

After you complete this lesson, you will be able to:

- Identify components of the editing interface
- Play clips
- Mark edit points
- Create a new sequence
- Add shots into a sequence by splicing and overwriting
- Remove shots from a sequence by lifting and extracting

The Editing Interface

The editing interface is where you review your footage and do your editing.

The interface consists of:

- Pop-up monitor
- Composer monitor
- Timeline

Pop-up Monitor

Pop-up monitors are windows, larger than the frames in Frame view, where you view and mark the footage you intend to use in your sequence. You can have several pop-up monitors open at the same time, so that you can view and compare several shots.

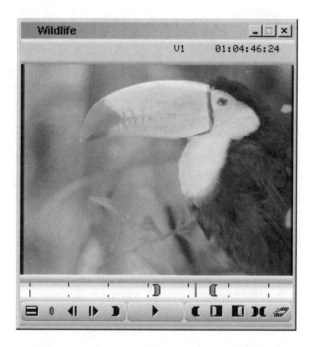

Pop-up monitor display

Composer Monitor

The Composer monitor displays your sequence. This is where edits are assembled and reviewed. A sequence is played in the Composer monitor the same way a clip is played in the pop-up monitor. The toolbar of buttons, Tool Palette Fast menu, and use of the blue position indicator in the Composer monitor and pop-up monitors are identical.

Blue position indicator

Tool Palette Fast menu

Toolbar of buttons

Composer monitor with components labelled

Timeline

The Timeline is a graphical representation of your sequence and the place where you do your editing. The Timeline window shows your sequence as bars of audio and video against a timecode line.

Timeline top toolbar —

Video —

Audio —

Timecode —

Bottom toolbar —

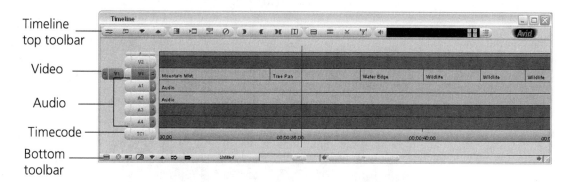

Timeline window with components labelled

Playing Clips

The basic editing procedure starts with loading a source clip into a monitor and playing the clip, so you can decide what portion of the clip you want to add to your sequence. As you will see, the system provides many ways to play and step through the clip.

Note: We'll cover Toolsets in more detail later in the book.

If you are using the Source/Record Editing toolset, you load clips in the Source monitor instead of the pop-up monitor. Throughout this book, we will refer mostly to Source monitor, and assume you are using the Source/Record Editing toolset. If we want to discuss pop-up monitors, we will explicit say so. Also, if you choose to use the Basic toolset, simply substitute pop-up monitor for Source monitor, wherever you see it in the text.

Loading a Source Clip

To load a source clip into the Source monitor:

1 Open the bin in which the clip resides.

Note: To load clips and other Avid objects listed in a bin, double-click the icon, not the name.

2 Click and drag the clip from the bin into the Source monitor, or double-click the desired clip image (Frame view) or clip icon (Text view).

The clip appears in the Source monitor, which is the window on the left in the Composer monitor.

The Composer monitor displays both Source and Record monitors in the Source/Record Editing toolset.

Source monitor

Source monitor

The Track Selector panel appears on the left side of the Timeline, indicating the video or audio tracks the loaded clip contains. In this example, the selected source tracks are the video track, V1, and audio tracks, A1 and A2.

Source Track Monitor buttons

Source Track buttons

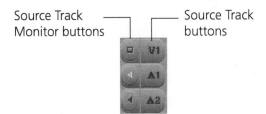

Working with Pop-up Monitors

You load a clip into a pop-up monitor just as you do into the Source monitor.

1 Choose the Basic toolset.

2 Double-click the desired clip image (Frame view) or clip icon (Text view).

The clip appears in the pop-up monitor.

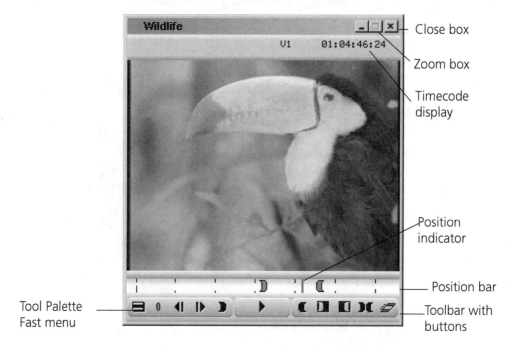

Pop-up monitor with components labelled

Opening Several Clips at Once

It may save you time to open several clips at once. To open several clips in pop-up monitors simultaneously:

Note: To lasso clips, position the cursor to the left of the first Clip icon you want to select, press the mouse button, and drag the mouse down and to the right until all the clips you want to select are highlighted, and release the mouse.

1 In an open bin, hold down the Control key (Windows) or Shift key (Macintosh) as you click on each clip, or lasso the clips if they're consecutive, to select them.

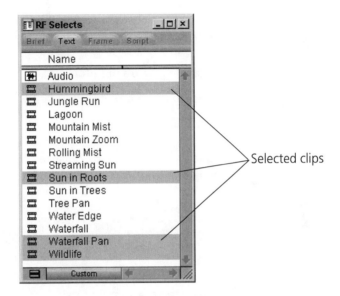

Selected clips

2 Alt+double-click (Windows) or Option+double-click (Macintosh) one of the selected clips.

A pop-up monitor appears for each clip.

Resizing a Pop-up Monitor

1 Move your cursor to the lower right corner of the pop-up monitor. The cursor turns into a bi-directional arrow.

2 Click and drag down and to the right (or up and to the left) to resize the pop-up monitor.

Closing Pop-up Monitors

While you are working on a project, it's a good idea to keep your desktop tidy by periodically closing pop-up monitors.

To close a single pop-up monitor:

1 Select the pop-up monitor you want to close.

2 Choose File > Close. You can instead, for Windows, click the close box (X) on the upper-right corner of the pop-up monitor; or for Macintosh, click on the small close box in the upper-left corner of the pop-up monitor.

Windows   Macintosh

Close box

To close all open pop-up monitors:

1 Select any pop-up monitor.

2 Choose Windows > Close All Pop-up Monitors.

Ways to Play Clips

The Avid system provides a variety of ways to play and step through footage. You should practice using all methods in your work before selecting the combination most comfortable for you.

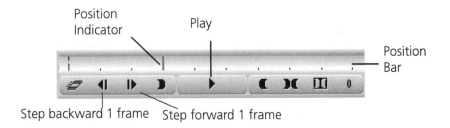

Source monitor toolbar with components labelled

Here are some basic ways to move through the clip, using buttons, their keyboard equivalents, and the blue position indicator.

- To play the clip, click the Play button below the Source monitor.

- To stop the clip, click the Play button again or press the space bar on the keyboard.

- To go to the start of the clip, press the Home (First Frame) key or click at the start of the position bar.

- To go to the end of the clip, press the End (Last Frame) key or click at the end of the position bar.

- Step through the footage forward or backward in 1-frame increments by:

  - Clicking the Step forward and backward 1 frame buttons

  - Pressing the 4 (forward) and 3 (backward) keys

- Step through the footage forward or backward in 10-frame increments by:

  - Pressing the Alt key (Windows) or Option key (Macintosh) while clicking the Step forward and backward 1 frame buttons

  - Pressing the 2 (forward) and 1 (backward) keys

- To scroll through the clip, click and drag the blue position indicator in the position bar.

- To move to a specific spot in the clip, click that spot in the position bar.

The position indicator automatically moves to that spot.

Motion Control Buttons and Keys

Note: Keyboard equivalents are indicated on the buttons.

The following table provides a list of motion control buttons and their keyboard equivalents that are covered in this lesson. (The buttons also indicate keyboard equivalents.)

Table 1   Motion Control Buttons and Keys

Function	Button	Key
Play		5
		˜ (Tilde)
Stop		5 again
		Space bar
Step forward 1 frame		4
		Right arrow
Step backward 1 frame		3
		Left arrow
Step forward 10 frames	Alt/Option +	2
		Alt+Right arrow (Windows)
		Option+Right arrow (Macintosh)
Step backward 10 frames	Alt/Option +	1
		Alt+Left arrow (Windows)
		Option+Left arrow (Macintosh)
Go to Start		Home
Go to End		End

Marking the Edit Points in a Clip

You define a shot that you want to add to the sequence by marking IN and OUT points in a clip.

One of the advantages of working in nonlinear editing is that you can loosely mark these IN and OUT points and refine them later in the editing process. When assembling the initial cut, you don't have to worry about being frame accurate; the Avid system provides several ways to fine-tune the edit after the shot has been added to the sequence.

To mark edit points in a clip:

1 Play a clip in the Source monitor, and stop at the start of the material you want to add to the sequence.

2 Click the mark IN button in the row of buttons below the Source monitor.

Mark IN  Mark OUT

3 Continue playing your clip and stop at the end of the material to be added to the sequence.

4 Click the Mark OUT button.

5 Play the clip from the IN to the OUT point by pressing the Play IN to OUT (6) key to confirm your marks.

6 Reposition an IN or OUT mark by placing the position indicator where you want the mark to be and then click the Mark IN or Mark OUT button. (You don't need to clear the previous mark first.)

Marking Buttons and Their Keyboard Equivalents

Note: Most of the buttons appear below the Source monitor. If they don't, you can map them from the Command palette, which will be covered later in the book, or use the keyboard equivalent.

The following table provides a list of Marking buttons and their keyboard equivalents. (The buttons also indicate keyboard equivalents.)

Table 2   Marking Buttons and Keys

Function	Button	Key
Mark IN		I
		E
Mark OUT		O
		R
Mark Clip		T
Play IN to OUT		6
Go to IN		Q
Go to OUT		W
Clear IN Mark		D
Clear OUT Mark		F
Clear Both Marks		G

Creating a New Sequence

You can create a sequence by defining a shot and making your first edit. Because this is nonlinear editing, this shot need not be the first one in your sequence—if you even knew which one that would be!

Note: You should create a separate bin to hold your sequences.

▶ Open or create the bin that will hold the sequence you are about to create.

Making the First Edit

1 Play a clip that you want to use in a new sequence and set the Mark IN and OUT points.

2 Click the Source Track buttons for the tracks you want to use for the edit.

Source Track buttons

3 To make your first edit, click the Splice button, which is the yellow arrow in the Tool palette's Fast menu.

Creating a New Sequence

1 If multiple bins are open when you click the Splice button, the Select a Bin dialog box appears. To choose the destination bin for your sequence, click the bin name and press Enter or Return, or click New Bin and press Enter/Return.

The new sequence appears in the selected bin, with its default name, *Untitled Sequence.n*. The sequence name also appears above the Record monitor.

2 Name your sequence by doing the following:

    a   If you don't see the bin in the monitor, choose it from the Windows menu.

    b   Click the sequence name to select it. It becomes highlighted in black.

    c   Type in the new name and press Enter.

3 Play the sequence in the Record monitor.

Note: The Source monitor is on the left side of the Composer monitor; the Record monitor is on the right side.

The sequence will not play in the Composer monitor (which consists of both the Source and Record monitors) if anything overlaps with it, or if the Composer monitor is on the wrong computer screen. In both cases, you will see a white bar flashing on the perimeter of the screen. Be sure to drag any overlapping objects to the side.

Note: We'll cover Toolsets in more detail later in the book.

If you are using the Source/Record Editing toolset, the sequence plays in the Record monitor. If you are using the Basic toolset, the Composer monitor contains only the Record monitor.

Adding Shots

You can add shots to the sequence by splicing or overwriting.

You typically use splicing to assemble shots in your sequence. You use splice edits to add the first shot, then the second shot, then the third shot, and so on. You also use splice edits to insert a shot between two other shots. Let's say you assemble ten shots and then decide to insert a shot between shots 6 and 7. You use splice edit to insert the shot.

You typically use overwriting to *replace* (write over) existing sections of the sequence with new material.

While you often splice during the first stage of editing and overwrite when you revise your initial cut, as you become experienced you'll use both operations as needed throughout the editing process.

Splicing

When you splice, footage from a clip is inserted into the sequence at a point you specify, without replacing material already in the sequence. Any shots in the sequence after the edit point ripple down, lengthening the sequence.

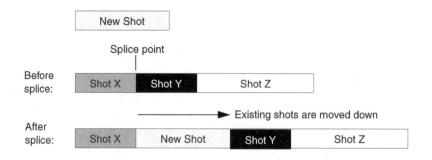

To splice a shot into your sequence:

1 Load your clip into the Source monitor.

2 Mark an IN and OUT in the source clip to define a shot.

If you don't mark the clip, the entire clip will be selected. (If the position indicator is not at the head of the clip, the mark IN will appear at the position indicator, and the mark OUT will appear at the end of the clip.)

3 Place the position indicator in the Timeline where you want to splice the shot into the sequence, and mark an IN.

If you don't mark an IN, the system splices the new shot into the sequence one frame before blue position indicator.

4 Click the Source and Record Track buttons for the tracks you want to use for the edit. The selected tracks are highlighted.

In this example, material from source tracks V1 and A1 will be edited onto tracks V1 and A1 in the Timeline.

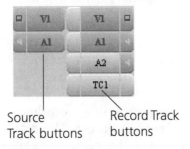

Source
Track buttons

Record Track
buttons

5 Click the Splice button, which is the yellow arrow in the Tool palette's Fast menu. The clip is spliced into the sequence at the Mark IN point.

Overwriting

When you overwrite, you replace (write over) existing sections of the sequence with new material. Overwrite edits do not change the length of the sequence unless the new footage extends beyond the existing sequence.

Three-Point Edits

The overwrite function is typically used to create three-point edits, where you mark three IN/OUT points, in one of the following combinations:

- Method 1: Overwriting a specific segment in the Timeline. You mark an IN *and* OUT in the Timeline, and you mark an IN *or* OUT in the clip

  This type of overwrite edit is very common, and is often used to create cutaways. For example, if your sequence contains a long clip of one person talking, you can add visual variety to the segment by overwriting other images over the "talking head." You mark the portion of the Timeline to overwrite, and mark an IN or OUT point in the clip. The system calculates the exact number of frames to write over the talking head.

- Method 2: Overwriting a specific segment of a clip into your sequence. You mark an IN *and* OUT in the clip, and you mark an IN *or* OUT in the Timeline.

  This type of overwrite is used when you know you want to add a particular shot into a sequence and it's less important to specify the exact segment to overwrite. For example, you would use this method if you want to insert a particular line of dialog or a sound effect.

To overwrite a shot in to your sequence, using the three-point edit:

1 Load your clip into the Source monitor.

Note: If you mark four IN and OUT points, the system defaults to the record OUT and ignores the source OUT.

2 Mark three IN and OUT points in the source clip and the Timeline, by doing one of the following:

- Mark an IN *and* OUT in the Timeline and mark an IN *or* OUT in the clip.

  The selected segment is highlighted in the Timeline. The insert shot will replace (overwrite) this segment.

  The system figures out how many frames to insert in the segment to replace the exact number of frames marked in the Timeline.

Note: If the clip does not have enough frames, this message is displayed: "Insufficient source material to make this edit."

- Mark an IN *and* OUT in your clip and mark an IN *or* OUT in the sequence.

  The marked clip is added into the sequence, at the IN or OUT point you marked.

3 Click the Source and Record Track buttons for the tracks you want to use for the edit.

4 Click the Overwrite button, which is the red arrow in the Tool palette Fast menu.

The marked section in the sequence is overwritten by the material you selected in the clip. The total length of the sequence does not change unless the inserted shot extends beyond the end of the sequence.

Adding Audio to Your Sequence

Adding audio to your sequence from a source clip is just like adding video.

Follow the steps for adding video to a sequence, but remember to turn off any video Track buttons in the track panel, and turn on desired audio Track buttons before you make the edit.

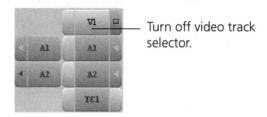 Turn off video track selector.

Removing Material from a Sequence

You can remove footage from your sequence, and either close or retain the gap that results.

Lifting and Extracting

- *Lifting* removes material from the Timeline and leaves video black or silence to fill the gap; it's often used if you want to maintain the rhythm of a sequence or the synchronization of the picture and audio tracks. This action is the inverse of overwriting; both operations maintain the integrity of the sequence.

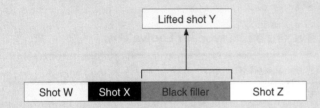

- *Extracting* removes material from the Timeline and closes the gap left by its removal. This action is the inverse of splicing; both operations affect the length of the sequence.

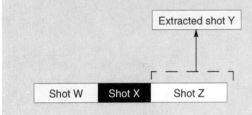

To lift or extract material from the sequence:

Tip: These buttons are also located in the Timeline top toolbar.

1 Mark an IN and OUT at the start and end of the material that you want to lift or extract.

Or use the Mark Clip button (or T key) to quickly select a whole clip for removal. (The Mark Clip button is found in the Timeline toolbar.) Based on the record tracks you have selected and the location of the blue position indicator, the Mark Clip function automatically finds the IN and OUT of a clip in the sequence.

2 Select the appropriate record tracks.

3 Lift or extract by doing one of the following:

- Click the Lift button or press the Z key to lift the selected material from the sequence and leave black or silence in the gap.

- Click the Extract button or press the X key to remove the selected material and close the gap.

Edit Buttons and Their Keyboard Equivalents

The following table provides a list of Edit buttons and their keyboard equivalents.

Table 3   Edit Buttons and Keyboard Equivalents

Function	Button	Key
Splice		V
Overwrite		B
Extract		X
Lift		Z
Undo		Control+Z (Windows) ⌘+Z (Macintosh)
Redo		Control+R (Windows) ⌘+R (Macintosh)

Essential Basic Tools

This section provides a number of basic tools and operations that you will use frequently as you edit.

Tool Palette

To display the Tool palette, click the Fast menu just below the line separating the Source and Record windows. The Tool palette can be *torn off* by dragging it anywhere on the monitor. It provides easy access to commonly used editing buttons. You are already familiar with some of these buttons; you will learn others in later lessons.

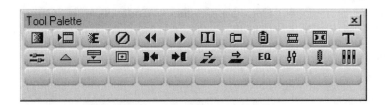

To display more or fewer buttons (and to display more empty buttons):

▶ Drag a corner of the Tool palette in or out.

Snapping to an Edit Point in the Timeline

You will often need to park the blue position indicator at the exact head or tail of a shot in the Timeline. One of the best and quickest methods to do this is to snap to a transition point. You never have to worry if you're a frame off. Also, the technique is not track sensitive, so you don't have to select a track first.

Tip: To mark a *series* of shots, Control+click (Windows) or ⌘+click (Macintosh) at the head of the first shot for the IN, and Control+Alt+click (Windows) or ⌘+Option+click (Macintosh) at the tail of the last shot for the OUT.

To snap to a transition point in the Timeline, do one of the following:

- Control+click (Windows) or ⌘+click (Macintosh) near the desired transition to snap to the *head* frame of the shot (or IN or OUT mark).

- Control+Alt+click (Windows) or ⌘+Option+click (Macintosh) near the desired transition to snap to the *tail* frame of the shot (or IN or OUT mark).

Undo/Redo

The Avid system allows you to undo and redo up to 32 previous editing changes. You can undo the previous operations, or a series of operations. Thus, if you perform a series of operations to perform one task, you can easily revert to the sequence as it was before you went down that path.

- To undo the previous operation, select Edit > Undo or press Control+Z (Windows) or ⌘+Z (Macintosh).

- To redo the previous operation, select Edit > Redo or press Control+R (Windows) or ⌘+R (Macintosh).

  Each undo removes the effect of the previous action; redo negates the previous undo. You can move forward and backward through your last 32 commands with undo and redo.

- To undo or redo everything back to a particular command, choose that command from Edit > Undo/Redo List. (The redo options, when present, are located at the top of the list.)

  The gray bar marks the place in the list where you are right now.

Zooming In and Out

The Zoom slider enables you to zoom in on a section of the Timeline centered around the blue position bar, and then zoom back to your original display.

1   Place the blue position indicator in the area you want to expand.

2   Drag the Zoom slider to the right.

Zoom slider

The Timeline expands horizontally to show more detail. If you zoom in far enough, the position indicator splits into a solid blue line and a dotted blue line (or "shadow"), marking the beginning and end of the current frame.

3   Move the Zoom slider back to the left to display the entire sequence.

Closing and Opening Tools and Windows

In the previous lesson, you learned how to locate the Project window if it is hidden from view. Other windows and tools that make up the Avid system can also be hidden from view or closed, just like any other Windows or Macintosh window. Since you might close these windows accidentally, you must know how to open and close them.

1   Click anywhere in the Timeline window to highlight it.

2   Choose File > Close.

The window disappears.

3   Choose Tools > Timeline.

The Timeline window reappears.

Review Questions

1 What are the main components of the editing interface?

2 Label the following buttons:

3 How do you load a clip into the Source monitor? (See "Loading a Source Clip" on page 43.)

4 When you create a new sequence, in what two places does the name appear? (See "Creating a New Sequence" on page 52.)

5 You have opened a bin and you want to change the name of the clip. Precisely where do you click on the clip before typing a new name? (See "Creating a New Sequence" on page 52.)

 binoculars LA

6 Provide the missing steps for this overwriting procedure: (See "Overwriting" on page 56.)

   a   Mark an IN and OUT in the clip.

   b

   c   Select the source and record tracks.

   d

7 What's the difference between splice and overwrite? (See "Adding Shots" on page 54.)

8 When would it be appropriate to splice? (See "Splicing" on page 54.)

9 When would it be appropriate to overwrite? (See "Overwriting" on page 56.)

10 If you just edited a shot by splicing it and now you want to remove it, but leave filler in its place, which of the following should you do?

   a   Select Edit > Undo.

   b   Mark the clip, then extract.

   c   Mark the clip, then lift.

11 How is lift similar to overwrite?

12 How is extract similar to splice?

13 How do you snap the position indicator to the head frame of an edit? (See "Snapping to an Edit Point in the Timeline" on page 62.)

14 What keys do you press to undo the last step? (See "Undo/Redo" on page 62.)

Exercise: Basic Editing

In this exercise, you begin editing a public service announcement (PSA) about preserving the rain forest. First you'll lay down a narration/music track, and then you'll start cutting video to the audio.

Narration begins: "If we don't save the rain forest, what will happen?"

Goals

- Create and name a sequence
- Mark clips and add them to a sequence
- Lift a clip, leaving a gap in the track
- Practice using new buttons and their keyboard equivalents
- Close and open tools and windows

Create the Rainforest Sequence

▶ The **Rainforest** project should already be open. If not, open it now by doing one of the following:

- Launch Avid Xpress Pro or Avid Xpress DV and select the Rainforest project in the Select Project dialog box. Click OK.

- If you are in a different project, click the close box in the Project window and select the Rainforest project in the Select Project dialog box that appears. Click OK.

Get Started

For the remainder of this and future lessons, you will view clips in the Source monitor instead of the pop-up monitor. So let's switch now to the Source/Record Editing toolset. (We will cover toolsets in detail in a later lesson.)

1 Choose Source/Record Editing from the Toolset menu.

From now on, when you double-click a clip, it loads in the Source monitor.

2 In the Project window, open the **RF Selects** bin. View the bin in Text or Frame view.

Splice the Audio Clip

Note: Tables of Motion Control, Marking, and Editing buttons and their keyboard equivalents appear at the end of the exercise.

Let's start by editing in the audio clip.

1 In the bin, press and hold the icon (Text view) or frame (Frame view) for the **audio** clip and drag it to the Source monitor. Release the mouse.

The clip opens in the Source monitor and has voice-over on track A1 and music on track A2. No picture appears because this clip only has audio. Notice that audio Track buttons A1 and A2 now appear in the Timeline.

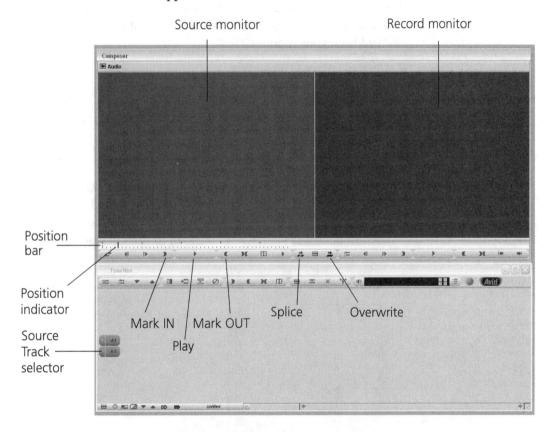

Composer monitor with components labelled

2 Click the Play button under the Source monitor.

Notice that a vertical blue line below the image scrolls along as the clip plays. This line is called the position indicator and the horizontal bar in which it is located is called the position bar.

3 The clip will play through to the end unless you press the space bar on the keyboard or click Play again.

4 Drag the position indicator forward and back in the position bar to see how quickly you can move through the clip.

5 To go to the first frame of the clip, click at the very beginning of the position bar or press the Home/First Frame key (between the main keyboard and the numeric keypad).

6 Click the Mark IN button.

7 Click the blue position indicator near the end of the clip. Click Play, and stop (by clicking Play again) at the end of the voice-over line, "And keep your promise."

8 Click the Mark OUT button.

You have now marked the audio you will use in the sequence.

 9 Click the Splice button, which is the yellow arrow in the Tool Palette's Fast menu.

If more than one bin is open, the Select a Bin dialog box appears.

10 If the Select a Bin dialog box appears, double-click **RF Sequences**. This is the bin in which your sequence will be stored. Remember, making that first edit is the first step in creating a sequence, so you need to tell the system where you want to store that sequence.

Congratulations! You've made your first Avid edit!

A graphical representation of your edit appears in the Timeline. The system will continue building this Timeline as you edit.

Name the Sequence: Rainforest v1

Now it is time to name your sequence.

1 Open the **RF Sequences** bin.

Your sequence bin pops to the front and contains your newly created sequence. By default, the system names it Untitled Sequence.01.

2 If the sequence name is not highlighted as above, click the name Untitled Sequence.01 once to highlight it.

3 Type **Rainforest v1**, and press Enter on the numeric keypad.

Play the Sequence

▶ Play through the sequence and listen to the audio track. The narration is transcribed for you.

Rainforest Narration

WOMAN

If we don't save the rain forest, what will happen?

CHILDREN

The trees will all fall down. (pause)

There won't be a place for the animals to live. (pause)

The plants that cure people will disappear. (pause)

The birds can't fly home. (pause)

Our planet will get too hot. (pause)

We won't be able to breathe. (pause)

Will I become extinct? (pause)

                    WOMAN

We promise our children the world. Let's show
them we mean it.... Adopt an acre of the rain
forest, and keep your promise.

Overwrite Video Over Narration

Now we'll start laying in some video on top of the lines of narration.

View Clips in the RF Selects Bin

1 Open the **RF Selects** bin.

2 Spend a few minutes screening the clips in this bin. Make a mental note of the clips that may fit some of the VO lines. For example, the **Hummingbird** video clip fits nicely with the VO, "The birds can't fly home."

You will now locate each individual line of voice-over, and edit a video clip for each one on the video track. Start anywhere in the sequence you like. Because this is non-linear editing, there is no need to start at the beginning of the sequence. Later in the exercise you will add video in the areas without voice-overs; for now, leave them black.

Prepare the Sequence

1 In the sequence, find a line of audio voice-over.

2 Click the Mark IN button under the Record monitor at the start of this line of VO.

3 Mark an OUT at the end of the line of VO.

4 Press the 6 (Play IN to OUT) key to confirm your marks.

Mark the Source Material

1 In the bin, double-click the video clip you want to edit over this VO line. (If you are editing over the first VO line, choose a shot with motion, such as **sun in roots**. It will be helpful to have a shot with movement for the next exercise.)

   The clip is loaded into the Source monitor.

2 Drag the position indicator to the right, then to the left, to locate the part of the clip you'd like to use.

   Notice that the video timecode display above the Source monitor updates as you scroll.

3 Mark an IN at the beginning of the section you'd like to use. If you want to use the head of the clip, mark the IN point at least 15 frames into the clip, so you can trim the shot or add a dissolve in a later exercise.

   You do not need to mark an OUT. The OUT will be determined by the duration of the marks you have placed in your sequence.

Perform the Overwrite

1 Turn off A1 and A2 Track button, because the next edits are video-only.

2 Click the Overwrite button, which is the red arrow in the Tool Palette Fast menu.

   In the Timeline you'll see two audio tracks, plus the section of video you just added.

3 Click the blue position indicator in the Timeline, a little before your newest edit.

4 Play through your edit.

5 Click Play again to stop playback, or press the space bar.

Repeat the Procedure

Note: If you make a mistake, you can undo it. To undo, press Control+Z (Windows) or ⌘+Z (Macintosh).

▶ Continue adding video to the other segments of voice-over in the sequence, by repeating the same procedure: mark a VO segment in the Timeline, locate appropriate video in the bin, load it into the Source monitor, and edit it over the audio.

! **You should have gaps between video segments where there is no narration.**

Overwrite Video on Your Own

Now we'll overwrite a few shots of video between the third and fourth voice-over lines.

1 Locate the line, "There won't be a place for the animals to live."

2 Hold down Control (Windows) or ⌘ (Macintosh) and click the mouse in a frame of black just after that VO.

Notice that a frame of black appears in the Record monitor and a bracket appears in the left corner. The bracket indicates that the position indicator is parked on the first frame of black.

There is about a four-second gap between this line and the next.

3 Overwrite three animal shots from the **Wildlife** clip into this gap, without leaving any space between the shots in the sequence.

Tip: If you like, zoom into the area.

Each time you overwrite a shot, think about whether to mark the IN and OUT points in the Source or in the Timeline. Why might you want to use the Mark Clip button in the Timeline for the last shot you overwrite?

The Mark Clip button is found in the Timeline top toolbar.

4 Play the section.

Fill in the Gap Between the First and Second VO Lines

Now fill in the gap between the first and second lines of voice-over. **Do not be concerned about editing to the music at this point; in the next exercise you will trim this section to a beat of the music.**

1 Place the blue position indicator within the black section between the first and second voice-over lines.

2 Click the Mark Clip button to mark this segment of black.

3 In the Source monitor, mark an IN or OUT in the clip you want to overwrite into the sequence.

4 Overwrite the clip.

5 Play the section.

Replace a Shot

Nonlinear editing makes it easy for you to experiment and try different shots at any time. Review the cut so far, and find a shot (or part of a shot) on the video track that you would like to replace.

1 Use the overwrite procedure to replace a shot or part of a shot in the sequence.

2 Play the segment, and if you do not like the results, try another clip.

Add a Slug

You realize you don't like the shot you added between the first and second voice-overs, but you don't have time to replace it. You can lift out the shot and the gap remains for you to fill in later. (Actually, you'll fill in the gap in the next exercise.)

1 Mark the second video clip in the sequence.

 2 Click the Lift button in the Timeline top toolbar or press the Z key to lift the selected material from the sequence and leave black in the gap.

What would happen to the Timeline if you extracted the segment instead of lifting it?

Close and Open Tools and Windows

It's easy to forget that the windows and tools that make up the Avid system can be closed or hidden from view like any other window. Since you might close these windows accidentally, you must know how to open and close them.

1 Click anywhere in the Timeline window to highlight it.

2 Choose File > Close.

The window disappears.

3 Choose Tools > Timeline.

The Timeline window reappears.

Note: If you cannot see your Project window, choose Tools > Project to bring it forward.

Unlike the other windows, the Project window must be open at all times. If you close the Project window, the entire project closes and the Select Project dialog box appears. So, only close the Project window if you want to open another project or quit the Avid application.

Close and Reopen Bins

1 Select your **RF Sequences** bin by clicking it, or if you cannot see it choose it from the Windows menu.

2 Choose File > Close Bin or click the bin's Close button (Windows) or Close box (Macintosh).

Windows   Macintosh

The bin disappears. But notice that your sequence is no longer in your Record monitor or in your Timeline. This is because the system allows you to see or work on a sequence only if the bin it resides in is open. Let's reopen that bin.

3 Open the RF Sequences bin.

4 Double-click the Sequence icon (showing three film frames) in the bin.

Your sequence is loaded back into the Record monitor and your Timeline is restored.

Additional Exercises

Try any of the following:

- Reload your **Rainforest** sequence into the Timeline and continue to overwrite video into the sequence. However, leave gaps between the two voice-overs, "If we don't save the rain forest…" and "The trees will all fall down"; and between the two voice-overs, "Our planet will get too hot" and "We won't be able to breathe." We will fill in those gaps in the next exercise.

- Replace one shot (video only) with another, using overwrite.

- Practice the motion control and mark buttons. These are listed in tables in the next section. Also, practice using keyboard equivalents to the buttons. The more familiar you become with the buttons and keys on this first day, the easier the future exercises will be.

Basic Editing (Outlined)

As you go through this exercise, it's important to start thinking "nonlinear." Don't worry about marking IN and OUT points exactly, and don't build the shots in consecutive order. Nonlinear editing makes it easy to experiment and change your mind; use these advantages to the fullest!

If necessary, refer to Lesson 2 or the detailed exercise for complete procedures.

Make sure you practice the following operations, buttons, and keys as you go through the exercise (see the table at the end of the exercise for appropriate buttons and their keyboard equivalents):

- Play, Stop, and Step buttons and keys
- Blue position indicator to navigate through the Timeline
- Control+click (Windows) or ⌘+click (Macintosh) to snap to the head of a shot in the Timeline
- Alt+Control+click (Windows) or Option+⌘+click (Macintosh) to snap to the tail of a shot in the Timeline
- Go to IN, Go to OUT
- Mark IN and OUT, and Mark Clip
- Splice
- Overwrite
- Lift
- Extract
- Undo

Create and Edit the Sequence

1 Open the **RF Sequences** bin; this is where you will store your sequence.

2 Open the **RF Selects** bin and load the **audio** clip in the Source monitor.

3 Mark an IN at the head of the **audio** clip, and an OUT after the voice-over line, "And keep your promise."

4 Click the yellow Splice button to make your first edit. (If a dialog box appears asking you to choose a bin, choose the **RF Sequences** bin.)

The new sequence appears in the Timeline, containing the **audio** clip on tracks A1 and A2.

5 Name the new sequence in the **RF Sequences** bin.

6 Play the audio track. To follow the narration, see "Rainforest Narration" on page 71.

7 Build the video track on track V1, using clips in the **RF Selects** bin, by doing the following:

   a Screen clips in the **RF Selects** bin.

   b Add video over each line of voice-over in the sequence by performing this procedure for each line of voice-over: mark a VO segment in the Timeline, locate appropriate video in the bin, load it into the Source monitor, turn on the correct Source and Record Track buttons, and edit the video over the audio.

   You should have gaps between video segments where there is no narration.

   c Overwrite video between the lines of voice-over in the sequence. (Make sure to turn on the correct Source and Record Track buttons.)

Note: If you make a mistake, you can undo it. To undo, choose Edit > Undo or press Control+Z (Windows) or ⌘+Z (Macintosh).

8 To remind yourself that Avid system windows behave like any window on a computer, close the Timeline window and then re-open it.

9 Close the **RF Sequences** bin and note the consequences.

10 Load the sequence you were editing into the Record monitor.

Lesson 3 **Fine-Tuning**

After you build the rough cut of your program, you can see where it drags, where you want to add emphasis, and how you want to build the rhythm of shots. Then you can go back to individual shots to tighten or extend them. You also add dissolves to smooth transitions and to modify the rhythm of a scene. This lesson covers techniques for fine-tuning a sequence by trimming, and how to add dissolves to a sequence. Additional techniques will be covered in later lessons.

Note: A table of Trim buttons and keyboard equivalents is found at the end of the exercise.

The only effects covered in this book are dissolves. If you would like to know more about creating and using effects, consider using *Avid Xpress Pro Effects and Color Correction*.

Objectives

After you complete this lesson, you will be able to:

- Locate an audio edit cue
- Trim footage
- Add dissolves

Locating an Audio Edit Cue

Locating an exact audio edit cue is crucial when working with audio. You may need to locate audio such as a specific word, sound effect, or the exact beginning or end of a phrase of music. The Avid system provides several tools to help you locate audio cues.

Monitoring Audio

Note: Selecting the speaker is different from selecting the track. You can deselect a track and still listen to it by turning on its Speaker icon.

In the Track Selector panel, you can determine which tracks will be edited into your sequence, as well as do patching and other functions. The little box next to each track selector controls how audio is monitored.

Monitoring Audio

- To monitor an audio track, the Speaker icon next to the desired track must be visible. If it's not, click the little box to the right of the desired track. (You can monitor up to eight tracks at once.)

- To solo a track, Control+click (Windows) or ⌘+click (Macintosh) the Speaker icon next to the desired track. The monitor box turns green.

- To prepare to scrub audio digitally, Alt+click (Windows) or Option+click (Macintosh) the Speaker icon next to the desired track. The Speaker icon turns gold.

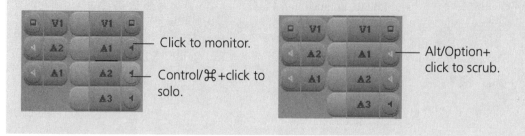

Monitoring audio by selecting the Speaker icon

Muting the Audio from Your Speaker

If you want to mute the volume from your speaker or headphones, you can use the Master Volume button.

1 From the Timeline top toolbar, click the Master Volume button.

Master Volume button

A red line runs through the Speaker icon, indicating the Master Volume button is muted.

2 Click the Master Volume button again to turn on the audio volume.

To adjust speaker volume (without Avid Mojo only):

You can also use the Master Volume button to adjust the volume from your speaker or headphones.

▸ From the Timeline top toolbar, click the Master Volume button and Alt/Option+drag the Volume Control slider to the level you prefer. Release the mouse.

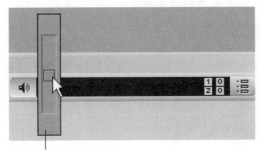

Volume Control slider

Digital Audio Scrub

The Digital Audio Scrub feature helps you locate an audio edit cue in either the source clip or the sequence. When you jog through footage using this feature you can hear the audio in a kind of slow motion, with the digital nature of the scrub giving the audio a stuttering quality.

To use Digital Audio Scrub:

1 Place your position indicator at the desired location in the source clip or sequence.

Tip: If you want to scrub only one track, solo that track.

2 Alt+click (Windows) or Option+click (Macintosh) the Speaker icon next to the track you want to scrub. The Speaker icon turns gold.

The Avid system uses as many tracks as possible to scrub, including tracks where the Speaker icon is not gold. As long as a track is on, it may be included for scrubbing. The gold icons indicate which tracks will be played if the system has to drop tracks during audio scrubbing. By default, the Avid system selects the top two audio tracks unless you make a selection.

3 Press the Caps Lock key to activate Digital Audio Scrub.

4 Press and hold the Step buttons to scrub around the edit cue to find it.

5 Turn off Caps Lock when finished scrubbing.

Using Caps Lock

For good work habits, always turn off Caps Lock when finished scrubbing. You can also use the Shift key as a temporary audio scrub that turns off automatically when you lift your finger from the Shift key.

Displaying Audio Waveforms

Waveform plots can help you visually locate points in an audio track for editing or trimming.

To display audio waveforms:

Timeline Fast menu

1 Choose Timeline Fast menu > Sample Plot.

- Sample plot displays the entire amplitude of the audio waveform.

Audio waveform displayed as a sample plot

Tip: Press Ctrl+period (Windows) or ⌘+period (Macintosh) at any time to stop the redraw.

2 Play the sequence to see the waveform and listen to the audio.

Improving the Visibility of the Waveform

- To enlarge the size of the plot without enlarging its track, press Ctrl+Alt+L (Windows) or ⌘+Option+L (Macintosh).

- To reduce the size of the plot without reducing its track, press Ctrl+Alt+K (Windows) or ⌘+Option+K (Macintosh).

Shuttling with J-K-L Keys

One of the most powerful and flexible shuttling tools is a three-key combination called *J-K-L*, because you use the J, K, and L keys on the keyboard. The L key functions as play forward, the J key functions as reverse playback, and the K key functions as a pause key.

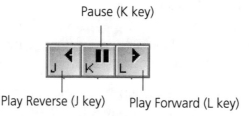

Pause (K key)

Play Reverse (J key)   Play Forward (L key)

J-K-L keys for shuttling power

You can use the J-K-L keys to play footage at standard speed, more slowly, or more quickly. This feature is also used to scrub audio; it provides an analog scrub with no stuttering quality.

To shuttle forward or backward, you have several options.

- Press the L key to play forward and the J key to play backward at standard speed (30 fps NTSC/25 fps PAL). Each additional press on the L or J key increases shuttle speed 2x, 3x, 5x, 8x. Press the K key to stop playback.

- Press the K key with either the L or J key to play forward or reverse at 8 fps (approximately quarter speed). Release the L or J key to stop playback.

- Hold down the K key and tap the L or J key to go forward or back one frame at a time.

- You can rock back and forth over an area of a clip by pressing the K key with the middle finger and alternately pressing the J and L keys.

- When you use the combination K/J or K/L, you can scrub a single audio track by soloing that track.

- The maximum speed at which the system can play audio is triple speed.

- In 1x forward speed (30 fps NTSC or 25 fps PAL), you can scrub all 8 audio tracks.

  At two times normal speed, you can scrub 8 tracks (Windows) or 2 tracks (Macintosh).

  At three times normal speed, you can scrub 2 tracks.

  You cannot scrub audio at higher than triple speed.

J-K-L Play Tips

Some editors use the J-K-L keys almost exclusively to move through footage and the I and O keys to mark footage so they can play and mark footage within a small area of the keyboard.

The J-K-L functionality can be assigned to different keyboard locations. Right-handed operators may want to move the operation to the left side of the keyboard. (Mapping buttons will be covered in a later lesson.)

Trimming

After you create a series of straight cuts, you can enter Trim mode to remove or add frames to the incoming or outgoing material on either side of the transition.

Trimming is one of the most powerful tools of your editing system. It will enable you to improve your sequence in a variety of ways. Good use of trimming can speed or relax the viewer's heartbeat, change your audience's reaction to a character, clarify (or mystify) an action, and undoubtedly enable you to go from a good to a great sequence.

Specifically, you can use trimming to:

- Move a transition point between two shots
- Fine-tune the length of a shot
- Smooth continuity of movement from shot to shot
- Create split edits
- Edit the picture to a beat of music, or create other correspondences between picture and sound

Trim mode creates a full-screen display that is dedicated to trimming.

Trim Mode

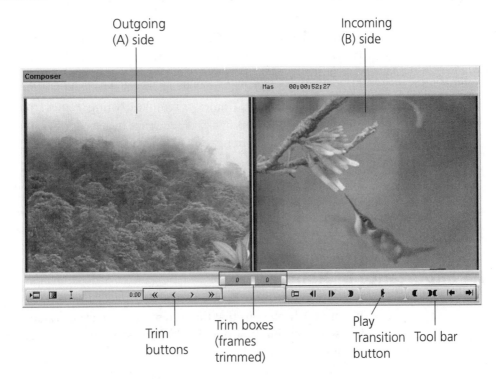

Outgoing (A) side

Incoming (B) side

Trim buttons

Trim boxes (frames trimmed)

Play Transition button

Tool bar

Trim mode interface

Different Types of Trimming

When you trim, you affect the outgoing (A) side or the incoming (B) side of the transition (using single-roller trimming), or both (using dual-roller trimming).

Explaining Single-Roller Trims

Single-roller trimming trims one side of a transition. Single-roller trims:

- Adjust the length of a shot.

- Reveal additional frames or remove existing frames from one side of a transition.

- Expand or shrink the duration of a clip in the sequence.

You use single-roller trims, for example, to "trim the fat" from a shot, to let another shot "breathe," or to smooth continuity of movement from shot to shot. You also use it to fix upcut audio, to shorten or lengthen a pause, and in general to improve the pace of a scene.

The Importance of Handle

It's intuitively obvious that the system can trim away frames from a clip in a sequence, but how does it add frames? Where does it get the frames?

Remember when you marked an IN and OUT in the source clip, and then added that segment to the sequence? The footage before the IN point and after the OUT point is still available. (Of course, if your IN and OUT points were at the very beginning and end of the source clip, you have no extra footage available for trimming. When we get to the capturing lesson, you'll be reminded to capture "loose" to avoid having nothing to trim.)

A source clip may be three minutes long. However, you may add a shot from that clip to the sequence that's only ten seconds long. That leaves 2 minutes and 50 seconds of extra material in the clip. That material can be added to the sequence by trimming.

This extra material that is not used in the sequence is called **handle**. Any media that exists as part of the clip **before** the shot used in the sequence is called **incoming handle**. Media that exists as part of the clip

after the shot used in the sequence is referred to as **outgoing handle**. The following illustration shows the incoming (before) and outgoing (after) handle for the *runners* shot in a sequence.

Handle: the frames in a clip before and after the shot in the sequence

Trimming the A and B Sides of a Transition

When you trim, you trim at an edit (also called cut point or transition) in a sequence. Each edit point is preceded and followed by a shot.

- The shot before the edit is the **outgoing shot** or **A Side** of the edit.

- The shot after the edit is the **incoming shot** or **B Side** of the edit.

Note: Do not confuse outgoing and incoming *shots* of an *edit* with incoming and outgoing *handle* of a *clip*.

Outgoing (A) side   Incoming (B) side

Displaying the outgoing and incoming images in Trim mode

One of the most important things to do when performing a single-sided trim is to focus on how you want the shot to change, and then know how to execute the change that you want.

For example, if a shot seems too long and you want to shorten it before the next shot comes, you need to know that you want to trim the **outgoing** shot by **removing** frames. You would therefore trim the A side to the left.

Trimming on the A Side

You can perform single-roller trim on the A side to extend or shorten the edit.

Trimming the A Side

- When you extend the edit on the A side:

  - The edit point moves to the right.

  - Frames are removed from the handle and added to the tail of the shot.

  - The sequence is lengthened.

- When you shorten the edit on the A side:

  - The edit point moves to the left.

  - Frames are removed from the tail of the shot and added to the handle.

  - The sequence is shortened.

The following illustrations show what happens when you use single-roller trim to shorten or extend the edit on the A side.

Single-Roller Trim:
Shortening the edit on the A side

Single-Roller Trim:
Extending the edit on the A side

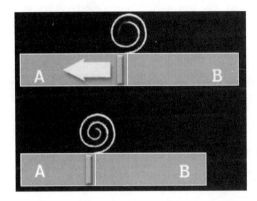 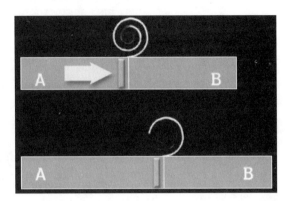

Trimming the A side of a transition

The following graphics illustrate what happens to the Timeline when you use a single-roller trim to extend the edit on the A side.

Before
Trimming

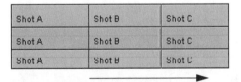

After
Trimming

Shot B is extended.

Shot C is unaffected yet pushed down.

Result of trimming the A side of a transition

Trimming on the B Side

Trimming the Outgoing (A) shot is fairly intuitive; trimming the Incoming (B) shot is not. Pay special attention to what happens when you trim the B shot. You can perform single-roller trim on the B side to extend or shorten the edit point.

Trimming the B Side

- When you extend the edit on the B side:
    - The edits downstream move to the right.
    - Frames are added to the head of the shot and removed from the handle.
    - The sequence is lengthened.
- When you shorten the edit on the B side:
    - The edits downstream move to the left.
    - Frames are removed from the head of the shot and added to the handle.
    - The sequence is shortened.

The following illustrations show what happens when you use single-roller trim to extend or shorten the edit on the B side.

Single-Roller Trim:
Extending the edit on the B side

Single-Roller Trim:
Shortening the edit on the B side

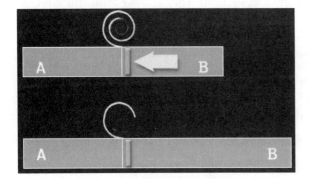
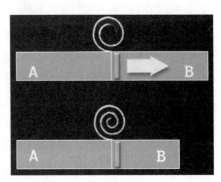

Trimming the B side of a transition

The following graphics illustrate what you see in the Timeline when you use a single-roller trim to shorten the shot on the B side.

Shot A	Shot B	Shot C
Shot A	Shot B	Shot C
Shot A	Shot B	Shot C

Before
Trimming

Shot A	Shot B	Sho
Shot A	Shot B	Sho
Shot A	Shot B	Sho

After
Trimming

Shot B is
unaffected.
Shot C is
shortened.

Result of trimming the B side of a transition

Examples of Single-Roller Trims

- A person makes a gesture at the end of the shot, but the gesture is not completed. To show the entire gesture; you want to extend the tail of the shot.

  a Select the transition in the Timeline between this shot and the following shot.

  b Click the picture of the outgoing (A side) frame.

  c Trim the tail of the outgoing shot by moving forward the appropriate number of frames.

- A person enters the frame but takes too long to reach a table in the middle of the room. You want to remove footage from the head of the shot.

  a Select the transition in the Timeline between this shot and the preceding shot.

  b Click the picture of the incoming (B side) frame.

  c Trim the head of the incoming shot by moving forward the appropriate number of frames.

Performing a Single-Roller Trim

This section explains how to enter Trim mode, make a single-roller trim, and exit Trim mode.

Entering Trim Mode

1 In the Timeline, park the position indicator near the transition you want to trim.

2 Click the Record Track buttons for the tracks you want to trim.

! **When you use single-rolling trimming with synced material, select all synced tracks to maintain sync.**

3 To enter Trim mode:

- Click the Trim Mode button in the Timeline toolbar or press the left bracket ([) key.

Performing a Single-Roller Trim

To perform a single-roller trim:

1 Click the picture of the outgoing (A side) or incoming (B side) frame.

Click A side or B side.

The pink Trim mode rollers in the Timeline move to the corresponding side to be trimmed, the mouse pointer becomes a Single-Roller icon, and the corresponding Trim box (in the Trim window) is highlighted.

Trimming the outgoing side

2 Use the Trim buttons to add frames to or remove frames from the selected material at the selected transition.

Trim Left
10 frames

Trim Right
10 frames

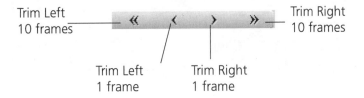

Trim Left
1 frame

Trim Right
1 frame

Trim buttons

3 To play the currently selected transition repeatedly, click the Play Loop button or press the 5 key.

The system plays the number of outgoing and incoming frames currently set in the Preroll and Postroll boxes in the Trim mode window.

4 To stop, click the Play Loop button again, or press the 5 key or space bar.

5 Trim additional frames until you like the result.

Exiting Trim Mode

To exit Trim mode and return to Source/Record mode:

▶ Click anywhere in the Timecode (TC1) track in the Timeline.

Dual-Roller Trimming

Dual-roller trimming affects both sides of a transition. Use dual-roller trimming to move the transition point earlier or later in the sequence, adding frames to one shot while subtracting the same number of frames from the adjacent shot. The combined duration of the two clips being trimmed does not change; and because both sides of the transition are equally affected, sync is maintained throughout the sequence.

The following illustrations show what happens when you use dual-roller trim to move the edit point earlier in the sequence.

Dual-Roller Trim: Before Trim

Dual-Roller Trim: After Trim Backward

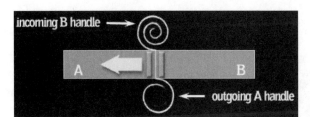

Using Trim mode to move a transition point

The following table explains what happens when you make a dual-roller trim. Unlike a single-roller trim, a dual-roller trim affects both the outgoing and incoming sides of a transition, and the length of the sequence does not change.

Table 4   Dual-Roller Trims

Trims Outgoing (A) Shot and Incoming (B) Shot	
Trim Backward	Removes frames from the tail, adds frames to the head, and the transition moves to the left; sequence length does not change.
Trim Forward	Adds frames to the tail, removes frames from the head, and the transition moves to right; sequence length does not change.

Entering Trim Mode

You enter Trim mode the same way as in single-roller trimming. (See "Entering Trim Mode" on page 100.)

Performing a Dual-Roller Trim

To perform a dual-roller trim:

1 When you enter Trim mode, you are automatically in dual-roller trimming. If you are in single-roller trim mode, click on the transition line between the frames to prepare for a dual-roller trim.

Click on the line between frames.

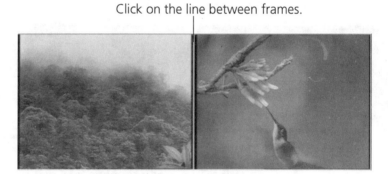

Both pink Trim mode rollers appear in the Timeline, the mouse pointer becomes a Dual-Roller icon, and both Trim boxes are highlighted.

 Trimming both sides

2 Use the Trim buttons to add frames to one side of the selected transition and remove them from the other.

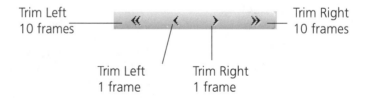

Trim Left 10 frames

Trim Right 10 frames

Trim Left 1 frame

Trim Right 1 frame

3 To play the currently selected transition repeatedly, click the Play Loop button or press 5.

4 To stop, click the Play Loop button again, or press the 5 key or space bar.

Exiting Trim Mode

You exit Trim mode the same way as in single-roller trimming. (See "Exiting Trim Mode" on page 98.)

Additional Trim Features

Now that you know the essential theory and practice of trimming, here are a few features to round out your knowledge.

Methods for Adding and Removing Frames

Use any of the following methods to trim by adding frames to one side of the selected transition and/or removing them from the other:

- Use the Trim buttons in the Trim window.

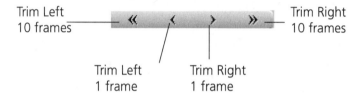

Trim Left
10 frames

Trim Right
10 frames

Trim Left
1 frame

Trim Right
1 frame

- Use the numeric keypad on the right side of the keyboard in one of the following ways:

  - Type a plus sign (+) and the number of frames (from 1-99) you want to move the edit forward, then press Enter.

  - Type a minus sign (-) and the number frames (from 1-99) you want to move the edit back, then press Enter.

  - Type a number larger than 99 to enter a timecode (for example, to enter 1 second and 2 frames, type 102). Or with Caps Lock off, type an f after a large number to enter it as a frame count (for example, to enter 200 frames, type 200, f, and press Enter).

!   **The (+) and (-) keys only refer to the direction of the trim. They do not necessarily indicate that frames will be added or removed. For example, a (+) operation on the B side of an edit will actually remove frames from the head of the B shot instead of adding them.**

- Trim using the Timeline:

  - Click a trim roller(s) in the Timeline, then drag the roller(s) forward or back in the sequence.

    If you are performing a one-sided trim, make sure the Trim cursor is pointed in the direction you want to trim.

  - Press and hold the Control (Windows) or ⌘ (Macintosh) key while dragging to snap to IN and OUT marks.

    Tip: You can use this method to snap to the previous or next transition.

    As you trim, the Trim boxes display the number of frames that have been trimmed from the outgoing and incoming sides of the transition.

The following table shows the equivalent methods for adding and removing frames, or to put it another way, moving backward and forward in time as you trim. The actions in the left column move a transition to the left in the Timeline; the actions in the right column move a transition to the right in the Timeline.

Table 5   Trimming Backward and Forward in a Clip

Moving Backward in Time	Moving Forward in Time
Negative (-) numbers	Positive (+) numbers
Drag Trim roller(s) left	Drag Trim roller(s) right

Scrubbing Audio While Trimming

Note: Don't forget to turn off Caps Lock when finished scrubbing.

▶ To scrub audio while you trim, press the Caps Lock key and solo the track you want to scrub.

Real-Time Effect Playback

Avid Xpress Pro and Avid Xpress DV can play most effects in real time (the exceptions are some motion and plug-in effects). In this book, we only cover video and audio dissolves.

Please note the following difference, depending on your system configuration:

- **Avid Xpress Pro without Avid Mojo and Avid Xpress DV:** Plays either real-time effects or outputs a DV signal (not both). This means you have to render all dissolves and other effects before outputting the sequence.

  If an external video monitor is connected to the system through the FireWire port, it will be blank when real-time effects are enabled. However, if your video card includes an S-Video preview connection, see the card manufacturer's manual on how to preview effects on an external video monitor.

- **Avid Xpress Pro with Avid Mojo:** Plays back all effects in real time and video output is always enabled.

Enabling or Disabling Real-time Effects (Avid Xpress Pro without Mojo and Avid Xpress DV):

You enable or disable real-time effect preview by toggling the Digital Video Out button on the right side of the Timeline toolbar.

▶ Click the Digital Video Out button in the Timeline toolbar.

Digital Video Out

Tip: Generally choose the first option until you are ready to output your sequence.

- Click so the button glows green (the default) if you want to preview real-time effects.

- Click so the button turns dark blue if you want to output your sequence.

Adding Dissolves

The Avid system uses the same basic method to create dissolves and fades. You can add a dissolve at any transition from Trim mode or from Source/Record mode.

To add dissolves at a transition point:

1 Place the position indicator on or near a transition in the Timeline.

2 Select the track(s) on which you want to add the dissolve.

 3 Click the Quick Transition button on the Timeline toolbar, or press \ (backslash) on the keyboard.

The Quick Transition dialog box appears.

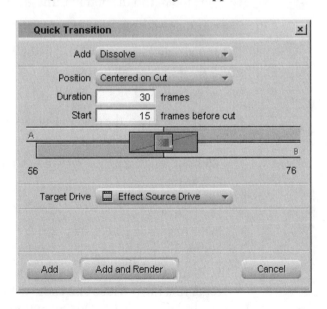

Adding and customizing dissolves in the Quick Transition dialog box

4 In the Quick Transition dialog box, specify the following fields:

- **Duration**: (number of frames to use for the dissolve's duration). The default is 30 fps for NTSC and 25 fps for PAL.

- **Position**: The position of the dissolve in relation to the cut: Starting, Centered, or Ending.

Tip: To fade up at the beginning of a sequence set the dissolve Position parameter to Starting at Cut. To fade down at the end of a sequence, set the dissolve Position parameter to Ending at Cut.

To add a dissolve, enough source media must exist on each side of the cut to last the duration of the transition. This extra media, as you know, is referred to as handle. If you attempt to add a dissolve where there is not enough handle, the system automatically adjusts to give you the longest possible transition. You can then adjust the duration or position, if desired, within the Quick Transition dialog box.

5 Choose the target drive where you want to store the media for rendered dissolves.

The default is Effect Source Drive, which stores the effect media file on the same disk as media for the clip on the A side of the transition.

6 (Without Avid Mojo) Click the Digital Video Out button on the Timeline toolbar so the button turns green.

7 Click Add or Add and Render.

The system can figure out which dissolves need to be added, and which need to be rendered.

When clicking Add and Render:

- With Avid Mojo, the system will not need to render video or audio dissolves.

- Without Avid Mojo, the system will render both types of dissolves.

When clicking Add:

- With Avid Mojo, the system will not need to render video or audio dissolves.

- Without Avid Mojo, the system adds the dissolves without rendering them. Video and audio dissolves play back if you enabled the Digital Video Out button.

Adding Audio Crossfades

Tip: Depending on the duration of the audio dissolves, the dissolves may have added undesired audio or cut off the desired audio. You may need to tweak the dissolves individually until you are satisfied.

On the Avid system, an audio crossfade is simply a dissolve applied to an audio transition. Audio crossfades will often eliminate pops in transitions. A crossfade of short duration (2-10 frames) can be used to smooth audio transitions. They may be especially important when making transitions between audio coming from different locations.

You can also select two useful options in the Audio Project settings: enable or disable real-time audio dissolves, and choose between two types of audio dissolves. To enable/disable real-time audio dissolves or change the type of audio dissolve:

1 Click the Settings tab in the Project window.

2 Open the Audio Project settings and click the Main tab.

3 Set Real-Time Audio Dissolves to Enable or Disable.

   You should disable real-time audio dissolves if you are experiencing audio delays during playback.

4 Set Dissolve Midpoint Attenuation.

   - **Const Power –3dB** (the default) uses constant power to maintain a consistent sound level through the midpoint of the dissolve. This setting is preferable, since it corrects the dip in gain created with the linear crossfade.

   - **Linear –6dB** uses a linear gradient to maintain a consistent amplitude through the midpoint of the dissolve. The gain dips midway through the crossfade, an action that you want to avoid.

! **If you will need to move your sequence to an older Avid system that does not have Constant Power dissolves, render the audio crossfades or they will become linear crossfades on the older system.**

5 Close the Audio Project settings.

Adding Dissolves from Trim Mode

If you are in Trim mode and want to add a dissolve to a transition you've been working on, add it in Trim mode. Also, if you have trimmed to the best of your ability and the transition is still a little rough, try adding a short dissolve to see if it helps.

To add a dissolve in Trim mode:

1 Enter Trim mode.

2 Select the transition and the track(s) where you want to add the dissolve.

3 Enter the duration in the Duration box and press Enter.

Position   Duration

This adds (and with Avid Mojo, renders) the dissolve at the selected transition and a Dissolve effect icon appears in the Timeline when you move the position indicator from that transition.

Without Avid Mojo, the dissolve plays as long as the Digital Video Out button is enabled (green).

4 If necessary, change the position by clicking the Position button and selecting the appropriate choice. (By default, the system creates a centered dissolve.)

Insufficient Handle

If you attempt to add a dissolve from the Trim window and there is not enough handle, the Insufficient Source dialog box appears.

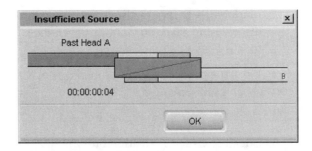

Insufficient handle to make a dissolve

The Insufficient Source dialog box shows you which side does not have enough handle and tells you how many frames are missing.

You can adjust the dissolve in the dialog box and click OK. Or you can adjust available handle on the clips using Trim mode, and then add the dissolve again with the new handles.

Deleting a Dissolve

To remove a dissolve from the Timeline:

1 In Source/Record mode, place the position indicator on the transition where you want to delete the dissolve.

2 Select the track that the dissolve is on.

 3 Select the Remove Effect button.

The dissolve is removed from the transition.

Adding Multiple Dissolves

To add a dissolve or audio crossfade to multiple transitions at once:

1 Mark an IN before the first transition where you want to add a dissolve and mark an OUT after the last transition where you want to add a dissolve.

2 Place the position indicator near one of the transitions within the IN and OUT marks.

3 Click the appropriate Track buttons.

4 Click the Quick Transition button.

5 Enter the duration and choose the relative position of the dissolve.

6 Check Apply to All Transitions.

7 Click Add and Render.

Review Questions

1 How do you solo an audio track? (See "Monitoring Audio" on page 82.)

2 In Trim mode, when only the B side is selected, and you enter +6 frames, will you add or subtract frames from the head of the shot? (See "Explaining Single-Roller Trims" on page 90.)

3 If the system is prepared to perform a single-roller trim, how can you activate dual-roller trimming at the same transition? (See "Dual-Roller Trimming" on page 99.)

4 What is one major difference between single-roller and dual-roller trimming?

5 A person completes a line of dialog, and you would like to add a brief pause before cutting to the listener. How would you trim the shot? (See "Explaining Single-Roller Trims" on page 90.)

6 Which Track buttons do you select if you want to trim V1 only but also want to monitor the audio only on track A2 as you trim? (See "Explaining Single-Roller Trims" on page 90.)

7 In the following table, two of the four boxes have mistakes; two are correct. Please identify the mistakes and correct them.

	Trim Outgoing (A) Shot	Trim Incoming (B) Shot
Trim Backward	Adds frames to the tail; transition moves to left and sequence is shortened.	Removes frames from the head; transitions downstream move to left and sequence is shortened.
Trim Forward	Adds frames to the tail; transition moves to right and sequence is lengthened.	Removes frames from the head; transitions downstream move to left and sequence is shortened.

8 Fill in the Frame counters to move the transition backward 20 frames without affecting the duration of the sequence.

9 What are these buttons?

10 How do you add multiple dissolves? (See "Adding Multiple Dissolves" on page 110.)

Exercise: Trim the Rainforest Sequence

In this exercise, you finish the Rain Forest PSA by fine-tuning your edits using dual-roller trim and adding dissolves.

Set up to make dual-roller trim

After dual-roller trim left: the first Wildlife shot is shorter, the second is longer. The length of the sequence does not change.

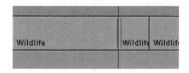

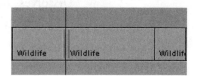

Note: If you prefer to work more on your own, follow the instructions in the outlined version at the end of the exercise.

Goals

- Use Digital Audio Scrub while trimming

- Use dual-roller trims to improve the rhythm of the video track

- Use dual-roller trims to cut the video to a beat of the music

- Fill in a gap between two shots by (dual-roller) trimming the shots toward each other

- Fade in the beginning of the sequence, and fade out the end (video track only)

- Create additional dissolves between shots

Fine-Tune the Sequence

In the first part of the exercise, you use dual-roller trim to fine-tune the Wildlife shots, make a cut occur on the beat of the music, and fill in a gap in the sequence.

Duplicate the Sequence

Before you start reworking the sequence, it's a good idea to *duplicate* it—this backup copy functions as a protection dub. If you make a mistake during the second cut, you can always go back to the original.

1 Open the **RF Sequences** bin.

2 Select the sequence (make sure to click its icon, not its name), and choose Edit > Duplicate.

A copy appears in the bin. The word Copy01 is appended to the sequence name.

3 Change the name of the copy to **Rainforest v2**.

4 Make sure Source/Record Editing is chosen in the Toolset menu.

5 Double-click the copied sequence to load it into the Record monitor.

Trim Wildlife Shots

Note: At the end of the exercise, you'll find a table of Trim buttons with keyboard equivalents that you might want to use as you work on this exercise.

In the last exercise, you added three shots from the Wildlife clip into your sequence. You can trim any of those shots, making them enter earlier or cut out later.

1 In the Timeline, lasso the transition of the **Wildlife** shot that you want to trim by positioning the cursor **above** the Timeline, pressing the mouse button, and dragging a lasso around the transition on only track V1. (Before lassoing, you may want to use the Zoom slider to zoom in on that section of the Timeline.)

The system enters Trim mode, and selects the transition you lassoed.

The Trim mode windows show the last frame of the outgoing shot on the left and the first frame of the incoming shot on the right. Notice the new buttons in the toolbar.

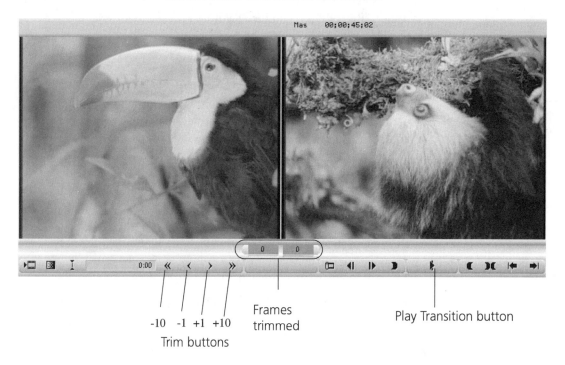

-10 -1 +1 +10
Trim buttons

Frames trimmed

Play Transition button

Trim mode toolbar with buttons labelled

2 Confirm that only the V1 Record Track button is on.

3 Click the Play Loop button, and decide whether you want to trim to the right or left.

4 To stop the playback loop, press the space bar or click the Play Loop button again.

5 Without pressing the mouse, move it over the highlighted transition, until it becomes a left-sided or right-sided roller (it doesn't matter which).

6 Press the mouse and drag the transition to the right or left, depending on what you want to trim. As you start to drag, the cursor becomes a hand. Notice the display that keeps track of the frames you have trimmed. Release the mouse.

Dragging to the right adds frames to the tail of the outgoing shot and removes frames from the head of the incoming one. Dragging to the left removes frames from the tail of the outgoing shot and adds frames to the head of the incoming one. In both cases, the duration of the video track remains the same.

7 Play the transition again and, if necessary, use the Trim Left and Right 1 Frame keys to adjust the trim.

8 When you are finished, return to Edit mode by clicking anywhere in the Timecode (**TC1**) track in the Timeline.

Exiting Trim mode by clicking in the Timecode track

9 Go to the area before the trim, and play through your cut.

10 Repeat the procedure to trim other **Wildlife** shots.

Cut to Music

Now, let's make a cut occur on a beat of the music.

1 Listen to the beginning of the sequence. Notice that at approximately
4 1/2 - 5 1/2 seconds into the sequence (between the first and second lines of voice-over), the music becomes rhythmic. Let's make the video cut to the first beat of this rhythmic passage.

2 Enter Trim mode at the **video** transition to the video for the voice-over line, "The trees will all fall down."

3 Click the Play Loop button. To stop the playback loop, press the space bar.

4 To prepare for audio scrubbing, Alt+click (Windows) or Option+click (Macintosh) the Audio Track Monitor button for track A2 (the music track) and press the Caps Lock key to turn on Digital Scrub.

5 Click the Trim 1 Frame key repeatedly until you add approximately 2/3 of a second to the head the incoming clip, so the cut occurs on the beat. With Digital Audio Scrub on, you should be able to hear a marked change in audio level, which indicates the beat of music.

Think before you act: Do you want to use the + or - Trim keys to make this trim? Why?

6 Play the transition again and, if necessary, use the Trim keys to trim the cut so that it occurs on the beat.

Trim Out Black Frames

This transition works, but now there are a few frames of black between the shot you just trimmed and the previous one. Let's trim out the black frames.

1 Drag a lasso around the previous edit, or press the A (Go to Previous Edit) key to move to the previous transition in Trim mode.

Notice that the incoming shot is a black frame.

2 Drag the Trim roller to the right until it won't move farther.

The incoming shot is no longer a black frame.

Tip: It's a good practice to turn off Digital Scrub when finished using it.

3 Press the Caps Lock key to turn off Digital Audio Scrub.

4 When you are finished, exit Trim mode.

5 Go to the start of the sequence, and play through your changes.

Trim Out Black Frames by Joining Two Clips

In some cases you may not want to fill a gap in the Timeline by adding another clip, but would instead prefer to simply join the two video clips on either side by making each a little longer. Let's try that for the gap between two voice-overs: "The planet will get too hot" and "We won't be able to breathe."

1 Place the position indicator on or near the **video** edit at the end of the VO line "Our planet will get too hot." to enter Trim mode.

2 Select track V1 and deselect all others.

3 Click the Trim button to enter Trim mode.

You are now set to perform a dual-roller trim at this transition.

4 Drag the Trim rollers to the right about halfway to the next edit.

5 Without leaving Trim mode, press the S (Go to Next Edit) key to advance to the next edit.

6 This time drag the pink rollers to the left, until the system prevents you from dragging any more.

7 Release the mouse.

The gap is now closed.

8 Click the Play Loop button.

9 Press the space bar to stop playback.

10 Continue trimming this edit to your liking.

11 Exit Trim mode, and play the section you just trimmed.

Trim to Bring in a Shot Earlier

Play the video edit with the corresponding audio "The birds can't fly home." It begins a little abruptly, so let's bring shot with the bird — or whichever shot you have put there — in a little earlier.

1 Enter Trim mode at the appropriate edit point.

2 Perform the appropriate dual-roller trim to bring the shot in earlier.

3 Play the trim.

4 Exit Trim mode, and play the section you just trimmed.

Add Dissolves

In this part of the exercise, you add fades and multiple dissolves.

Fade Up

In this part of the exercise, you will fade up the beginning of the sequence, on the video track.

1 Use the Home/First Frame key to go to the start of your sequence.

2 Make sure only the V1 Record Track button is on.

 3 (For systems without Avid Mojo) Click the Digital Video Out button on the Timeline toolbar to enable Real-Time Preview of Video Effects. The button turns green.

 4 Click the Quick Transition button on the Timeline toolbar.

The Quick Transition dialog box appears.

5 For the Position parameter, choose Starting at Cut.

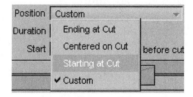

6 For the Duration parameter, use 30 frames (NTSC) or 25 frames (PAL).

7 Click Add.

Will you be able to play the fade?

Fade Down

Follow a similar procedure to fade down the video track at the end of the sequence. (Choose Ending at Cut for the Position.)

Add Multiple Dissolves

Add dissolves on at least two consecutive transitions on track V1.

1 Mark an IN before the first transition where you want to add a dissolve and mark an OUT after the last transition where you want to add a dissolve.

2 Select only the V1 Record Track button.

3 Place the position indicator near one of the transitions within the IN and OUT marks.

4 Click the Quick Transition button.

A dialog box appears.

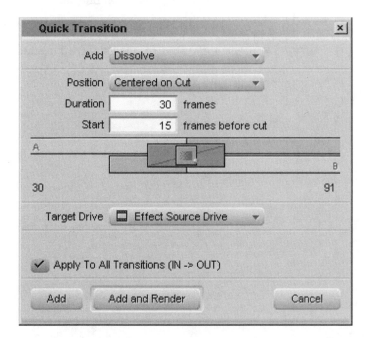

5 Choose the position, Centered on Cut.

6 Enter a duration.

7 Check the Skip Real-Time Effects and Apply to All Transitions check boxes.

8 Click Add.

9 Play that portion of the sequence to see the results.

Additional Exercises

Try any of the following:

- If gaps remain in the sequence, fill them by using one of the following methods:

    - Overwrite shots into the sequence to fill the gaps.

    - In some cases you may not want to fill a gap in the Timeline by adding another clip, but would instead prefer to simply join the two video clips on either side by making each a little longer. Use Trim mode to extend the shots on both sides of the gap.

- Continue trimming this edit to your liking, by dragging the Trim roller and using the Trim buttons.

- Replace one clip with another using Overwrite.

- Add a dissolve from within Trim mode.

Periodically play through your cut.

Fine-Tune the Sequence (Outlined)

! Use Digital Audio Scrub when you perform some of the trims.

1 Create a duplicate of the **RF sequence** you began in the last exercise. Name the duplicate sequence.

2 Perform at least two dual-roller trims to further improve the rhythm of the video track and to cut the video to a beat of the music.

3 Practice navigating from edit to edit within Trim mode by using the A (Go to Previous Edit) or S (Go to Next Edit) keys.

4 Periodically exit Trim mode and play through your cut.

5 When you finish using Digital Audio Scrub, turn off Caps Lock.

Now, see how to fill a gap in the sequence by extending shots in Trim mode:

1 To prepare, lift the last one or two seconds of any shot in the sequence. Then, trim the material back in the sequence by dragging the Trim rollers in the Timeline.

2 Lift an unwanted shot. Fill the gap in the Timeline by joining the two video clips on either side by making each a little longer. Do this by dragging the Trim rollers in the Timeline.

In this exercise, performing single-roller trims is optional because this isn't the best sequence to use single-roller trims. Do you know why? (Stop and think before you read on.) Because single-roller trims will remove the correspondence between the video and the voice-over segments that you created in the previous exercise. You might want to practice single-roller trims toward the end of the sequence to avoid loss of sync in the earlier part of the sequence.

Create Dissolves

In this part of the exercise, you add a fade in and out and several dissolves to the sequence.

1 Fade up the V1 track at the beginning of your Rain Forest sequence.

2 Fade out the V1 track at the end of the sequence.

3 Add dissolves to two or more consecutive transitions on the V1 track.

4 Add a dissolve from within Trim mode.

Use Trim Buttons

The following table lists various buttons (and their keyboard equivalents). Practice using them now, because recognizing them and understanding what they do will help you during the rest of the book, and also make you a more productive and efficient editor.

Table 6   Trim Keys and Buttons

Function	Button	Key
Enter Trim mode		[(left bracket)
Trim Left 1 frame		, (comma)
Trim Right 1 frame		. (period)
Trim Left 10 frames		M
Trim Right 10 frames		/
Play transition		5
Exit Trim mode		1, 2, 3, 4

Lesson 4 **Additional Editing Tools**

This lesson presents some powerful tools to aid you in the editing process, including ways to change settings, use the SuperBin and toolsets, create subclips, and storyboard edit a series of clips.

Objectives

After you complete this lesson, you will be able to:

- View and change settings
- Navigate effectively through the sequence
- Map buttons to the keyboard or a Command palette
- Use the SuperBin
- Use toolsets
- Create subclips
- Perform storyboard editing

Viewing and Changing Settings

Tip: User settings can be copied to a removable disk and used on another system. However, keep in mind that you might not be able to use your settings on an earlier version of the Avid system.

The Settings button in the Project window opens a list of features that you can customize and save for your particular work style, for example, you can change the automatic saving frequency.

To view or change a setting:

1 Click the Settings button in the Project window.

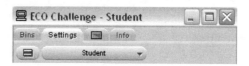

The Project Settings window opens.

2 Double-click the name of a setting to open a window that lists the options you can adjust.

For example, double-click Bin settings and Auto-Save interval to change the frequency with which the Avid system automatically saves your work.

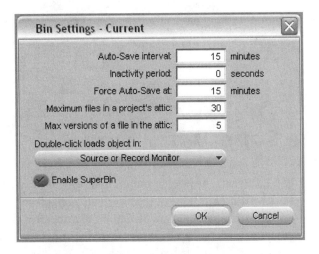

Bin settings options

Creating Multiple Versions of Settings

You can create multiple versions of a single setting file to accommodate different tasks. For example, you might have one setting for capturing and another for editing.

1 Activate the Project window and click the Settings button.

2 Choose All Settings from the Project Window Fast menu.

3 Single-click the setting name you want to duplicate to highlight it.

4 Choose Edit > Duplicate, or press Control+D (Windows) or ⌘+D (Macintosh) to create a copy of the setting called "Untitled."

5 Double-click the setting to open the dialog box, and reconfigure.

6 Close the dialog box and retitle the setting by clicking on the custom name.

7 Activate the setting by clicking once in the check mark column on the left side of the Project window.

Click here to activate an alternate version of the setting.

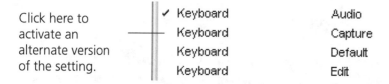

✓ Keyboard	Audio
Keyboard	Capture
Keyboard	Default
Keyboard	Edit

Using the SuperBin

Earlier in the book, you learned how to open bins by double-clicking the Bin icon. The Avid system also enables you to make efficient use of the screen real estate by using the SuperBin. The SuperBin feature lets you open multiple bins in a single Bin window, keeping them open with only one bin visible at a time.

To enable the SuperBin:

1 Click the Settings tab in the Project window.

2 Double-click Bin in the Settings list.

The Bin Settings dialog box appears.

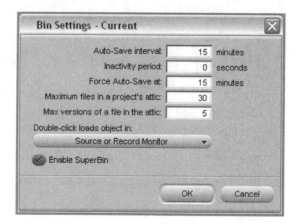

3 Click Enable SuperBin, and click OK.

4 Click the Bins tab in the Project window.

To open bins in the SuperBin:

1 Close all open bins.

2 Click a Bin icon in the Project window.

The bin opens in the SuperBin. The SuperBin icon appears in the upper-left corner, and the title is SuperBin: *bin name*.

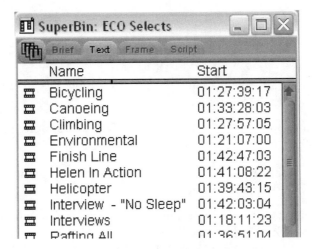

SuperBin: to make efficient use of screen real estate

Ways to Use the SuperBin

- To view a previously opened bin in the SuperBin, click the SuperBin icon and choose the bin from the menu of open bins. You can also click the open bin in the Project window.

  The bin reappears in the SuperBin.

- To move bins in and out of the SuperBin, double-click the open bin's icon in the Project window.

- To move clips and sequences into the SuperBin, drag the clip or sequence from an open bin window into the SuperBin.

- To move clips and sequences from the SuperBin into another bin, drag the clip or sequence from the SuperBin to a Bin icon in the Project window.

- To copy clips and sequences between the SuperBin and another bin, press the Alt key (Windows) or Option key (Macintosh) as you drag.

- To close one or more bins in the SuperBin, select the bin(s) in the Project window. Then right-click (Windows) or Shift+⌘+click (Macintosh) anywhere in the Project window and choose Close Selected Bins. If no other bins are in the SuperBin, the SuperBin closes.

- To delete one or more bins in the SuperBin, select the bin(s) in the Project window. Then right-click (Windows) or Shift+⌘+click (Macintosh) anywhere in the Project window and choose Delete Selected Bins. If no other bins are in the SuperBin, the SuperBin closes.

Additional Navigation Tools

Moving From One Transition to Another in the Timeline

 By default, the Go to Previous Edit button (or A key) and Go to Next Edit button (or S key) go to the first frame of each clip in the sequence on the selected tracks. These buttons are found below the Record monitor. These buttons work in Source/Record mode and Trim mode.

If you press the Alt (Windows) or Option (Macintosh) key while clicking the button, the position indicator moves to the head of the closest clip regardless of track selection.

Using the Clip Name Menu

Both the Source and Record monitors have Clip Name menus.

Source Monitor Clip Name Menu

The Clip Name menu on the source side lists the clips you recently loaded into the Source monitor, along with several other options. You can load multiple clips into the Source monitor at the same time, then access each one through the Clip Name menu.

1 Open the bin.

2 Do one of the following to select the clips you want to load into the Clip Name menu:

- In Frame view, Shift+click or lasso the clips.

- (Windows) In Text view, Control+click the clips, or click the first and Shift+click the last in a sequence of clips.

- (Macintosh) In Text view, Shift+click or lasso the clips.

3 Press one of the highlighted clips, and drag it to the Source monitor and release the mouse.

The clips are loaded, one after the other, in the Source monitor.

4 Click and hold the clip name to display the clips, which are listed in alphabetical order in the Clip Name menu. Choose the one you want to view in the Source monitor.

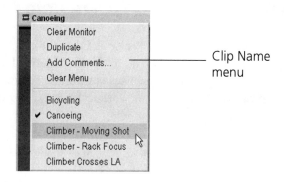

Clip Name menu in the Source monitor

Record Monitor Clip Name Menu

The Clip Name menu on the record side lists the sequences you recently loaded into the Record monitor along with the same options that are in the source side menu.

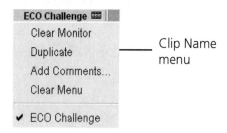

Clip Name menu in the Record monitor

Using the Timecode Display

Above the Source and Record monitor is a Timecode display that shows data about the source of the frame currently displayed in the monitor. This display lists timecode data about the sequence and also about the source clips that make up the sequence.

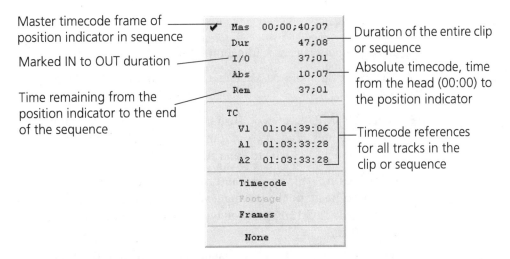

Master timecode frame of position indicator in sequence

Marked IN to OUT duration

Time remaining from the position indicator to the end of the sequence

Duration of the entire clip or sequence

Absolute timecode, time from the head (00:00) to the position indicator

Timecode references for all tracks in the clip or sequence

Timecode display options

To adjust the Timecode display, press the timecode display and choose a timecode type from the pop-up menu. The first five timecodes give you information about the sequence loaded in the Timeline.

- Mas (M on the interface): displays the location of the position indicator on the sequence's Timecode track (known as Master timecode)

- Dur (D): displays the duration of the entire clip or sequence

- I/O (IO): displays the marked IN to OUT duration

- Abs (Ab): displays the time from the head (00:00) to the position indicator (known as Absolute timecode)

- Rem (R): displays time remaining (from the position indicator to the end of the sequence)

- Below the dotted line, the source timecode references for all tracks in the clip or sequence are listed.

Seeking Frames

After loading a clip or sequence into a monitor, you can go to a specific frame by typing its video timecode. You can also move forward or backward from your current position in a clip or sequence by entering a frame offset.

Finding a Frame

1 Load a clip or sequence into a monitor.

2 Make sure the monitor is active (the active monitor has the brighter position bar).

3 Enter the SMPTE timecode using the numeric keypad, typing the hours, minutes, seconds, and frames, omitting leading zeros. Example: type 1230200 to enter 01:23:02:00.

Or, if you find a timecode that starts at the same hour as the current timecode, just type the last digits. For example, if the current timecode is 1:05:12:13 and you type 423, the system finds the frame at 1:05:04:23.

As you start typing, an entry field opens in the middle of the monitor, showing the numbers you type. (The system inserts the colons.)

4 Press Enter on the numeric keypad.

The position indicator locates the specified frame.

! **Whenever you use the numeric keypad, you must press Enter on the numeric keypad after typing the number. Do not use the Enter key on the main keyboard.**

! **The system beeps if it can't find specified timecode number in the clip or sequence. Check the Timecode display and make sure the appropriate timecode is shown.**

Check the Timecode Display

The monitor's timecode display determines the way the system references the numbers you type into the monitor. For example, if you want to reference the V1 (video) timecode of a clip, you must select V1 in the timecode display. If you instead display I/O timecode, the system won't be able to find a frame using the following method.

Typing a Frame Offset

You can also use the "frame offset" feature to move the position indicator from its current frame forward (or backward) a specified number of frames. (This procedure is similar to the method for adding and removing frames using the numeric keypad in Trim mode, covered in the previous lesson.)

To type a frame offset with a clip or sequence loaded in a monitor:

1 Make sure the monitor with the clip or sequence is active.

2 Use the numeric keypad on the right side of the keyboard and type a plus sign (+) before the number to move forward or a minus sign (-) before the number to move backward from the current position.

3 Enter the number of frames for the offset by doing one of the following:

   • Type numbers between 1-99 frames.

   • Enter 100 or a higher number to move forward or backward a specified number of seconds and frames.

   • With Caps Lock off, type an f after a large number to enter it as a frame count (for example, to enter 200 frames, type 200, then f).

   When going forward or backward, enter one less frame than desired, since the system counts the current frame. For example, if you want to move forward 3 seconds and 10 frames, type 309.

4 Press Enter.

5 If you press Enter again, the system remembers the last entry and advances the same number of frames.

Match Frame

The Match Frame function locates the frame currently displayed in the Record monitor, by loading the master clip that contains it into the Source monitor, and locating the frame with the blue position indicator. An IN point is marked at that location to prepare for making an edit.

This function is useful when you need to view earlier or later source footage from a clip in the sequence, or when you need to re-edit a clip into your sequence.

1 Move to the frame in your sequence that you want to match.

2 Select the track in the track panel that you want to match and deselect higher tracks.

3 Click the Match Frame button in the Tool palette (the Fast menu below the Source/Record monitors).

You can also use Match Frame to locate the frame currently displayed in the *Source* monitor. You would use this, for example, if a subclip is currently in the Source monitor and you want to locate the same frame in the master clip.

With the subclip in the Source monitor, press the Alt/Option key with the Match Frame button to load the master clip into the Source monitor.

Useful Application for Match Frame

If a portion of a clip is in your sequence, and you want to see what you left out, park at the beginning or end of the clip and use Match Frame to load the master clip into the Source monitor.

Mapping User-Selectable Buttons

The Command palette provides a central location for all user-selectable buttons. You can map buttons to any row of buttons, Command palette, or the keyboard. You can also map menu commands to various buttons and keys.

The Command palette groups buttons by editing category: Move, Play, Edit, Trim, FX, Color Correction, Other, and More. Tabs are displayed for each category and the buttons that perform those functions are displayed within each tab. You will find the following Command Palette windows most useful in these lessons.

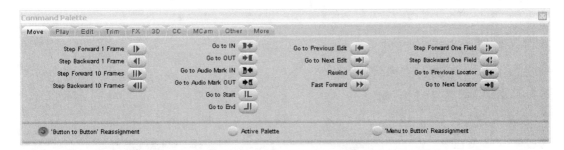

Move tab of the Command palette

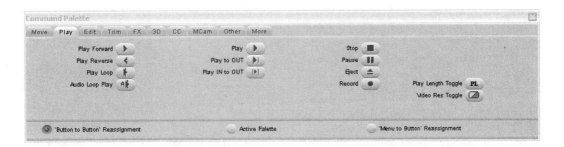

Play tab of the Command palette

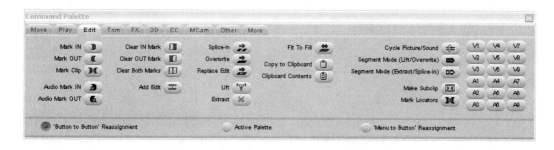

Edit tab of the Command palette

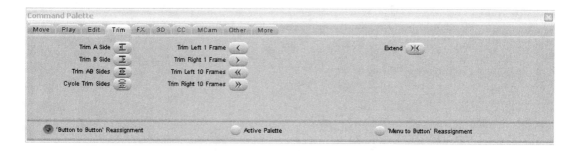

Trim tab of the Command palette

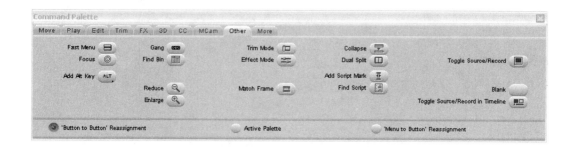

Other tab of the Command palette

Mapping a Button to a Button or Key

You probably realize by now that there are often several ways for you to perform an action on the Avid system. This versatility gives you incredible freedom to work in the way that's best for you.

The ability to customize buttons and the keyboard is one of the most crucial ways that you can tailor the Avid system to the way you work.

To remap buttons or keys using the Command palette:

1 Open the Keyboard settings from the Project window if you want to map a button to the keyboard.

2 Choose Tools > Command Palette.

The Command palette appears.

Click a tab.

Click the Button to Button Reassignment radio button.

3 Click the **Button to Button Reassignment** button if it's not selected.

4 Click the tab for the category that contains your user-selectable button.

Tip: If you hold the Shift key down when you drag the button to the Keyboard palette, you can map to Shift+[key]. This also works for other modifiers in addition to Shift.

5 Click and drag the button from the Command palette to the Keyboard palette or to a location on a row of buttons, for example, under a monitor or in the Tool palette.

(Windows only) You can't map to the F1 key.

6 Close the Command palette when you are finished.

As you get used to editing on the system and find that you constantly use certain features, you might want to map them to keys on the keyboard.

Saving Your Keyboard Settings

All of your interface modifications are saved as User settings and can be copied to a removable disk and used on another system. However, keep in mind that you might not be able to use your settings on an earlier version of the Avid system.

Mapping a Menu Command to a Button or Key

In addition to mapping a *button* from the Command palette, you can also map a *menu command* to a button or key.

To map menu commands:

1 Open the Keyboard settings from the Project window if you are going to map a menu item to the keyboard.

2 Choose Tools > Command Palette.

   The Command palette appears.

3 Click the **Menu to Button Reassignment** button.

Click the Menu to Button Reassignment button.

4 Click a button on the keyboard or a row of buttons.

   The pointer changes to a small white menu when it's over the keyboard.

5 Choose a command from a menu.

The initials for the command appear on the button.

Menu command (in this example, Tools>Command
Palette) mapped to keyboard

Customizing the keyboard

6 Close the Command palette when you are finished.

Using Toolsets

You can use predesigned work environments, called toolsets, to set up your desktop to perform some frequently used tasks. You can also link toolsets to settings.

1 Choose one of the following options from the Toolset menu or press the keys listed:

- Basic (the default) (Shift+F8)

  This toolset displays a basic set of windows: Project window, bin(s) (if open), the single-monitor Composer window, and the Timeline.

- Color Correction

  This toolset displays the Color Correction tool.

- Source/Record Editing (Shift+F9)

  This toolset displays the following windows: the Project window, the SuperBin (if activated) in Frame view, the Source/Record monitor, and the Timeline.

- Effects Editing (Shift+F10)

  This toolset displays tools used to create effects.

- Audio Editing (Shift+F11)

  This toolset displays tools used to adjust audio.

- Capture (Shift+F12)

  This toolset displays tools used to Capture media.

2 (Option) To customize a toolset:

Tip: If the bins are in Frame view and you prefer Text view, place one bin in Text view, and choose Toolset > Save Current. Any bin you open will now be in Text view.

a Choose the toolset you want to customize from the Toolset menu.

b Arrange, add, and remove windows on the desktop.

c Choose Toolset > Save Current.

Any time you return to this toolset this arrangement appears.

3 To remove the customization, choose Toolset > Restore Current to Default.

4 To return to the toolset for editing, choose Toolset > Source/Record Editing.

Displaying the Single or Dual Monitor

If the single Composer monitor is displayed and you want to display the Source/Record dual monitor, hold the mouse over the left edge of the Composer monitor. When the cursor becomes a double-sided arrow, click and drag the left edge to the left. When you release the mouse, the Source/Record monitor is displayed. (If it isn't, repeat and drag farther to the left.)

To return to the single monitor, drag the mouse in the opposite direction.

Linking Toolsets to Other Settings

You can link the current toolset to custom settings or to unnamed settings.

To link a toolset to another setting:

1 Give all settings you want to associate with a setting the same name.

For example, you might want to associate the Audio toolset with one or more other settings, which you name "audio."

✓ Interface	audio
Interface	default
Interface	digitize
✓ Keyboard	audio
Keyboard	default
Keyboard	digitize

2 Choose the toolset you want to link from the Toolset menu.

3 Choose Link Current to from the Toolset menu.

The Link Toolset dialog box appears.

4 Choose Link to Named Settings from the Links to Current Toolset pop-up menu.

143

5 Type the name of the other setting(s) to which you want to link the toolset.

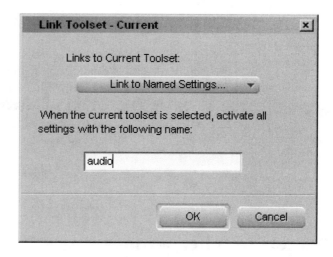

Linking toolsets to settings

6 Click OK.

The active toolset is linked to the custom setting you specified.

Subclipping and Storyboarding

Mastering subclipping and storyboarding will help you work more efficiently on the Avid system. Subclipping enables you to divide long clips into useful pieces. Storyboarding lets you move clips around in Frame view so that you can display a useful arrangement; it also gives you the ability to rapidly assemble a rough cut.

Creating a Subclip

Subclipping is used to divide portions of one clip into shorter clips, called subclips. The original master clip used to create a subclip remains intact. In addition, a subclip edited into a sequence can be expanded to reveal more material from the original master clip. Subclipping is a great tool for organizing your footage into manageable units and for creating storyboards.

Tip: Before you start creating subclips, adjust the Bin window to its largest size. This gives you the maximum target area to use to drag clips back to the bin.

To create a subclip:

1 Load the clip into the Source monitor.

2 Play the clip.

3 Mark an IN where you would like the subclip to begin and an OUT where you would like it to end.

4 To confirm the marks, press the Play IN to OUT (6) key.

5 Create the subclip:

Tip: To create a subclip, you can also click the Make Subclip button in the Tool Palette, or map the Make Subclip button from the Command palette (Edit tab) to the keyboard, and use it.

- Alt+drag the *picture* from the Source monitor to the destination bin.

A new item appears highlighted in the bin, called *clip name.Sub.n*, where *n* is the number of subclips you have created from that clip. Notice that the subclip icon is a small version of the clip icon.

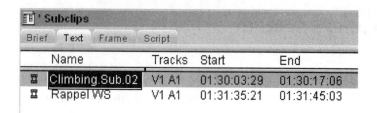

	Name	Tracks	Start	End
⊞	Climbing.Sub.02	V1 A1	01:30:03:29	01:30:17:06
⊞	Rappel WS	V1 A1	01:31:35:21	01:31:45:03

Naming subclips in the bin

! **If the icon looks like a regular master clip you did not press the modifying key while dragging the picture from the Source monitor. Dragging the picture without pressing this key results in the entire master clip being copied to your bin.**

Subclipping a clip does not restrict your access to the material in the master clip when trimming or performing other editing functions.

6 Name the subclip.

When creating subclip names, it's just as important to follow a good naming scheme as when creating clip names. This will help you keep track of your footage and make the subclip easy to locate when needed.

Useful Applications for Subclipping

Use subclipping to:

- Break up an interview into one subclip per question.

- Break up a dialog scene into separate passages of dialog.

- Isolate interesting cutaways.

- Create storyboards.

Creating a Storyboard

Tip: Storyboarding can be used effectively with subclipping, particularly if the master clips are long and will be used more than once in the storyboard.

You can storyboard clips in your bin and edit them into the sequence in the order your storyboard indicates, in one operation. You simply mark the parts of the clips you want to use, arrange them in the bin, and then make the batch edit.

1   Place the bin in Frame view.

2   Arrange the clips in your bin, from left-to-right and top-to-bottom, in the order you want them to appear in your sequence. If you need to make more room available in your bin, reduce the size of the clips by pressing Control+K (Windows) or ⌘+K (Macintosh).

Tip: To move to the next and preceding clip in the bin, press the Right and Left Arrow keys.

3   For each clip:

   a   Play or jog through the clip using any motion control keys on the keyboard, including Play (5), Step (1, 2, 3, and 4), J-K-L, and Home and End keys.

   b   Press the IN (I) and OUT (O) keys at the start and end of the material you want to use in your sequence.

!   **You must press the I and O keys while the footage is playing.**

!   **If you need to select source tracks, Alt+click (Windows) or Option+click (Macintosh) the clip name and select the source tracks from the menu that appears.**

4   Choose one of the following to prepare the sequence:

   • If you are adding the clips to an existing sequence, mark an IN point or place the position indicator at the location in the Timeline where you want to add the storyboarded clips and turn on the desired Record Track buttons.

   • Otherwise, create a new sequence. (Choose Clip > New Sequence, and if prompted choose a bin.)

5   In the bin, select all the desired clips by Shift-clicking each one individually, or by dragging a lasso box around them all.

6 To splice the clips into the sequence:

- Drag the clips to the position indicator (or edit point or IN/OUT mark) in the Timeline. (If you have created a new sequence, drag the clips into the Timeline window.)

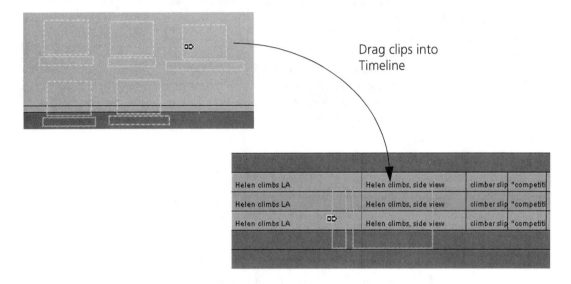

Drag clips into Timeline

Creating a storyboard of clips in the Timeline

When the clips are dragged over the Timeline, the cursor changes to a yellow arrow.

The clips are automatically spliced into your sequence at the position indicator.

Red arrow

To overwrite instead of splice the clips into the sequence, select the red arrow at the bottom of the Timeline before you drag the clips. The cursor changes to a red arrow.

Useful Applications for Storyboarding

Use storyboard editing to:

- Scan easily through a bunch of clips (by storyboard editing them into a sequence). Save the sequence so you can scan through the clips at any time.

- Quickly assemble a rough cut.

- Quickly assemble a long string of talking heads.

- Assemble an entire long program from multiple sequences for output and to time the show. To do this most effectively:

  a Number each "act" of your show so they are in story order in Text view.

  b Load each act into the Source or Record monitor, select all tracks, and remove IN and OUT marks.

  c Create a new sequence.

  d Display the bin in Frame view, and arrange the sequences in "act" order.

  e Storyboard edit the acts into one long sequence.

- Quickly add one or more clips into the Timeline. If you don't care about the order of the clips, you can also use this technique with the bin in Text view.

Review Questions

1 How do you customize specific features (menus, buttons, and so on) of the Avid system to suit your work preferences? (See "Viewing and Changing Settings" on page 126.)

2 When you change a setting, how can you use the setting on a different Avid system? (See "Viewing and Changing Settings" on page 126.)

3 How would you go to a frame in the sequence one second before the current location of the blue position indicator? (See "Seeking Frames" on page 134.)

4 How would you map the Clear IN button to a blank button in the Tool palette? (See "Mapping a Button to a Button or Key" on page 139.)

Exercise: Subclips and Storyboards

Note: If you prefer to work more on your own, follow the instructions in the outlined version at the end of the exercise.

In this exercise you begin a sequence that you'll continue to build in later exercises. This sequence uses documentary footage from "ECO Challenge, Utah," an annual multi-activity sporting competition. The finished sequence will be a 40-second advertising spot promoting the Canyonlands Outdoor Adventure School in Utah.

You'll use subclipping to divide clips into subclips, and then storyboard edit the subclips into a brief montage that will be used as the opening of a sequence. The exercise illustrates how storyboarding can be used to quickly create a rough cut.

Create subclips.

Arrange subclips into a storyboard.

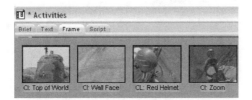

Edit the storyboard into a sequence.

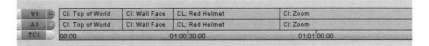

Goals

- Change User settings
- Map buttons and menu commands
- Subclip ECO Challenge clips
- Create a short montage of ECO Challenge activities by storyboard editing your subclips

Change Auto-Save Interval in Bin Settings

The Auto-Save interval regulates the frequency with which the Avid system automatically saves your work. The default is 15 minutes.

To change the Auto-Save interval:

1 Open the ECO Challenge project.

2 Click the Settings tab in the Project window.

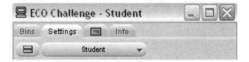

The Project Settings window opens.

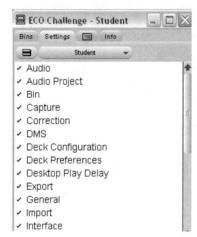

3 Double-click the Bin settings.

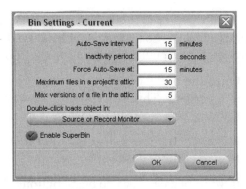

4 Change the Auto-Save interval, which regulates the frequency with which the Avid system automatically saves your work. Click OK.

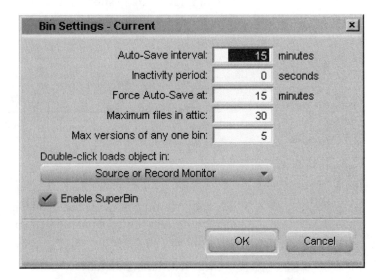

5 Click the Bins tab in the Project window.

Map Buttons to Tool Palette and Keys

Before subclipping and storyboarding, let's map some commands to buttons and keys. You'll then be able to use them in this and later exercises. First, you'll map buttons to the Tool palette.

1 Open the Tool Palette Fast menu. Drag your mouse off to the right of the palette. This will "tear off" the menu and leave it as a free standing palette of buttons when you release the mouse.

Make sure the Tool palette does not overlap with the Source or Record monitor or the image won't play back smoothly.

If the Tool palette has no blank buttons, drag one of its edges or corners to enlarge it and display blank buttons.

2 Choose Tools > Command Palette.

The Command palette appears.

3 Click the **Button to Button Reassignment** button if it's not selected.

Click the Button to Button Reassignment button.

4 Click and drag the following buttons from the Command palette to a blank button in the Tool palette (the specific Command Palette tab is indicated in parentheses):

- Clear IN Mark (Edit tab)

- Clear OUT Mark (Edit tab)

- Add Locator (More tab)

Map Fill Window Menu Command to F8 Key

The Fill Window Menu command can be used to arrange the clips neatly. This command will be useful when you create your storyboard later in the exercise. You'll map this menu command to a key on the keyboard.

1 Open the Keyboard palette from the Settings option in the Project window.

2 In the Command palette, click the **Menu to Button Reassignment** button.

Click the Menu to Button Reassignment button.

The pointer changes to a small white menu when it's over the keyboard.

3 Click the F8 button on the Keyboard palette.

4 Choose Bin > Fill Window.

The initials for the command appear on the button.

Menu command
mapped to keyboard

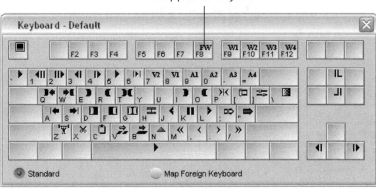

5 Close the Command palette and Keyboard palette.

6 Now, whenever you want to use the Fill Window command, press the F8 key. (You must be in Frame view to use this feature.)

Activate the SuperBin

You need to enable the SuperBin in the Bin settings before you can open bins into the SuperBin.

1 Click the Settings tab in the Project window.

2 Double-click Bin in the Settings scroll list.

The Bin Settings dialog box appears.

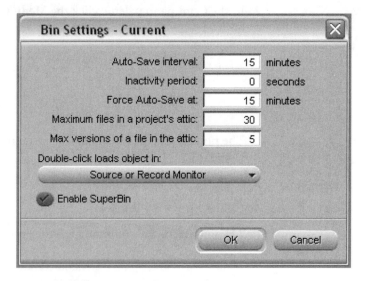

3 Click Enable SuperBin, and click OK.

4 Click the Bins tab in the Project window.

Practice Opening Bins in the SuperBin

To open bins in the SuperBin:

1 Close any open bins.

2 Click once on the **ECO Selects** Bin icon.

The bin opens in the SuperBin. The SuperBin icon appears in the upper-left corner, and the title is SuperBin: *bin name*.

SuperBin icon ———

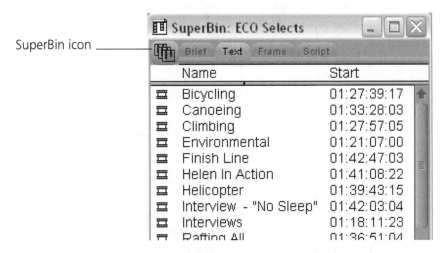

Name	Start
Bicycling	01:27:39:17
Canoeing	01:33:28:03
Climbing	01:27:57:05
Environmental	01:21:07:00
Finish Line	01:42:47:03
Helen In Action	01:41:08:22
Helicopter	01:39:43:15
Interview - "No Sleep"	01:42:03:04
Interviews	01:18:11:23
Rafting All	01:36:51:04

3 Create a new bin and name it **Activities**. This bin will hold the subclips you are about to create.

Now two bins are open (look at the Bin icons in the Project window to confirm), but only the last one you opened is visible.

4 To view **ECO Selects** bin (still open) in the SuperBin, click the bin in the Project window.

5 Do you want to continue using the SuperBin? If not, close it, change the Bin setting, and open bins by double-clicking.

Subclip Climbing Clips

When you are editing you want to know the content of your shots quickly. Subclipping is a great tool for giving you faster access to the contents of longer shots. In this part of the exercise, you will create subclips of a long clip, **Climbing**, to make the material more manageable.

After creating the subclips, you will storyboard edit some of them into a video montage of approximately 15 seconds.

Create Subclips

The Climbing clip is quite long, and contains separate shots. Let's create five subclips for this clip.

1 Load the **Climbing** clip from the **ECO Selects** bin into the Source monitor.

2 Mark an IN and OUT point for the first shot in the Climbing clip. Practice using the J-K-L keys to move through the clip. *Don't worry about being frame accurate; subclipping can be done quickly. Remember you still have access to the entire clip when you trim.*

3 Alt+drag the *picture* from the Source monitor to the **Activities** bin. Release the mouse.

A subclip appears in the bin. Its name is **Climbing, Sub.01**.

Tip: Consider naming all subclips of the same subject with the same prefix. For example, begin climbing subclips with "cl." The reason will be clear when we discuss sorting and sifting.

4 The subclip name is highlighted, so type a name and press Enter. Choose a meaningful name, for example: "**cl: rotate & zoom out on climber.**"

5 Create subclips for at least four additional shots in the Climbing clip, renaming each subclip when it appears in the bin.

Storyboard Edit a Short Montage

In the previous section, you made your footage more accessible by creating subclips. For this part of the exercise, you will use some of these subclips to create a **15-second montage of climbing shots**. In the next exercise you will add narration and music under this montage, and it will be the beginning of your ECO Challenge sequence.

This section takes you through the following steps: First, you will decide which subclips you want to include in the montage, and organize them into a storyboard. Then, you will mark the sections you want to use. Finally, you will edit the subclips as a batch into a new sequence.

When building the video montage, do not worry about choosing the perfect shots. Remember, this is a practice exercise. It is more important to take the time to understand what you are doing and have fun!

Arrange the Subclips into a Storyboard

1 Create a bin to hold your ECO Challenge sequence. Name it **ECO Sequences**. Leave the bin open.

2 Make sure the **Activities** bin is in Frame view. (With SuperBin, you can no longer see the ECO Sequences bin, but it is open.)

3 If you want to change the frame size, click once in the bin to highlight it and press Control+K (Windows) or ⌘+K (Macintosh) to shrink or Control+L (Windows) or ⌘+L (Macintosh) to enlarge.

4 Move the subclips you want to use to a clear area at the bottom of the bin, positioning them from left to right, and top to bottom, in the order you want them to appear in the sequence. You should use at least five subclips in your montage. (The montage should be approximately 15 seconds, but don't worry, we also give you time to shorten or lengthen the montage at the end of the exercise.)

   You can quickly arrange clips in a storyboard, without paying attention to neatness or lining up frames exactly.

5 Press the F8 key to line up the subclips.

Mark IN and OUT Points in the Storyboarded Subclips

For each subclip you will use in your storyboard:

1 Play or step through the clip using any motion control keys on the keyboard, including Play (5), Step (1, 2, 3, and 4), J-K-L, and Home and End keys.

2 Press the IN (I) and OUT (O) keys at the start and end of the material you want to use in your sequence. (Do not worry about being frame-exact. You will have a chance to trim the clips in the next section.)

! **You must press the I and O keys while the footage is playing.**

Edit the Storyboard into a New Sequence

1 Select all of the subclips in your storyboard by dragging a lasso around them. Press and hold the mouse button in the gray space just to the left of the left-most subclip, then drag down and to the right. A box forms as you move.

2 Release the mouse button when the box touches all the storyboarded subclips.

The storyboarded subclips are all highlighted.

Tip: Closing the bin that holds the sequence will achieve the same result.

3 There should not be a sequence in the Timeline. If there is one, clear it by choosing Clear Monitor from the Clip Name menu in the upper-right corner of the monitor.

4 Drag one of the subclips into the (empty) Timeline window. All the other subclips follow. Release the mouse.

5 If the Select a Bin dialog box appears, choose the **ECO Sequences** bin.

6 A new sequence appears in the Timeline, with all the subclips from your storyboard. The sequence is stored in the ECO Sequences bin. (If the sequence appears instead in the Activities bin, move it into the ECO Sequences bin.)

7 Name the sequence **ECO Challenge v1**.

8 Play the sequence.

Revise the Sequence

Now you should shorten or lengthen your montage to 15 seconds.

1 To display the entire duration of the sequence in the Timecode display, press the Timecode display above the Record monitor and choose Dur from the pop-up menu.

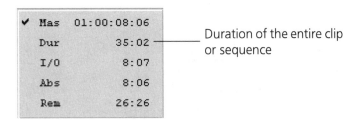

Duration of the entire clip or sequence

2 If it is exactly 15 seconds in duration, you're finished.

Use single-roller trimming to shorten or lengthen the transitions. Here is the basic procedure. Refer back to the Trimming lesson if you need more instruction.

1 Play the sequence and decide on a shot you want to shorten or lengthen. Plan how you will trim the shot: Which transition will you trim? Will you trim the incoming or outgoing shot? Will you trim forward or backward?

2 Enter Trim mode at the appropriate transition.

3 Click the picture of the outgoing (A side) or incoming (B side) frame.

The pink Trim Mode rollers in the Timeline move to the corresponding side to be trimmed, the mouse pointer becomes a Single-Roller icon, and the corresponding Trim boxes above the Timeline are highlighted.

4 Use the Trim buttons (or another method you learned) to add frames to or remove frames from the selected material at the selected transition.

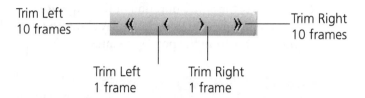

Trim Left
10 frames

Trim Right
10 frames

Trim Left
1 frame

Trim Right
1 frame

5 Play the transition.

6 Stop play.

7 Adjust the trim further, if necessary.

8 When you are satisfied, press the A (Go to Previous Edit) or S (Go to Next Edit) key go to another transition while staying in Trim mode. (Or if you prefer, exit Trim mode and enter it again at another transition.)

9 Trim other transitions by repeating this procedure.

10 Exit Trim mode.

Additional Exercises

Try any of the following:

- Map additional buttons and menu items to the keyboard. In particular, map the following buttons (the Command Palette tabs are identified) to keys:

  - Make Subclip (Edit tab)

  - Fast Forward (Move tab)

  - Rewind (Move tab)

  - Match Frame (Other tab)

- Practice the navigational tools introduced in Lesson 4.

- Practice trimming using the J-K-L keys, particularly by holding down the K key and using the J and L keys to trim frame-by-frame.

- Change other User settings you would find helpful.

Subclips and Storyboards (Outlined)

Change Settings

1 Open the ECO Challenge project.

2 In the Bin settings, change the Auto-Save interval from 15 to 10 or 20 minutes.

3 Change any other User settings you would find helpful.

Customize your Keyboard

1 Map the Clear IN, and Clear OUT buttons (and any others) from the Command palette to a blank button or key on the keyboard.

2 Map the Fill Window menu item from the Bin menu (and any others) to a key on the keyboard. You can use this key later to neaten your storyboard of clips in the bin.

Create the SuperBin

▶ Activate the SuperBin (in Bin settings) and practice using it. Then if you prefer using the standard bin, close the SuperBin and change the Bin setting.

Subclip

In this section you will subclip and storyboard a long clip, **Climbing.** You will use some of the subclips in a 15-second montage that will play at the start of the ECO Challenge sequence you will work on for several exercises.

1 Create a new bin to hold the subclips and name it **Activities**.

2 Create at least five subclips for the **Climbing** clip, giving them meaningful names. The clip is found in the **ECO Selects** bin.

Practice using two methods for creating subclips.

Storyboard the Subclips

1 Arrange the subclips you want to use in a storyboard, and use your Fill Window key to neaten the storyboard. You should use at least 5 subclips for the 15-second montage.

2 Mark the sections you want to use by doing the following:

a Play or step through the clip using the motion keys.

b Press the IN and OUT keys at the start and end of the material you want to use in your sequence.

3 Drag the subclips as a batch into the (empty) Timeline window.

4 Create a new sequence and store it in a bin that will hold your ECO Challenge sequences.

5 Practice trimming using the J-K-L keys, particularly by holding down the K key and using the J and L keys to trim frame by frame.

Revise the Sequence

1 Display the entire duration of the sequence in the Timecode display above the Record monitor.

2 If the montage is not exactly 15 seconds long, use single-roller trimming to shorten or lengthen the sequence. (See the Trimming lesson if you need further guidance.)

Lesson 5 **Saving Your Work**

This lesson shows you how to save and back up your projects.

Objectives

After you complete this lesson, you will be able to:

- Save projects
- Back up projects and bins

Saving Bins

When you are working on a computer-based editing system, it is important to save and back up your work. Although the Avid system automatically saves for you at regular intervals, you should get into the habit of explicitly saving your bins to protect your work in case of power outages or other mishaps.

Auto-Save

The Avid system automatically saves changes to your work every 15 minutes. When this occurs, any open bins are updated with changes you have made since the last save and copies of these bins are placed in the Avid Attic.

Explicit Saves

An explicit save is one where you, the user, manually save something you are working on. An asterisk (Windows) or diamond (Macintosh) in the title bar of your bin indicates that a change has been made since your last save.

Windows (asterisk)   Macintosh (diamond)

Unsaved bin symbol

Saving a Bin

When you explicitly save a bin, a backup copy is made and placed in a storage area and your original bin file is updated.

To save a bin:

1 Click the bin to activate it.

2 Choose File > Save Bin, or press Control+S (Windows) or ⌘+S (Macintosh).

   If you save the SuperBin, all bins opened in it are saved.

   The Save Bin command is dimmed if the active bin has already been saved.

Saving All Bins in a Project

Note: If your goal is to save changes to the sequence you are working on, make sure you know which bin it is in, and save that bin. If you are not sure and don't want to take the time to locate the sequence, save all your bins.

1 Click the Project window to activate it, but don't select any individual bins listed in the window.

2 Choose File > Save All, or press Control+S (Windows) or ⌘+S (Macintosh).

   The system saves all the open bins for the project as well as your settings.

Retrieving Bins from the Avid Attic

The Avid Attic is a folder on the system's internal drive where backup copies of bins in a project are stored. Each project has its own folder within the attic folder, and the backup bin files are stored in the appropriate project folder. Whenever you save or auto-save, a backup copy is placed in the project folder within the Avid Attic folder, with '.bak' and a number added to the bin name. Each new backup is placed in this folder until the number of copies in the folder reaches a maximum (which you can set). Once the maximum is reached, subsequent backup files replace older versions of the same file.

The Avid Attic folder is useful when you have lost information in a bin, or if you wish to return to an earlier version of your sequence.

To retrieve a bin from the Avid Attic folder:

1 (Option) From within the Avid application, move any needed clips from the bin you will replace to another bin, and delete the bin you will replace.

2 Close all open bins.

3 If you are experiencing any technical problems, quit the Avid application.

4 Open the Avid Attic folder using the following navigation:

- (Windows) C:\Program Files\Avid*Avid application*\Avid Attic

- (Macintosh) Avid internal drive\Users\Shared\Avid Attic

5 Open the folder for the project.

6 Identify the bin you wish to retrieve by its name and Last Modified date (in this case the date and time the bin was saved into the Avid Attic).

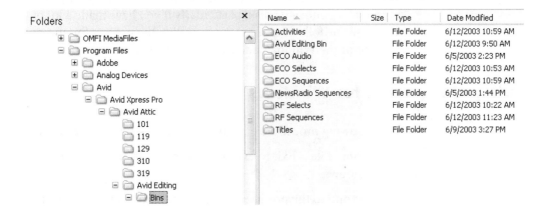

Navigating to the Avid Attic

7 Make a copy of the bin, by doing one of the following:

- (Windows) Press Control+C (Copy), click anywhere in the folder, and then press Control+V (Paste).

- (Macintosh) Press ⌘+D.

8 Rename the copy.

9 Drag that bin into the appropriate Project folder in the Avid Projects folder.

10 Drag the original bin from the Project folder to the trash.

11 Return to the Avid application. If you previously quit the application:

  a Launch the Avid application.

  b Open the project.

  c Open the backup bin by choosing File > Open Bin.

  d In the dialog box that appears, navigate through the project folders until you locate the backup bin and select it.

! **If you did not close the bin for which you are retrieving a backup (step 2), you will get an error message stating that you cannot have more than one copy of a bin open at the same time.**

Ending the Session

When you end the session, it's a good idea to back up your project and bins onto a removable disk, particularly if you have made a lot of changes. The following procedures outline the process for ending the session for the Windows and Macintosh systems.

Ending the Session for Windows

The following procedure explains how to back up your project to disk:

1 Choose File > Exit to exit the Avid application and return to Windows.

2 Respond to the prompt asking if you want your work saved.

The system saves the project, closes the Avid application, and puts you back to the desktop.

Tip: If you have a large Project folder, consider backing up to a removable drive, such as a CD-ROM drive.

3 Insert a backup disk into the disk drive.

4 If the disk is unformatted, format it by double-clicking the "My Computer" icon and choosing File > Format.

5 Open the C: drive.

6 Open the Program Files folder, Avid folder, and Avid Projects folder.

7 Copy the entire project or selected bins to the backup disk.

Tip: You can also right-click the appropriate folder, select Copy, and right-click the destination drive and select Paste.

- If backing up the entire project, drag the Project folder with bins and projects enclosed to the floppy disk.

- If backing up selected bins, double-click the Project folder that contains the bin(s) you want to back up, and drag the Bin icon(s) to the floppy disk.

Note: For safety, you should save at least a week's worth of work on separate disks rather than backing up on a single disk.

8 When the system finishes copying the files, eject the disk.

Ending the Session for Macintosh

1 Choose File > Quit.

The system saves the project and closes the Avid application.

Tip: If you have a large Project folder, consider backing up to a removable drive, such as a CD-ROM drive.

2 Insert a backup disk into the disk drive.

3 If the disk is blank, click Initialize both times the prompt appears in the dialog box, and name the disk if prompted.

4 Open the Avid drive.

5 Open the Avid Projects folder.

Note: For safety, you should save at least a week's worth of work on separate disks rather than backing up on a single disk. In other words, you have a "Monday" disk, "Tuesday" disk, and so on.

6 Back up the entire project or selected bins.

- If backing up the entire project, drag the Project folder with bins and projects enclosed to the backup disk.

- If backing up selected bins, double-click the Project folder that contains the bin(s) you want to back up, and drag the Bin icon(s) to the backup disk.

7 When the system finishes copying the files, eject the disk.

Review Questions

1 How do you explicitly save the sequence you are working on? (See "Explicit Saves" on page 166.)

2 What does an asterisk or diamond in the title bar of your bin indicate? Circle one of the following. (See "Explicit Saves" on page 166.)

   a That the active bin was just saved by the Auto-Save feature.

   b That the bin has been altered since your last save.

3 You have been working on a sequence for several hours and decide you want to go back to an earlier version. How can you find that sequence? (See "Retrieving Bins from the Avid Attic" on page 168.)

4 You need to abruptly end your session. Do you need to explicitly (manually) save your work before leaving the Avid application? Please explain. (See "Ending the Session" on page 170.)

Exercise: Back Up Your Project

In this exercise, you back up your project and bins. You should do this at the end of each session, whether for these lessons or in your own work. It is one of the most important safety precautions you can take to preserve your work.

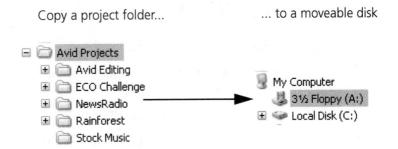

Copy a project folder...   ... to a moveable disk

Goal

- Back up your project

End the Session

When you are ready to end the session, back up your Rainforest and ECO Challenge projects (and bins) onto a floppy disk (or CD-ROM). The following procedures outline the process for ending the session for the Windows and Macintosh systems.

Back Up Two Projects (Windows)

To back up the **Rainforest** and **ECO Challenge** projects:

1 Choose File > Exit to exit the Avid application and return to Windows.

2 Respond to the prompt asking if you want your work saved.

The system saves the project, closes the Avid application, and puts you back to the desktop.

3 Insert your backup disk into the disk drive.

4 If the disk is unformatted, format it by double-clicking the "My Computer" icon and choosing File > Format.

5 Open **C:\Program Files\Avid*Avid application*\Avid Projects folder.**

6 To back up the entire **Rainforest** and **ECO Challenge** projects, drag both Project folders with bins and project files enclosed to the floppy disk (3 1/2 Floppy (A:) in Windows Explorer or "My Computer").

7 When the system finishes copying the files, eject the disk.

Back Up Two Projects (Macintosh)

To back up the **Rainforest** and **ECO Challenge** projects:

1 Choose File > Quit.

The system saves the project and closes the Avid application.

2 Insert your backup disk into the disk drive.

3 If the disk is blank, click Initialize both times the prompt appears in the dialog box, and name the disk if prompted.

4 Open the Avid drive.

5 Open the **Avid Projects folder**.

6 To back up the entire **Rainforest** and **ECO Challenge** projects, drag Project folders with bins and project files enclosed to the backup disk.

7 When the system finishes copying the files, eject the disk.

Lesson 6 Editing Dialog

Working with synced dialog requires that you pay close attention to your edits, especially when trimming. The Avid system provides a host of tools to help you maintain sync and to regain sync should you lose it.

This lesson stresses a problem-solving approach to the intricacies of working with dialog and audio.

Objectives

After you complete this lesson, you will be able to:

- Trim dialog
- Create split edits
- Prevent breaking sync and regain sync

Trimming Dialog

In this section, we review single-roller trim and present a new way to trim using J-K-L functionality.

Adjusting Dialog Rhythm Using Single-Roller Trim

You use single-roller trimming to trim the shots in a scene until you like the rhythm of the dialog (at this point, you are not considering the visuals). This focus on dialog cutting is often referred to as the radio edit. The dialog should flow smoothly, with an appropriate speed and rhythm for the scene. Remember, single-roller trims reveal or remove frames from the outgoing or incoming shot of a transition.

To review single-roller trim:

1 Enter Trim mode.

2 Activate the Record Track buttons for the synced tracks.

3 Click the picture of the outgoing (A side) or incoming (B side) frame.

4 Add frames to or remove frames from the selected material at the selected transition by using the Trim buttons (or any other method you have learned).

5 Click the Play Loop button or press the 5 key.

6 To stop, click the Play Loop button again, or press the 5 key or space bar.

7 Exit Trim mode.

J-K-L Trimming

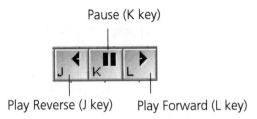

Pause (K key)

Play Reverse (J key)   Play Forward (L key)

There are many ways to trim a transition in Trim mode. Some editors use the Trim buttons, the numeric keypad, or drag the pink rollers in the Timeline. Although these methods can be useful, they are not very dynamic because you must play your edit first, stop, and then trim.

Another more visual method that allows you to watch and trim at the same time is called J-K-L trimming. This method is powerful because it plays your incoming and/or outgoing material beyond the edit in the Timeline, allowing you to see your source material. Trimming with J-K-L keys also allows you to scrub audio as you trim.

J-K-L play works in Trim mode just as it does in Source/Record mode, except that you actually trim frames as you go forward or back.

Activating the J-K-L Trim Setting

J-K-L trimming is deselected by default, so you need to activate it in Trim settings.

1 Double-click Trim in the Settings scroll list in the Project window.

The Trim Settings dialog box opens.

2 Click the Features tab.

3 Select J-K-L Trim.

A check mark appears next to the option. You can now trim with the J-K-L keys.

Tip: You can use this technique to extend or trim long sections of clips quickly, for example, trimming in additional interview material while you watch it in real time, or faster than real time.

To use J-K-L Trim:

1 Enter Trim mode.

2 Place rollers at the appropriate points.

3 If you want to trim back from the edit, press the J key alone or J-K combination. At the desired frame, press the K key (or press the space bar) to stop playback and perform the trim.

4 If you want to trim forward from the current edit, press the L key alone or K-L combination. At the desired frame, press the K key (or press the space bar) to stop playback and perform the trim.

   The system tracks the overall number of frames you have trimmed from either side in the outgoing and incoming trim boxes.

5 If you are not sure which way you want to trim, press the J key to back up a little, and then press the L key to take you forward again. Press the K key to choose your new edit.

   J-K-L trim will never completely trim away a shot. It will stop when one frame of the clip remains. If you trim away too much material, just reverse your direction to add more of the shot back in again.

You can trim back and forth over the transition by pressing the K key with the middle finger and pressing the J and L keys alternately.

Also, when using dual-roller trimming you can switch back and forth between monitoring the incoming or outgoing audio at any time by moving your cursor between the A side and B side of the monitor. (You cannot do this while performing a trim, just while setting it up.) The green light below the monitor indicates which audio is being monitored and which side is displayed.

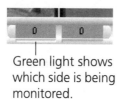

Green light shows which side is being monitored.

Green light (in Trim mode) for monitoring audio

Creating Split Edits

After you have trimmed the dialog of a scene using single-roller trimming (or J-K-L trimming), the dialog sounds good. However, the sequence is still a series of straight cuts, where the video and audio start and end at the same point. This can be monotonous for the viewer. Also, if you look at the visuals, you will undoubtedly see things to correct at the beginning and end of shots, such as an incomplete action or an inappropriate expression.

Split edits to the rescue! You use split edits to trim the audio and video separately, to vary the rhythm of a dialog scene and to fix problems. A split edit (also called an L-cut or overlap cut) is one in which the video and audio start or end at different points. For example, you might use a split edit to linger on Character A's reaction while hearing Character B begin to respond. You can create a split edit by using dual-roller trimming or the Extend function.

Split edit operation

Creating Split Edits Using Dual-Roller Trims

1. Start by editing a sequence using straight cuts.

2. Enter Trim mode at the transition where you want the split edit to occur.

3. Turn off the Track button(s) for either audio or video, depending on whether you want to extend the video over the audio or the audio under the video.

4. With both sides of the transition selected, slide the edit point right or left on the Timeline.

   You can also use any other trim method to adjust the edit point.

5. Play your edit while still in Trim mode.

6. Exit Trim mode.

Creating Split Edits Using the Extend Function

The Extend function allows you to create a split edit without going into Trim mode. With this feature, you slide an edit point left or right in the Timeline, thus trimming frames from one side of the transition and adding them to the other. The Extend function prevents you from losing sync, and also enables you to mark the edit point on-the-fly.

1 Start by editing several straight cuts together.

2 Turn off the Track button(s) for either audio or video, depending on whether you want to extend the video over the audio, or the audio under the video.

3 Play the edit that you want to split and decide where you want the video or audio edit to begin or end.

Tip: To create a split edit on-the-fly, map the Extend button (Command palette, Trim tab) to Shift+I or Shift+E (and to Shift+O or Shift+R). This will allow you to mark the IN (or OUT) mark on-the-fly, and then press Shift+I (or one of the other combinations) to make the edit.

4 If you want the edit to start earlier than it does, mark an IN at that point. If you want it to end later than it does, mark an OUT at that point.

In this example, video will be extended to the mark OUT.

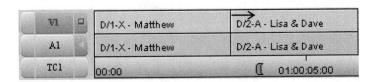

Extend edit to the mark OUT

In this example, audio will be extended to the mark IN.

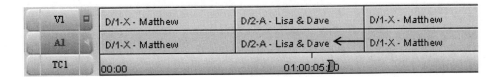

Extend edit to the mark IN

5 Map the Extend button (Command Palette, Trim tab) to a button in the Tool palette.

6 Select the Extend button in the Tool palette to trim the edit back to the IN or forward to the OUT.

Using Trim Versus Extend Edit

You can create split edits using either Trim mode or Extend edit. The choice of which one to use is largely a matter of personal preference. Here are some points to consider:

- You might prefer Extend edit because it involves fewer keystrokes.

- You can use Extend edit to create split edits on-the-fly (see the previous tip) while doing your final run-through.

- Use Trim mode if you are fine-tuning your program (in Trim mode) and want to create a split edit.

Maintaining Sync

Working with dialog and other synced sound brings with it the possibility of losing sync. If you understand the common ways of breaking sync and the tools the Avid system provides to keep sync, you can save yourself a lot of time and avoid problems.

Common Ways to Break Sync

- Trim only one side of a transition, without selecting all tracks.

- Extract frames from only the video or audio track.

- Splice in only audio or video.

- Move only audio or video when using Segment mode (to be covered in the next lesson).

Ways to Prevent Breaking Sync

- When trimming a single track, always trim with both sides of the transition selected.

- Whenever you add to or subtract frames from one track, also add to or subtract them from the other. It is especially helpful to remember this rule when trimming, splicing, or extracting.

- Alternatively, whenever you want to add to or subtract frames from one track, use lift or overwrite instead of extract or splice.

- Work with sync locks turned on.

Trimming with Sync-Locked Tracks

Sync-locking tracks enables you to lock several tracks of audio in sync with one another, or lock the audio to the video. When it is enabled, sync lock is applied to the entire sequence.

Sync lock maintains sync by preventing you from removing footage from only some of the locked tracks. This feature will also add filler to non-selected locked tracks to maintain sync when you add material. (If filler is added to an audio track, you will probably need to fill the gap with "nat" sound.)

Sync-locked tracks only aid single-roller trims, because dual-roller trims cannot break sync between tracks.

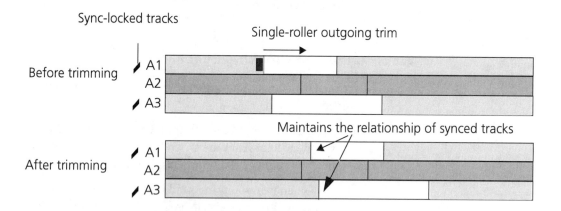

Trimming with sync locks on

To trim with sync-locked tracks:

1 In the Timeline, click the Sync Lock button (in the Track Selection panel) for each track that you want to keep in sync. The Sync Lock icon appears next to each track.

Sync Lock button

Click here to lock all tracks.

Turning on sync lock

2 Enter Trim mode and perform any necessary single-roller trims. You will see following results:

Tip: Click the box to the left of the Timecode (TC1) Track button to lock all tracks.

- When you lengthen the A side or B side of an edit with sync locks turned on, any sync-locked tracks whose segments are not included in the trim will have "filler" added to maintain the sync relationship.

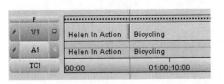

Before trimming forward, two tracks are sync-locked.

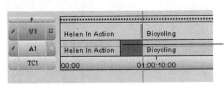

After the trim, filler is added, maintaining sync.

- When you shorten the A side or the B side of an edit with sync locks turned on, the system prevents the edit from happening. The Avid system does not allow you to remove material to maintain sync. Instead you receive an audible alert sound indicating that the system cannot maintain the sync relationship without sacrificing the integrity of other edits.

Tip: You might want to use sync lock while you are learning to use the Avid system. It can also be useful in complex sequences that have extensive sound effects or video effects (because these tracks tend to have a lot of filler).

3 Turn off sync lock by clicking the Sync Lock button. (The icon disappears.)

Sync locks are automatically disabled when you end the editing session.

Explanation of the Way Sync Lock Works

Here's an explanation of why the system lets you add, but not remove, material when using sync locks:

- Adding filler to other tracks to maintain sync is an obvious change to the Timeline. The editor should notice the change and be able to make a fix, if necessary.

- Removing material from the other tracks is not easily detected by an editor and may go unnoticed. The system prevents an editor from making this mistake and forces the editor to make a conscious decision about how to fix the edit.

Fixing Broken Sync Using Sync Breaks

Note: Sync breaks show the amount that two tracks from the same clip are out of sync, for example, the video is out of sync with the sync sound, or audio from the same source master clip.

By default, the Timeline displays sync breaks whenever they occur during editing. These appear at break points as positive or negative numbers indicating the number of frames out of sync. Sync-break offset numbers appear only in the affected track(s).

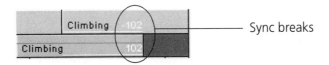

Sync breaks

Detecting out-of-sync frames using sync breaks

! **Sync break information is not displayed if the audio and video tracks come from different sources.**

Using Trim Mode to Correct Sync

In Trim mode, you can restore the frames to sync by performing one or more single-roller trims on the out-of-sync track(s). To reverse the sync break, you trim the exact number of sync-break frames displayed in the Timeline. Dual-roller trims do not remove sync breaks.

To fix broken sync:

1 Enter Trim mode at the first transition that displays a number.

2 To determine whether the video or audio is out of sync, listen to the area before and into the material that goes out of sync (it may help to close your eyes and pay attention to the rhythm of the audio). If both audio and video are out of sync, first adjust one and then sync up the other.

3 Using single-roller trim, add or subtract the appropriate number of frames.

   • If the number shown in the Timeline is negative, you know that track is delayed by that number of frames. You will need to add to one side of the edit on one track.

   • If the number shown in the Timeline is positive, it is ahead of the other track by that many frames. You will need to remove frames from one side of the edit on one track.

! **Simply removing the white numbers does not mean the original edit has been fixed. A sync break can be fixed while altering the original edit. To make sure that your sequence is in sync, play it and carefully review the repaired section for errors.**

Review Questions

1 To create a split edit, would you use a single-roller or dual-roller trim? (See "Creating Split Edits" on page 181.)

2 Describe a situation where you would want to hold on Character A's image while cutting to Character B's dialog.)

3 Describe a situation where you would want to hold on Character A's dialog while cutting to the visual of Character B.)

4 Identify the two ways of performing a split edit. (See "Creating Split Edits" on page 181.)

5 How can you trim dynamically? (See "J-K-L Trimming" on page 179.)

6 Which type of edit are you more likely to break sync with: a splice or an overwrite edit? (See "Maintaining Sync" on page 185.)

7 What's wrong with this single-roller trim set-up?

F			
V1	□	Canoeing	Bicycling
A1	◄	Canoeing	Bicycling
TC1		00:00	01:00:10:00

8 You are cutting a dialog sequence, and so far you have been cutting tight on the dialog. At the climax of the sequence, a character hears shocking news. You would like to show the person's reaction before he speaks. To add footage to the head of the shot (underline the appropriate choices):

    a Select the transition in the Timeline between this shot and the [*preceding/following*] shot.

    b Select the Trim window for the [*outgoing/incoming*] shot.

    c Trim the head of this shot by [*adding/removing*] the appropriate number of frames (typing a *negative/positive* number).

9 A person speaks a line of dialog, followed by one word of the next sentence. To remove the extraneous word (underline the appropriate choices):

    a Select the transition in the Timeline between this shot and the [*preceding/following*] shot.

    b Select the Trim window for the [*outgoing/incoming*] shot.

    c Trim the tail of this shot by [*adding/removing*] the appropriate number of frames (typing a *negative/positive* number).

Exercise: Edit Dialog

You are developing an educational CD-ROM that uses "real-life" situations to teach students math and science. Your assignment is to edit a dialog scene that takes place in a hospital's Trauma Room, a room in the Emergency wing. The scene's characters include Susan and Fred, a doctor and nurse working in the Trauma Room; Jennifer Bates, an unconscious patient; and Mrs. Bates, Jennifer's mother.

This exercise has two parts: You begin by quickly editing the scene; then you trim the shots to improve the rhythm of the dialog and to create split edits.

"Trauma Room" scene

Goals

- Create a rough cut of the "Trauma Room" scene
- Trim the sequence to improve the rhythm of the dialog
- Create split edits to improve the rhythm of the scene

Get Started

1 Open the **Trauma Room** project.

2 Create a new bin and name it **Trauma Room Sequences**. Do not close the bin.

3 Open the **Trauma Room Selects** bin.

4 Watch all of the scene's clips.

There are several basic shots: Master Shot, Fred's single, and Susan's single. There are also a few cutaway (B-roll) shots.

To create a new sequence:

1 Choose Clip > New Sequence.

In the dialog box that appears, choose the **Trauma Room Sequences** bin.

2 Name your new sequence something meaningful like Trauma Room Cut 1.

Load Clips into the Source Monitor

You can load multiple clips into the Source monitor at the same time, then access each one through the Clip Name menu.

1 In the **Trauma Room Selects** bin, select all of the clips.

The clips are highlighted in the bin.

2 Press one of the highlighted clips, and drag it to the Source monitor and release the mouse.

The clips are loaded, one after the another, in the Source monitor.

3 Click and hold on the clip name above the Source monitor to display the Clip Name menu, and choose one of the clips from the menu.

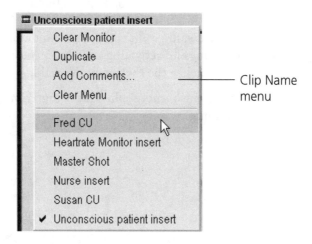

The clip you chose appears in the Source monitor.

Assemble the Sequence

To build this sequence, mark and splice each line of dialog and edit it into the sequence.

Note: Mark your IN and OUT points quickly. Remember you can edit rough and then fine-tune later.

1 Using the script at the end of the exercise as your guide, mark an IN and OUT point for Susan's first line of dialog. Practice using the J-K-L keys to locate the beginning and end of the dialog. *Don't worry about being frame accurate; initial assembling can be done quickly. After you edit the first cut, you will trim it.*

2 Splice the clip into the new sequence.

3 Repeat the process for the next line.

4 Finish assembling the rough cut.

Editing Dialog for the Trauma Room Scene

While you will not be given specific tasks in this part of the exercise, you should perform the following activities:

Note: Do not use sync locks for this exercise. If you lose sync, fix it by using Trim mode or Undo.

1 Before creating split edits, use Trim mode (using single-roller trimming and activating all Record Track buttons) to trim the shots until you like the rhythm of the dialog.

2 Create one or more split edits using Trim mode (dual-roller trimming).

Script for "Trauma Room"

This dialog comes from the shooting script. The characters ad lib a good deal, however, so the words they speak may be different from the words on the page.

```
                    ACT ONE

                    SCENE D

INT. TRAUMA ROOM IN A HOSPITAL EMERGENCY ROOM

(Susan, Fred, Mrs. Bates, Jennifer Bates)

Susan, the doctor, and Fred, the nurse, examine
Jennifer, while Mrs. Bates (Jennifer's mother)
stands by.

                    SUSAN

What's up?

                    FRED

I'm just getting her vitals in. She's 110
pounds, age 15, and respiration is 28.

                  MRS. BATES

Is 28 high?

                    SUSAN

Yes, 28's higher than normal.

                    FRED
Pulse is 125.

                  MRS. BATES

How's that? I mean is 125 a good pulse or what?
```

SUSAN

Mrs. Bates, we need to look at the entire
situation before we can make a decision....
Anything else, Fred? How's her blood pressure?

FRED

BP's 90 over 60.

SUSAN

90 over 60, okay. What about her temperature?

FRED

Temperature is 38 Celsius.

SUSAN

38 Celsius, fine. Anything else?

FRED

Yeah, not responding to stimuli.

SUSAN

Right, let's move on this right away. I want a
glucose reading with a finger stick, a
complete blood count, and a chem 7 panel.

FRED

Glucose, blood count, and a chem 7. Got it.

SUSAN

Oh, and Fred, check the blood gases, too. I'm
going to run down to the lab and see if I can't
light a fire under these guys to get them done
stat. And Fred? Make sure she doesn't go into
a coma.

Lesson 7 **Working in the Timeline**

For basic editing, you load clips into the Source monitor and edit the material into a sequence in the Record monitor. To revise and fine-tune the sequence, you can edit in the Timeline.

This lesson explains the different ways you can use the Timeline to edit.

Objectives

After you complete this lesson, you will be able to:

- Use locators
- Add and patch tracks
- Edit segments in the Timeline
- Slip and slide segments in the Timeline

Using Locators

You can add locators to your sequence at any time. Locators are electronic bookmarks that allow you to find and identify specific frames during editing. You can enter text into the comment field attached to each locator. While you can add locators to your clips or sequences, editors find many more uses for them in sequences than in clips.

Useful Applications for Locators

You can use locators in your sequence to:

- Identify shots that will be added later.

- Provide the correct spelling for titles.

- Identify where music cues or sound effects will need to be added at a later time.

- Include notes for a colorist, audio mixer, or graphic artist.

- Identify all remaining tasks. Thus, when all of your locators are gone, the program should be finished.

Adding Locators

To add locators to a sequence or clip:

1 Open a clip or sequence.

2 If you want to add locators to your sequence, map an Add Locator button from the More tab of the Command Palette to a button in the Tool Palette or to a key.

3 Cue to the frame where you want to add the locator.

4 To add a locator to a clip in the Source monitor, click the Add Locator button in the toolbar under the Source monitor. To add a locator to the sequence, map the Add Locator button to a button and click it.

An oval appears at the bottom of the frame in the monitor, in the position bar (on the highest highlighted track), and if you have added the locator to the sequence, in the Timeline.

Locator

Displaying a locator in the Source or Record monitor

5 To add comments, click the Locator oval in the Record or Source monitor image. The Locator window appears, allowing you to view and enter information for the current locator or other locators found in your sequence.

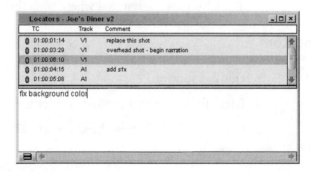

Displaying locators and comments in the Locator window

6 Type the information. The amount of information you can enter is unlimited.

7 Close the window.

The information is stored with the marked frame, and the first line of the information appears at the bottom of the monitor.

fix background color

Locator text displayed in the Source or Record monitor

Moving to Locators

▶ Use the Fast Forward and Rewind buttons in the Tool Palette to move to the next or previous locator. You can also use the Go to Previous Locator or Go to Next Locator buttons if they are mapped (from the Move tab of the Command palette) to a button or key.

Track buttons are ignored when using these options.

Removing Locators

To remove a locator:

1 Go to the frame that contains the locator.

2 Press the Delete key on the keyboard. The locator is removed.

Adding and Patching Tracks

You can edit up to 24 audio tracks and up to 24 video tracks in the Timeline.

Typically, you create a new sequence by splicing video and audio from your source tracks into the Timeline. For example, you might start a new sequence by splicing a clip with source tracks V1, A1, and A2 to the Timeline. The material is spliced to record tracks V1, A1, and A2. The sequence automatically creates the record tracks when you make that first edit. In fact, each new sequence displays V1 and A1-A4 by default.

However, you may at some point need to add more tracks than are contained in your sequence. You need to manually add these tracks. For example, you can add tracks A5 and A6 to the sequence.

In addition, you may need to patch video or audio from tracks on the source to different tracks on the record. For example, after you add tracks A5 and A6 to the sequence, you can patch A1 from your source clip to A5 in the sequence and patch A2 in your source clip to A6 in your sequence.

Adding Tracks

Adding the Next Audio or Video Track

To add the next audio track:

Tip: You can also right-click (Windows) or Shift+⌘-click (Macintosh) the Timeline window and choose New Audio Track (among other options).

▶ With a sequence in the Timeline, choose Clip > New Audio Track, or press Control+U (Windows) or ⌘+U (Macintosh).

For example, if the sequence currently includes tracks A1-A4, the system adds track A5.

To add the next video track:

▶ Repeat the above, substituting Video for Audio, and Y for U.

Adding a Specific Audio or Video Track

Sometimes you will want to add a specific audio or video track. For example, your sequence currently uses tracks A1-A2, but you want to put all audio effects on tracks A5 and A6.

To add a specific audio track:

1 While holding down the Alt (Windows) or Option (Macintosh) key, choose Clip > New Audio Track, or press Control+Alt+U (Windows) or ⌘+Option+U (Macintosh).

A dialog box appears, allowing you to select a specific track.

Adding an out-of-sequence track in the Add Track dialog box

2 Select A (Audio) and the desired track from the two pop-up menus and click OK.

An empty track is added to your Timeline.

To add a specific video track:

▶ Repeat the above, substituting Video for Audio, and Y for U.

Patching Tracks

Patching tracks enables you to edit a source track onto a different track in the sequence. For example, you would patch source track A1 to record track A5 if the audio is on track A1 in the source clip, but you want to add it to track A5 in the Timeline.

To patch a track from a source clip to a different track in the sequence:

▶ Click the source track and drag the arrow to the record track on which you want to make the edit.

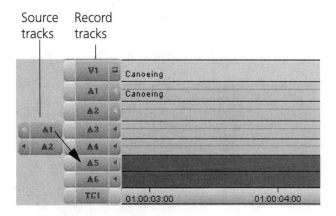

Using the mouse to patch tracks

The source track you selected jumps next to the record track and is highlighted.

Configuring the Timeline

While editing in the Timeline, you can choose from a wide range of display options in the Timeline menu.

To display the Timeline menu:

1 Click and hold the Fast menu button in the bottom-left corner of the Timeline.

Timeline Fast menu

2 Choose an option from the Timeline Fast menu.

Display options in the Timeline Fast menu

For example, you can display or hide the duration for each shot, show more or less detail in the Timeline, or display the entire sequence or only a selected section of it.

The following table describes some of the options.

Table 7   Display Options in the Timeline Menu

Timeline Menu Item	Function
Clip Frames	Displays the start frame for each clip edited into the sequence.
Clip Names	Displays the name of the clip. This option cannot be turned off.
Clip Durations	Displays the length of the clip as a straight cut, without the additional material required for transition effects.
Comments	Displays comments you entered for each shot using the Add Comments command from the Record Monitor menu.
Source Names	Displays the source tape name for each shot.
Media Names	Displays the file names for the media files associated with each shot.
Dupe Detection	Automatically locates every instance in sequence of duplicated frames on video tracks.
Render Ranges	Displays a red line under unrendered or partially rendered effects, depending on the submenu option you select.
Sample Plot	Represents audio as a sample waveform.
Audio Clip Gain	Displays current level, as adjusted in Audio Mix tool.
Audio Auto Gain	Displays current gain, as adjusted by keyframes.
Clip Color	Allows you to assign colors to clips in the Timeline, to indicate shots that should be grouped together.
Track Color or Background Color	Allows you to specify colors for tracks (if tracks are selected) or a background color for the Timeline if no tracks are selected.
Zoom Back	Returns the Timeline display to the last-zoomed level. To return to your original display level, Zoom Back repeatedly until the Zoom Back option is disabled in the menu.

Table 7   Display Options in the Timeline Menu (Continued)

Timeline Menu Item	Function
Zoom In	Provides a cursor for drawing a box around the area in the sequence to be expanded. You can zoom into any area in the Timeline as many times as necessary to expand the view of the zoomed information in that section.

Enlarging and Reducing a Track

There are two ways to change the width of a track.

Method 1:

1 Click the selector for the track that you want to resize.

Click additional Track buttons, or choose the Edit > Select All to select all tracks for resizing.

2 Deselect the Source and Record selectors for the tracks you do not want to modify.

3 To enlarge, repeatedly press Control+L (Windows) or ⌘+L (Macintosh).

4 To reduce, repeatedly press Control+K (Windows) or ⌘+K (Macintosh).

Method 2:

▶ Press the Control (Windows) or Option (Macintosh) key and place the cursor at the bottom boundary of the track in the Track Selector panel. When the cursor becomes a double-sided arrow, drag it down.

You need not select the track for this to work, making this is a good choice when you only want to adjust one track.

Saving a Customized Timeline View

After you have customized a Timeline view, you can save it so you can use it again. The Timeline that you save contains the following display features:

- All tracks shown in the sequence
- Track sizes
- Clip names
- Clip frames
- Audio waveforms
- Track panel
- Track and background colors

Saving a View

To save a customized Timeline view:

1 Press the Timeline View button that may be called *Untitled* and choose Save As.

Timeline View
button

A dialog box appears.

2 Type a name for the view you are saving and press Enter.

The Timeline View is placed in the User settings.

3 To see a list of all the Timeline views used in the project, press the Timeline View button.

> ### Useful Applications for Timeline Views
>
> Create a Timeline view, with expanded audio tracks and volume displayed, that you can use to work on your audio.
>
> Create a Timeline view with Sample Plot turned on.

Changing to a Different View

▶ To change to a different view, press the Timeline View button and select the view you want to use.

Editing Segments in the Timeline

You can reposition one or more segments in the Timeline using the Segment Mode buttons found below the Timeline.

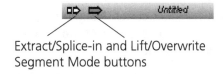

Extract/Splice-in and Lift/Overwrite
Segment Mode buttons

- Extract/Splice-in (yellow Segment Mode button) rearranges the order of segments within the Timeline.

- Lift/Overwrite (red Segment Mode button) repositions a segment in the Timeline, leaving black filler or silence at the original location, and placing the shot at the new location.

!   **Do not confuse these buttons with the Splice and Overwrite buttons.**

!   **Segment Mode Editing mode ignores sync locks, so it is very easy to put your sequence out of sync when working in this mode.**

Extracting and Splicing-in Segments

Extract/Splice-in can be used to move a selected segment forward or backward in the sequence. The Extract/Splice-in procedure extracts a segment, closes the gap, and splices in the segment at its new position.

The total duration of the sequence does not change when you use Extract/Splice-in segment editing.

To reposition one or more segments using Extract/Splice-in:

1 To prepare to Extract/Splice-in, do one of the following:

- Click the yellow Extract/Splice-in Segment Mode button to highlight the button. Then click a segment you want to edit.

Note: Drawing a lasso *right to left* around segments in the Timeline enables Slip and Slide mode (to be covered later in the lesson).

- While in Source/Record mode, lasso the area you want to reposition by drawing a lasso from *left to right* around the entire segment(s).

The cursor changes to a Segment pointer.

Climbing		Ride And Run		Climbing	
Climbing		Ride And Run	▭⇨	Climbing	

Selecting segments in Segment mode

2 To include additional segments within the Segment Mode edit, press the Shift key and click or lasso additional *adjacent* segments.

Once a single segment is selected, you can Shift+lasso from left or right or right to left to add other segments. Once a segment has been selected, you will not be forced into Slip and Slide mode by lassoing from left to right.

Note: Default Snap-To Edit, a Timeline setting, enables you to indicate how clips are moved in Segment Mode editing. With the option selected, the clip snaps to an existing transition endpoint. With the option deselected, the clip moves freely to any position on the track. This option is deselected by default.

3 Drag the segment horizontally and/or vertically to a new position. (If you selected multiple adjacent segments, you only need to drag one of the selected clips; the others will follow.)

Drag the segment to the left or right.

Climbing		Ride And Run		Ride A ▭⇨ning		
Climbing		Ride And Run		Climbing		

Moving segments in Segment mode

The Avid system extracts the selected segment from its old position, closing the gap left by its removal, then splices the material back into the sequence at the new location.

The insertion point is located at the frame before the head of the segment you're dragging into position.

4 Click the Extract/Splice-in Segment Mode button again to leave Segment mode and return to Source/Record mode.

Useful Application for Extract/Splice-in

Use Extract/Splice-in to rearrange shots in a sequence.

Lifting and Overwriting

Tip: It's often better to use the Lift/Overwrite Segment Mode button when you move from track to track. If you don't, dragging to a different track will pull up all later segments on the track you're moving from, and push down all segments on the track you're moving to.

If you use the Lift/Overwrite (red) Segment Mode button instead of the Extract/Splice-in button, the lifted segment replaces material at the new position, while leaving filler in its previous position.

The total duration of the sequence is unaffected unless you place the segment you're moving beyond the end of the sequence.

Useful Application for Lift/Overwrite

Use Lift/Overwrite to:

- Move sound effects on an audio track.

- Move a title to a new location on the Timeline.

- Move audio segments from one track to another to create an audio overlap.

- Lift a shot from the sequence, holding its place with filler until you choose the replacement shot.

Removing Segments Using Segment Mode

In an earlier lesson, you learned how to extract and lift material from the sequence. You can also use Segment mode to remove clips from a sequence, either closing or retaining the gap that results.

To remove material from the Timeline using Segment mode:

1 Click one of the Segment Mode buttons at the bottom of Source/Record monitor.

- Extract/Splice-in (yellow) will extract the selected segments.

- Lift/Overwrite (red) will lift the selected segments.

2 Select a clip in the Timeline, and Shift-click additional clips on the same or other tracks. They do not have to be adjacent.

Note: If there is an effect or Audio Gain Automation on any selected segment, this action will remove it and not the clip. Select the clip again and press Delete to remove the clip.

3 Press Delete to extract or lift the selected material, *depending on the Segment Mode button you selected.*

4 Click the Segment Mode button again to deselect it.

Slipping and Sliding Segments

In addition to Trimming and Segment Mode editing, the Avid system has two more functions that allow you to alter the position or contents of various shots within your Timeline: slipping and sliding. Slipping and sliding are forms of trimming, where two consecutive transitions are trimmed simultaneously.

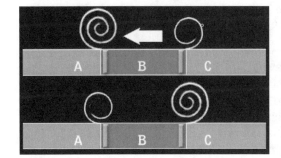

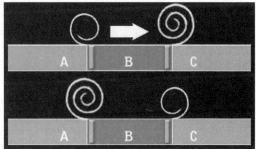

Changing the contents of a shot with Slip mode

Changing the position of a shot with Slide mode

Slipping a Shot

You can slip a shot in your sequence, keeping its duration and its position in the Timeline the same, but changing its contents to earlier or later material in the master clip.

To slip a shot:

1 While in Source/Record mode, drag a lasso around the entire segment in the Timeline, from right to left.

(Windows) Or, while in Trim mode, right-click in the Timeline window and choose Select Slip Trim from the menu.

Notice the four new pictures at the top of the monitor.

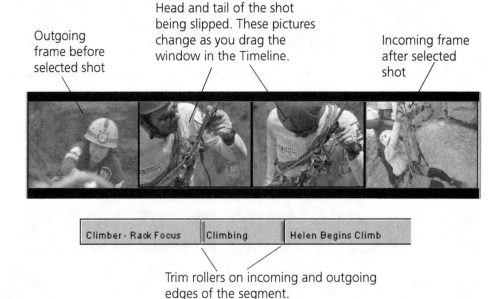

Outgoing frame before selected shot

Head and tail of the shot being slipped. These pictures change as you drag the window in the Timeline.

Incoming frame after selected shot

Climber - Rack Focus   Climbing   Helen Begins Climb

Trim rollers on incoming and outgoing edges of the segment.

Setting up for a slip operation

The first picture is the outgoing frame before the selected shot; the last picture is the incoming frame after the selected shot. The middle two pictures are the head and tail of the shot you are slipping.

2 In the Timeline, press one of the selected heads or tails (it doesn't matter which), with the tail of the Trim Mode cursor pointed toward the center of the segment you are sliding, then drag the selected material to the left or right.

Notice that the first and last pictures remain static as you drag, because you are not changing the position of the shot in the sequence. The middle two pictures (the first and last frames of the selected segment) change, because you are changing the content of the shot itself.

- Dragging right reveals later material.

- Dragging left reveals earlier material.

3 Release when you are satisfied with the change.

The following illustration shows what happens when you slip to the right.

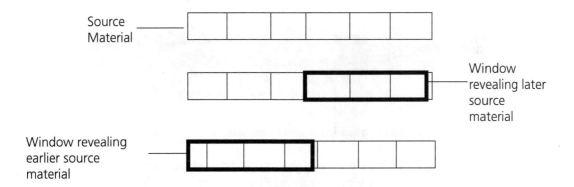

Source Material

Window revealing later source material

Window revealing earlier source material

Sliding a Shot

Sliding is similar to slipping, but instead of changing the content of the shot, you change its position in the sequence. The end result is that your shot's position is changed (slid) in the sequence.

To slide a shot:

1 While in Source/Record mode hold the Shift+Alt (Windows) or Option (Macintosh) key and drag a lasso from right to left around the material you want to slide.

   (Windows) Or, while in Trim mode, right-click in the Timeline window, and choose Select Slide Trim from the menu.

   The same four pictures at the top of the monitor that we saw in Slip mode are also displayed.

   In the Timeline, the Trim rollers are located on the outgoing and incoming frames preceding and following the segment.

Outgoing Frame _____

	Helen going up	"boyscout jamboree"
	Helen going up	"boyscout jamboree"
	Helen going up	"boyscout jamboree"

_____ Incoming Frame

Setting up for a slide operation

2 In the Timeline, press one of the selected heads or tails (it doesn't matter which), and drag left or right.

   • Dragging to the right moves the segment to a later master timecode.

   • Dragging to the left moves the selected segment to an earlier master timecode.

3 Release when you are satisfied with the change.

Sliding vs. Segment Editing

The Slip and Slide display is very similar to the Segment Mode display. Sliding a clip is similar in many ways to performing a Segment Mode edit, but there are important differences between the two functions.

- Segment Mode Lift/Overwrite leaves a gap in the sequence at the original location of the clip that is moved.

- Segment Mode Extract/Splice-in inserts a clip at a new location. If the insertion point is not at an existing edit, the remaining frames of the shot are moved downstream.

- Sliding does not allow you to skip over other clips to an entirely new location in the sequence. Sliding is essentially a two-sided trim with a clip (or clips) in the middle.

- J-K-L play does not apply to Segment mode.

Review Questions

1 Describe how you might use locators. (See "Using Locators" on page 200.)

2 If your Timeline displays tracks A1-A4, how would you display track A5? (See "Adding and Patching Tracks" on page 203.)

3 Once you have customized your Timeline to display your preferred colors and track sizes, how do you save this view? (See "Configuring the Timeline" on page 206.)

4 Describe two methods for enlarging and reducing the track size. (See "Enlarging and Reducing a Track" on page 208.)

5 In Segment mode, how can you select multiple segments? (See "Editing Segments in the Timeline" on page 211.)

6 When Segment editing, what modifier key, if any, do you hold to snap the head of a segment to a transition? (See "Extracting and Splicing-in Segments" on page 211.)

7 Scenario: You are editing a three-shot sequence, and the first and third shots are perfectly positioned. However, you would like to see an earlier portion of the second shot. Do you slip or slide the second shot? (See "Slipping and Sliding Segments" on page 215.)

8 What are the key differences between using Segment Mode editing and using the Slide function? (See "Sliding a Shot" on page 218.)

Exercise: Work in the Timeline

Note: If you prefer to work more on your own, follow the instructions in the outlined version at the end of the exercise.

In this exercise, you continue to edit the advertising spot promoting the Canyonlands Outdoor Adventure School in Utah that you began previously. The sequence will have voice-over narration, music, and some sync sound in the form of interviews with participants. After adding these elements, you will manipulate shots in the sequence by rearranging and slipping them.

In future exercises, you will continue to work on this sequence by adjusting audio levels and pan, and adding titles.

Rearrange shots in a sequence.

V1		Two men ru	Rappel down,	Rappel WS	Rappel across - awa
A1		Two men ru	Rappel down,	Rappel WS	Rappel across - awa
A2		Narration for ECO Challenge spot			
A3		Music for ECO Challenge spot			
TC1		00:00	01:00:05:00		01:00:10:00

Slip a clip.

| Climbing | Ride and Run | Helen Climbs - LA |
| Climbing | Ride and Run | Helen Climbs - LA |

The two middle frames display the first and last frame of slipped clip.

Goals

- Lay down the audio track for the ECO Challenge sequence
- Create a short montage
- Move segments in the Timeline using Segment Mode editing
- Slip a shot in the Timeline

Work in the Timeline

For this exercise you continue to build the ECO Challenge sequence you created in the subclipping and storyboarding exercise. Because you have already practiced many of the tools that you need to cut this job, we provide less detailed instruction than in previous exercises. In some cases, however, it is necessary to follow specific instructions in order to demonstrate certain editing features.

Get Started

1 In the **ECO Challenge** project, open the **ECO Sequences** bin.

2 If your **ECO Challenge** sequence is not loaded in the Timeline, please do so now.

3 Here is a transcription of the script you will use for the sequence.

ECO Challenge Narration

VOICE-OVER

Are you looking for a challenge? Do you want to test your physical and mental endurance to their limit? Then come to beautiful Southern Utah and the Canyonlands Outdoor Adventure School.

The Canyonlands Adventure School offers week-long, intensive expeditions where you'll master the skills required for rappelling, hiking, mountain biking, whitewater rafting, and horseback riding.

The Canyonlands OUTDOOR Adventure School: 1-800 OUT-DOOR.

Lay Down the Narration and Music

In this section you will lay down the narration and music tracks and continue building the video track.

Edit the Narration onto Track A2

1 Open the **Audio** bin and load the **Narration for ECO Challenge Spot** clip into the Source monitor.

2 Listen to the narration, and then press T to mark the entire clip.

3 If your sequence has only one audio track, choose Clip > New Audio Track to add the A2 audio track to the sequence.

4 Patch source track A1 to record track A2.

5 Make sure only source A1 and record A2 tracks are selected.

6 Place the position indicator at the head of the sequence and clear IN and OUT marks, if present.

7 Click the red Overwrite button to edit the narration.

Notice that the Timeline now has the narration on A2, and that the sequence now extends beyond the montage.

Edit the Music onto Track A3

Now you will add a music bed under the narration using a three-point edit.

1 Play the **Music for ECO Challenge Spot** clip (which is in the **ECO Audio** bin) and mark an IN at the beginning of the clip. (There is no need to mark an OUT at the end.)

2 Mark an IN in the beginning **of your sequence** and an OUT at the end.

3 If your sequence has only two audio tracks, choose Clip > New Audio Track to add the A3 audio track to the sequence.

4 Patch source track A2 to record track A3.

5 Make sure only source A2 and record A3 tracks are selected.

6 Click the Overwrite button.

7 Play the sequence.

The music cuts off at the end. We will fix that later, in the section "Free-Style Editing" on page 228.

Note: Don't forget to turn on the monitor when you want to listen to the music.

8 The music is louder than the narration. You may want to deselect the track A3 monitor for now.

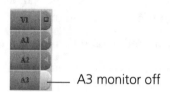 —— A3 monitor off

9 Save this Timeline view by pressing the Timeline View button (perhaps called *Untitled*) and choose Save As. Type a name for the view, such as Standard. In the next exercise, you will create an additional view. This step will enable you to return to this view whenever you like.

Timeline View button

Add a Short Montage of Activities

Now, you'll build a short montage. Later you will slip some of the shots to change their content.

▶ Using clips from the **ECO Selects bin**, build a series of video-only shots over this voice-over narration: "RAPPELLING, HIKING, MOUNTAIN BIKING, WHITEWATER RAFTING, AND HORSEBACK RIDING."

Consider the following as you build this montage:

- You can solo the narration track to isolate that audio.

- There are several ways you can add video-only shots. Which way will you use?

Fine-Tune the Sequence

In this section you will fine-tune the sequence by moving segments in the Timeline and slipping edits.

Move Segments in the Timeline

Now experiment a little by swapping the order of any two clips in your opening climbing montage. If you think you might prefer your existing cut, how can you return to it after you swap the two clips? (There are at least two ways.)

Get Started

First, let's turn on Default Snap-To Edit, a Timeline setting, so the clip snaps to an existing transition endpoint.

1 Select the Settings tab in the Project window.

2 Open the Timeline settings and click the Edit tab.

3 Select Default Snap-To Edit and click OK.

4 Click the Bins tab in the Project window.

To move a segment:

1 Select the yellow Extract/Splice-in arrow at the bottom of the Timeline.

2 Shift-click the clip (on tracks V1 and A1) in the Timeline you want to swap to highlight it.

3 To snap the clip to the head of the other clip, drag the clip to the right or left. When the clip you're moving snaps to the insertion point, release the mouse.

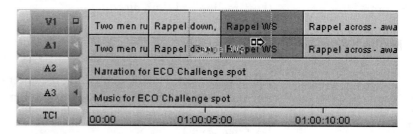

Moving a segment in Segment mode

The order of your two clips is swapped.

4 Deselect the Extract/Splice-In button.

5 Play your sequence to view the result.

6 Swap any other shots in the montage.

Slip the Ride and Run Shot

To prepare for this part of the exercise, we'll add a section of the Ride and Run clip.

1 In your sequence, park the position indicator on the first frame of black after the opening climbing montage. Clear any IN and OUT marks.

2 Load the **Ride and Run** clip from the **Selects** bin into the Source monitor.

3 Mark an IN and OUT to isolate the rider's dialog: "SUPER! COULDN'T BE BETTER! THIS IS SO AWESOME! THIS IS SO EXCITING!"

4 Set the Track Selector panel to record V1 and A1.

5 Click the Overwrite button.

6 Play the section.

We don't need to include all of the rider's exclamations. So let's slip the shot a little later to omit the word, "Super!" Slipping it allows you to keep the duration of the clip the same, and maintain the timing of the edits downstream.

Note: If you accidentally lasso your clips from left to right, you will end up in Segment mode. Click the highlighted Segment Mode button at the bottom of the Timeline to exit this mode and start again.

1 Enter Slip mode by dragging a lasso from upper right (starting **above** the Timeline) to lower left around tracks V1 and A1 of the **Ride and Run** clip.

Make sure you lasso both V1 and A1 or you will go out of sync in the next step.

The system enters Slip mode where you can now view the first and last frames of the clip.

First frame   Last frame

2 Slip the clip to later material using the Trim buttons or the numeric keypad. (Slip approximately +1/2 second for good results).

3 Press 5 to play the result.

4 Press 5 again to stop.

Practice Slipping on Your Own

Here, you'll slip some of the shots in the short montage you created over the dialog, "rappelling, hiking, mountain biking, whitewater rafting, and horseback riding," to change their content. We provide suggestions, but feel free to make your own decisions about what to slip.

1 Slip several of the shots to change the content of the shot without changing its duration. Here are some suggestions:

a For the bikers shot, change from bikes coming toward the camera to bikes moving away (early in the clip), or vice versa.

b For the rafters, change from them successfully riding the raft to falling off, or vice versa.

c Slip a shot a little to improve the movement or pacing within the shot or the rhythm from shot to shot.

2 Play through your changes and make adjustments as desired.

Free-Style Editing

You've now completed the structured part of this exercise. Spend the remaining time continuing to build the sequence making your own editorial decisions. In addition to adding shots into the sequence, practice moving segments in the Timeline, and slipping and sliding clips.

Also, as we mentioned earlier, the music ends abruptly. You can use Match Frame to see if there is a better end to the music (listen around 2 seconds after the current ending). (See the lesson, "Additional Editing Tools," for information about Match Frame.) Add this music to the end of the sequence and extend the video so the video and audio tracks end at the same time.

Finally, you can add (multi-color) locators to your sequence and write comments for them.

In the next exercise, you will finish the audio by adjusting audio levels and pan.

Work in the Timeline (Outlined)

If you want to refer to the more detailed exercise for more information, see "Work in the Timeline" on page 222.

Get Started

1 In the **ECO Challenge** project, open the **ECO Audio** bin.

2 Edit the **Narration for ECO Challenge Spot** voice-over narration onto track A2 of the ECO Challenge sequence begun earlier. (For the printed narration, see "ECO Challenge Narration" on page 222.) (If necessary, add track A2 to your sequence, and then patch the audio from source A1 to record A2 track.)

3 Edit the **Music for ECO Challenge Spot** clip onto track A3.

4 Edit a video-only track over this voice-over, using clips in the **ECO Selects** bin: "RAPPELLING, HIKING, MOUNTAIN BIKING, WHITEWATER RAFTING, AND HORSEBACK RIDING."

Work in the Timeline

1 Rearrange, add, or remove shots or segments that play over the voice-over and music. When you rearrange, add, and remove shots in the sequence, here are some things to think about doing:

- Increase the continuity of movement between shots.

- Increase the conflict of direction between shots. (For example, a shot with movement from left to right is followed by a shot with movement from right to left. Or a high angle shot is followed by a low angle shot.)

- Replace natural audio in track A1. You can do this anywhere you don't see people's lips moving. Hint: Mark the clip you want to change in the Timeline, make sure you select the correct tracks, and use an overwrite edit.

- Improve pacing and rhythm.

2 Move at least one shot earlier or later in the sequence.

3 Extract or lift at least one shot from the sequence using the Segment Mode buttons. If you lift a shot, replace it with another.

4 Slip the content of a shot to improve the shot-to-shot movement.

5 Slide a shot to reposition it in the sequence.

You may use any of the following tools to further refine the sequence, but you should particularly practice the tools learned in the previous lesson.

- Extract or Lift to remove material from the sequence

- Overwrite to replace shots in the sequence

- Trim to fine-tune shots in the sequence

- Extract/Splice to rearrange shots in the sequence

- Lift/Overwrite to move shots but maintain other relationships in the sequence

- Slip to maintain the position of a shot in the sequence, but change its start and end point

- Slide to move a shot within the sequence

Lesson 8 **Working with Audio**

Most of the editing techniques used when editing the video track can also be used on the audio track. As described in previous lessons, you can quickly:

- Cut and trim sound
- Create split edits

This lesson focuses on ways to optimize the audio quality by regulating the stereo balance of the speakers for each track and adjusting audio levels within a specific segment of a sequence.

Objectives

After you complete this lesson, you will be able to:

- Adjust audio level and pan with the Audio Mix tool
- Adjust audio gain with keyframes
- Perform real-time recording with the Automation Gain tool

Introduction

Level and pan can be set in the Audio Mix tool. In addition, the Audio Gain Automation tool allows you to graphically manipulate levels and change levels in real time within a clip or segment.

Typical Audio Gain Workflow

1 Use the Audio Mix tool to adjust the overall volume of an entire clip or track.

2 (Optional) Use Audio Gain Automation recording to adjust gain in real time.

3 Add and manipulate audio gain keyframes to fine-tune the volume of different sections of the audio in the sequence.

Adjusting Level and Pan in the Audio Mix Tool

Use the Audio Mix tool to set the level and pan for a clip, sequence, or multiple clips within a sequence.

❗ **Changes made in the Audio Mix tool affect the *entire* clip in the Source monitor, or the *entire* segment on which your blue position indicator is parked in the sequence.**

To set level and pan:

Tip: If you know an entire clip is too loud or soft, adjust the clip before editing it into the sequence, especially if you know you will use the clip repeatedly in the sequence.

1 Do one of the following:

- Load the clip into the Source monitor.

- To set pan or level for a segment in a sequence, load the sequence into the Timeline and park in the segment you want to adjust.

2 (Option) If you are setting level in the sequence and want to display the level in the Timeline:

a Expand the audio track.

b Choose Timeline Fast menu > Audio Clip Gain.

A straight line appears in the selected audio track, showing the current volume level for that track in the Audio Mix tool.

Opening the Audio Mix Tool

There are two ways to open the Audio Mix tool.

First Method

▶ Choose Tools > Audio Mix.

The Audio Mix tool appears.

233

Second Method

The second method uses the Avid system's Audio Editing toolset, one of its predesigned work environments.

1   Choose Toolset > Audio Editing, or press Shift+F11.

The Audio Editing toolset appears.

2   Rearrange, open, or close Audio tools to customize the display as you wish.

3   Choose Toolset > Save Current.

Any time you return to the Audio Editing toolset this arrangement appears.

4   To remove the customization, choose Toolset > Restore Current to Default.

5   To return to the toolset for editing, choose Toolset > Source/Record Editing.

Working with the Audio Mix Tool

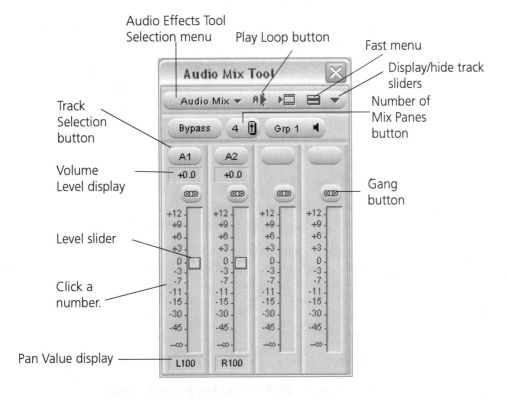

Audio Effects Tool
Selection menu

Play Loop button

Fast menu

Display/hide track sliders

Track Selection button

Number of Mix Panes button

Volume Level display

Gang button

Level slider

Click a number.

Pan Value display

Audio Mix tool with components labelled

The Audio Mix window is divided into four or eight panes. It can only display tracks that exist in the sequence, or tracks that were captured with the source clip.

1 Click the Number of Mix Panes button to switch between displaying four or eight tracks. (If you display four tracks, you can display the first four or second four tracks.)

2 Click the Track Selection button for the audio track to be adjusted.

3 (Option) To link (gang) tracks together so they are adjusted in tandem, click the Gang buttons on the desired tracks.

4 Click the Play Loop button. The system repeatedly loops through the selected area as follows:

- If you have IN and OUT marks on your sequence, it loops over the selected area.

- If there are no IN or OUT marks, it loops over the smallest audio clip on a selected track, identified by the position indicator.

If you adjust the level while playing, the new level will go into effect in the next go-around.

To adjust level for a track:

▶ Move the sliders up or down, type a number in the Volume Level display, or click a number next to the slide panel.

To type a number in the Volume Level display, click in the Volume Level display and type a number (negative number to decrease the level) in the numeric keypad.

Tip: Alt+click (Windows) or Option+click (Macintosh) a Volume Level slider to set the level to unity (0).

 —— Volume
Level display

Volume level displayed in the Audio Mix tool

To adjust pan for a track:

Tip: Alt+click (Windows) or Option+click (Macintosh) a Pan slider to set the pan to MID.

▶ Click and hold the Pan Value display to open a pop-up slider, and move the slider left or right.

 Pan Value display

Pan values displayed in the Audio Mix tool

Setting Global Pan and Level

The Global Pan and Level options apply the current pan or level settings to all clips on entire track(s) in a sequence. To set this option:

1 Clear any IN or OUT marks from the Timeline.

2 (Option) If you want to modify multiple tracks, click the Gang button for each track you want to modify.

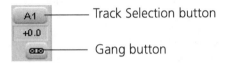

      ——— Track Selection button

      ——— Gang button

3 Adjust the pan or level for the track in the Audio Mix tool.

4 Click the Track Selection button(s) for the track(s) you want to modify.

5 Press the Audio Mix Fast Menu button for the desired track and choose Set Pan (or Level) on Track - Global. (If the menu is grayed out, click the Track Selection button(s) and try again.)

Global options in the Audio Mix Fast menu

Pan or level will be adjusted for the entire track or multiple ganged tracks.

Setting Pan and Level Using Marks

You can set level and pan for clips contained within marked IN and OUT points, or from the beginning of a clip with an IN point to the end of the sequence.

To set this option for clips contained within IN and OUT points:

1 Mark an IN and OUT in the sequence around the clip or clips you want to affect.

2 Make sure the position indicator is within the IN and OUT marks and within an audio clip (not filler) on the track(s) you are adjusting.

3 (Option) If you want to modify multiple tracks, click the Gang button for each track you want to modify.

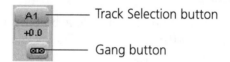

Track Selection button

Gang button

4 Adjust the pan or level for the track in the Audio Mix tool.

5 Click the Track Selection button(s) for the track(s) you want to modify.

6 Choose Audio Mix Fast menu > Set Pan (or Level) On Track - In/Out. (If the menu is grayed out, click the Track Selection button and try again.)

In/Out options in the Audio Mix Fast menu

The system sets the level or pan from the beginning of the segment with the IN mark to the end of the clip with the OUT mark.

Adjusting Audio Gain with Keyframes

Audio Gain Automation (also called audio rubberbanding) allows you to change the volume of a segment by adding and manipulating gain keyframes (break points) in the Timeline.

When you add a keyframe, the system adds the point at the level currently set for that track in the Audio Mix tool. Audio gain keyframes are **additive** to the values set in the Audio Mix tool. This allows you to adjust the values separately.

Preparing the Timeline

To prepare the tracks to add and manipulate keyframes:

1 In the Timeline, select the audio track(s) you want to adjust. Also, select the speaker monitors for the tracks you want to hear.

2 Expand the audio track(s) you want to adjust.

Tip: To display audio gain meters and keyframe information superimposed over a waveform plot in the Timeline, choose Timeline Fast menu > Sample Plot.

3 Choose Timeline Fast menu > Audio Auto Gain.

A straight line appears in the selected audio track, showing the current gain level for that track in the Automation Gain tool.

4 To view the clip gain values in the Timeline at the same time, choose Timeline Fast menu > Audio Clip Gain.

Adding Keyframes

To add a keyframe to the sequence:

Tip: The Add Keyframe button is mapped to the keyboard on the N key. To map the button to another key, see the FX tab of the Command palette.

1 Place the position indicator where you want to add the keyframe in the sequence.

2 Select the track(s) where you want to add the keyframe(s).

3 Click the Add Keyframe button in the Tool Palette.

Adjusting Keyframes

Use the following methods to adjust the gain on a selected track or tracks:

To raise or lower the level, do one of the following:

- Click and drag a keyframe up or down to increase or decrease the gain at that point. If there is a keyframe at the same position on another enabled track, it moves also.

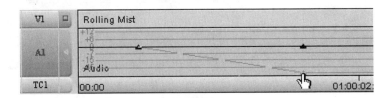

Dragging a keyframe to adjust level

If the Automation Gain window is open, you see that the corresponding Volume slider moves.

- To snap to the decibel lines, hold the Control (Windows) or ⌘ (Macintosh) key while you drag the keyframe.

- If the Automation Gain window is open, you can click in the Volume Level box and type a number (negative number to decrease the level) in the numeric keypad.

 —— Volume
Level box

To change the start or end of a ramp:

1 Move the cursor over the keyframe you want to move. When the cursor becomes a hand:

Note: You cannot move one keyframe on top of another or past another.

2 Press the Alt (Windows) or Option (Macintosh) key, and then click on the keyframe and drag it left or right.

This moves the keyframe horizontally earlier or later in the Timeline.

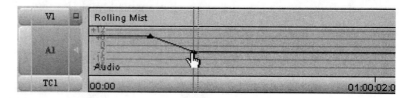

Alt/Option+dragging a keyframe to adjust the audio ramp

Deleting Keyframes

To delete a single keyframe:

1 Move the cursor over the keyframe until the cursor turns into the pointing hand. (Make sure the position indicator is not parked on the keyframe.)

2 Press the Delete key.

If there are identical keyframes in other active tracks the system deletes them also.

To delete groups of keyframes:

1 Do one of the following:

- Mark an IN and OUT surrounding the area.

- Mark the entire segment with the Mark Clip button (T key).

2 Select the appropriate audio tracks.

3 Move the cursor over one of the keyframes until the cursor turns into a pointing hand.

4 Press the Delete key.

All the keyframes are deleted.

Typical Scenarios for Adjusting Gain with Keyframes

These are typical scenarios for adjusting the gain on a selected track or tracks:

- To adjust gain evenly throughout a segment, on all enabled tracks:

  a   Add a single keyframe in the segment.

  b   Click a keyframe and drag it up or down to increase or decrease the gain within the entire segment.

- To create a gradual increase or decrease within a segment, on all enabled tracks:

  a   Add two keyframes in the Timeline: one at the start of the change in level and the other at the end.

  b   Click a keyframe and drag it up or down to increase or decrease the gain at that point.

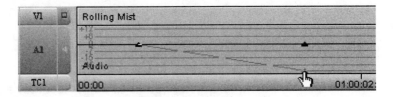

Using two keyframes to adjust level gradually

- To adjust the gain in a marked portion of the Timeline, on all enabled tracks:

  a Add four keyframes in the Timeline:

  – Just before the change in level begins

  – Just after the change in level begins

  – Just before the change in level ends

  – Just after the change in level ends

  b Add an IN mark between keyframes 1 and 2, and an OUT mark between keyframes 3 and 4.

  c Drag keyframe 2 or 3 up or down.

  Notice how the keyframes outside the IN/OUT marks do not move.

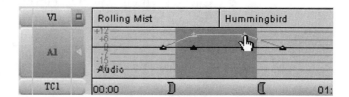

Using keyframes to adjust level for a portion of the sequence

Automation Gain Real-Time Recording

You can use Audio Gain Automation recording to adjust gain in real time. If you want to use this feature, it's often best to perform this procedure *after* setting overall levels in the Audio Mix tool and *before* adjusting keyframes, as described in the previous section.

1 (Option) Prepare the Timeline as in "Preparing the Timeline" on page 239.

If you adjust audio gain on a track in your sequence and do not display any volume information, a little pink triangle appears in each clip to which audio gain adjustments have been made.

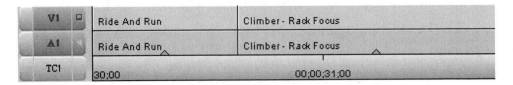

Sequence in the Timeline with pink triangles displayed

2 Mark IN and OUT points on the area you want to adjust. If you don't set IN and OUT marks, you can adjust the entire sequence.

3 Choose Tools > Automation Gain.

The Automation Gain tool appears.

Audio Effects Tool
Selection menu

Play Loop button

Fast menu
Displays track
sliders

Trash icon

Record
button

Preroll and postroll

Number
of Panes
button

Track
Selection
button

Volume
Level box

Gang
button

Level Slider

Click a
number.

Pan

Automation Gain tool with components labelled

4 (Option) Type a number in the Preroll and Postroll boxes to play frames before and after the automation gain adjustments. For example, type 2 for two seconds.

5 Click the Track Selection button(s) for the audio track(s) to be adjusted.

6 (Option) To link (gang) tracks together so they are adjusted in tandem, click the Gang buttons on the desired tracks.

7 Click the Record button or press the B key to start recording your actions.

8 Adjust the Level sliders as you listen.

9 If you want to stop recording, click the Record button again.

10 If you want to abort the process and try again, click the Trash icon.

During Audio Gain recording, the system adds volume keyframes to the audio in the Timeline. Because it records every movement of the sliders, there are usually more keyframes than you need.

To decrease the number of keyframes:

1 Click the Track Selection button to enable the Automation Gain Fast menu.

2 Choose Filter Automation Gain on Track In/Out from the Automation Gain Fast menu.

The system removes approximately 10 percent of the keyframes while maintaining the overall shape of the curves.

3 Repeat the previous step until you have decreased the number of keyframes to an acceptable level.

You should remove as many excess keyframes as possible while still maintaining the desired volume changes.

Now you can adjust keyframes manually to fine-tune the levels.

Deleting All Keyframes

To delete all keyframes, thereby undoing the changes in levels made in Audio Gain Automation:

1 Remove any IN/OUT points on the track.

2 In the Automation Gain Tool, choose Remove Automation Gain on Track from the Automation Gain Fast menu.

Review Questions

1 Where in the Audio Mix tool would you go to apply a level to an entire track? (See "Setting Global Pan and Level" on page 237.)

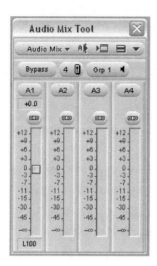

2 How would you start ramping up the music a little earlier? (See "Adjusting Keyframes" on page 241.)

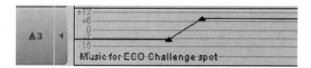

3 You want to raise the audio level for the portion between point A and point B, but you want the level before A and after B to remain the same. The levels will gradually increase and then gradually diminish. How would you do that? (See "Adjusting Keyframes" on page 241.)

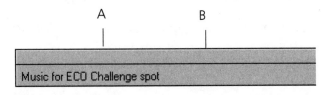

4 How do you reduce the number of keyframes after changing levels using the Audio Gain Automation Record function? (See "Automation Gain Real-Time Recording" on page 245.)

Exercise: Fine-Tune Audio

Now that you have fine-tuned the structure of the ECO Challenge advertising spot, it's time to work on the audio. You will adjust levels for entire clips and for portions of clips.

Raising the level for an entire clip using the Audio Mix tool:

Track A2 unadjusted

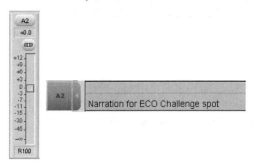

Track A2 level raised in the Audio Mix tool

Track A2 level raised

Raising the level for a portion of a clip using keyframes:

Step 1

Step 2

Step 3

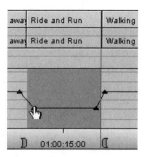

Note: If you prefer to work more on your own, follow the instructions in the outlined version at the end of the exercise.

Goals

- Center pan using the Audio Mix tool

- Adjust levels using the Audio Mix tool

- Adjust levels using keyframes

- Use the Record feature of Audio Gain Automation

Get Started

1 In the **ECO Challenge** project, open the **ECO Sequences** bin.

2 Duplicate the sequence you worked on in the previous exercise, and name the duplicate.

3 Load the duplicated sequence into the Timeline.

Use the Audio Editing Toolset

1 Choose Toolset > Audio Editing, or press Shift+F11.

Let's customize the display.

2 Adjust the interface so that the only Audio tool displayed is Audio Mix. **If the tool is not displayed, choose it from the Tools menu.**

Tip: When you want to return to the toolset for editing, choose Toolset > Source/Record Editing.

3 Choose Toolset > Save Current.

Any time you return to the Audio Editing toolset this arrangement appears.

Center Pan

If you are sharing your system with someone, it is sometimes difficult to hear one of the speakers. You might want to center pan all of the audio tracks. Let's do that now.

To center pan all audio tracks using the Audio Mix tool:

1 Clear any IN or OUT marks from the Timeline.

2 In the Audio Mix tool, click the Gang button for tracks A1, A2, and A3.

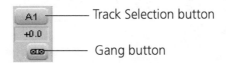
Track Selection button
Gang button

3 Press the Alt (Windows) or Option (Macintosh) key and click in the Pan Value display for one of the tracks. All boxes now display **MID**.

4 Click the Track Selection buttons for tracks A1, A2, and A3.

5 Choose Audio Mix Fast menu > Set Pan on Track - Global.

Pan will be adjusted to the midpoint for the ganged tracks.

Adjust Audio Levels

In this part of the exercise, you will adjust audio levels using Audio Mix and add and manipulate keyframes.

Adjust Audio Levels in the Audio Mix Tool

First, adjust the audio playback level of the narration on A2.

1 Play the sequence and listen first to the narration in relation to the music. It's too low. We'll use the Audio Mix tool to increase the level for the entire narration track.

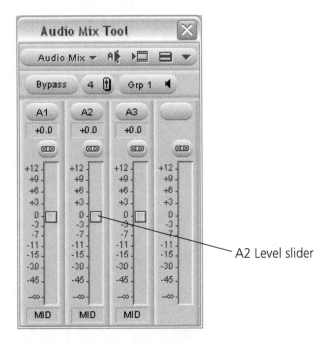

A2 Level slider

2 Drag the Level slider for track A2 up to raise its audio level. The new level is applied to the entire track (because it's a single clip).

3 Listen to part of the sequence. Continue to modify the level until you like the result.

Now let's raise the overall level of the rider's comment to the camera in the Ride and Run clip. (The music will still be too loud; you'll adjust that next.)

1 Place your blue position indicator in the **Ride and Run** clip.

2 In the Audio Mix tool, drag the A1 Level slider up a few decibels.

3 If you can't hear well over the music track, what can you do? (If you said, "Solo the A1 track," you're right!)

4 Play the result, and adjust as necessary.

Adjust Levels Using Audio Automation Gain

One key task in an audio mix is to adjust the levels of the dialog in relation to music. In the ECO Challenge sequence, the music overwhelms the Ride and Run sync audio. Let's adjust the audio level for just that segment of the music (we'll soon get to the rest of the music track). We will add and adjust audio gain keyframes to accomplish this task.

First, set up the Timeline to prepare for working with Audio Gain Automation keyframes.

Set Up the Timeline

To set up the Timeline:

1　Choose Timeline Fast menu > Audio Auto Gain.

2　To expand the music track, first click anywhere in the Timeline window. Then place the cursor just below the A3 Track button. When the cursor becomes a double-sided arrow, press and drag down the bottom boundary of the A3 Track button.

How else could you expand track A3? Why might this second way not be the best method for this situation?

Adjust Level for a Section of the Music Track

Now you can adjust the level of the music in relation to the Ride and Run clip.

1 Play the music under the **Ride and Run** clip. It's too loud. Let's lower it.

2 Select only the A3 Record Track button; deselect other tracks.

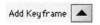

3 For each of the following keyframes, place the position indicator where you want to add the keyframe in the sequence and click the Add Keyframe button (in the Tool palette), or press the *N* key.

   - Keyframe 1: Just before the Ride and Run clip begins

   - Keyframe 2: Just after the Ride and Run clip begins

   - Keyframe 3: Just before the Ride and Run clip ends

   - Keyframe 4: Just after the Ride and Run clip ends

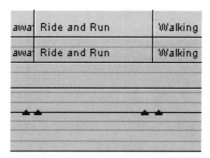

4 Add an IN mark between keyframes 1 and 2, and an OUT mark between keyframes 3 and 4.

5 Drag keyframe 2 or 3 down to lower the level. To snap to the decibel lines, hold the Control key (Windows) or ⌘ key (Macintosh) as you drag the keyframe.

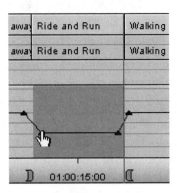

6 Listen to the segment and adjust as necessary.

Work on Your Own

You've now completed the structured part of this exercise. Spend the remaining time going over the audio levels and making further adjustments using the Audio Mix tool and by adding and manipulating keyframes.

Also, if you want to make adjustments to a significant section of the music track using the Automation Gain record feature, see the procedure and suggestions below.

In a later lesson, you will be introduced to titles, and you will have the opportunity to complete this spot.

Audio Automation Gain Recording

Previously in this exercise you used keyframes to lower the music level under the **Ride and Run** audio. If you like, you can adjust the levels for the rest of the music track "on-the-fly" by using the Audio Automation Gain tool's record feature.

1 Listen to the sequence and decide where you want to raise and lower the music level.

2 Mark an IN at the point where you would like the audio level to change, and an OUT at the point after the clip where you would like to end your changes. (You can of course also "record" one section of the music track at a time, rather than all at once. And remember you already fixed the music track under Ride and Run; there is no need to change that section.)

Use Automation Gain Recording

1 Make sure the Automation Gain window is still open.

Record button

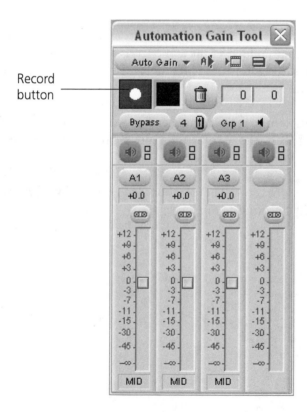

2 Click the Record button to start recording your actions from the IN to OUT mark.

3 As you listen to the audio, adjust the track A3 Volume slider to raise and lower the level of the music track.

When you finish, you see that there are more keyframes than you need.

4 To decrease the number of keyframes:

a Click the Track Selection button for track A3 to enable the Fast menu.

b Choose Automation Gain Fast menu > Filter Automation Gain Control In/Out.

The system removes approximately 10 percent of the keyframes while maintaining the overall shape of the curves.

5 Repeat the previous step until you have decreased the number of keyframes to an acceptable level.

Adjust Level by Adding and Manipulating Keyframes

Now you can raise or lower the volume in a portion of the music clip.

1 Play through the sequence and find a portion of the A3 track that you want to further adjust.

2 Select only the A3 Record Track button; deselect other tracks.

3 Add four keyframes and manipulate them, as you did for a section of the music. If you need assistance, see "Adjust Level for a Section of the Music Track" on page 256.

4 To move a keyframe earlier or later in the Timeline:

a Move the cursor over the keyframe. When the cursor becomes a hand:

b Press the Alt (Windows) or Option (Macintosh) key, and then click on the keyframe and drag it left or right.

5 Play the clip and adjust further as necessary.

6 Listen to the end of the music track. If it still ends abruptly, use keyframes to fade the music out at the end.

7   When finished, choose your standard view from the Timeline view menu to return to the Timeline view with reduced audio tracks and no displayed audio data.

Fine-Tune Audio (Outlined)

If you want to refer to the more detailed exercise for more information, see "Exercise: Fine-Tune Audio" on page 250.

Get Started

1   In the **ECO Challenge** project, duplicate the **ECO Challenge** sequence you worked on in the previous exercise, name the duplicate, and load it into the Timeline.

2   Display the Audio Editing toolset and customize it so Audio Mix and Automation Gain are the only audio tools displayed.

3   Save this customized display.

Optimize Audio

First you want to prepare for using the Audio Mix tool and Audio Gain Automation keyframes by doing the following:

1   In the Timeline, expand the audio tracks and display Audio Clip Gain and Audio Auto Gain.

2   Raise or lower the levels for entire clips or tracks using the Audio Mix tool.

3   Add and manipulate keyframes or use the Record function in the Audio Automation Gain tool to dip and swell the music, so the music plays better with the rest of the audio in your sequence. (If you use the Record function, be sure to adjust keyframes afterward.) For example, you might:

   • Lower the level for the music that plays under the voice-over narration

   • Exaggerate a swelling of the music by raising the level

   • Dip the music to hear the audio on tracks A1 and A2 more clearly

4 Add and manipulate keyframes to adjust the narration, sync audio, and music.

5 Change the pan for the music and/or narration track.

Lesson 9 **Capturing Media**

When you use the Avid system to edit material, you are not working with the actual physical source tapes. Instead, you are working with captured clips and media files that contain the audio and video information captured from the source tapes.

This lesson describes and demonstrates the process of logging and capturing material.

Objectives

After you complete this lesson, you will be able to:

- Set capture options
- Set audio levels
- Capture individual clips
- Log and batch capture clips

Setting the Capture Options

To set your capture options and begin capturing, you must first:

1 Open the bin where you want to store your clips.

Tip: If you like, you can also use the Capture toolset (see the Toolset menu). If the single-monitor Composer monitor is displayed for that Toolset, that should be fine.

2 With that bin highlighted, choose Tools > Capture.

You can also type Control+7 (Windows) or ⌘+7 (Macintosh).

The screen displays the Capture tool.

Record button

Toggle between capture and log

Deck button

Audio tool

Passthrough Mix tool

Click to activate tracks to record.

Press to choose your target bin.

Single/ Dual Drive Toggle

Resolution Pop-up

Deck pop-up menu

Press to select the target drive(s).

Click here to choose a new tape.

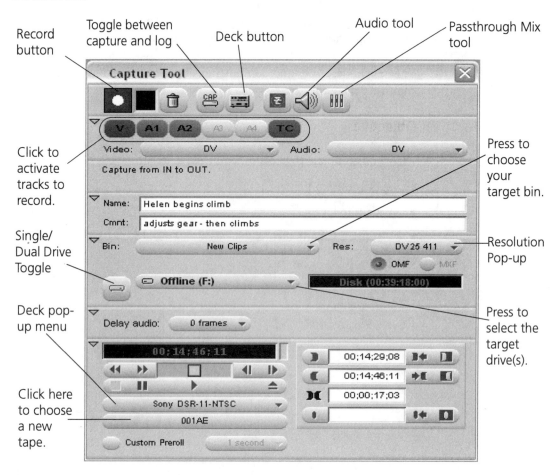

Capture tool with components labelled

Working in the Capture Tool

The Capture tool provides all the controls you need to capture your footage in digital form. To set up the tool, you will select:

- Source deck (or camera)
- Source tape name
- Tracks to capture
- Video and audio formats
- Target bin for storing the clips
- Target drive(s) for storing the captured media

Selecting the Deck or Camera

(Avid Xpress DV/Pro without Avid Mojo) If your source material is not Mini-DV (also known as IEEE 1394 or FireWire) you will need to convert the signal with a third-party analog to digital transcoder. In this case, you will need to control the device with serial control.

1 Physically connect the deck (or camera) you will use.

2 If no deck/camera appears in the Capture tool, choose Deck menu > Check Decks. This works if the Avid system knows that the deck exists, but the deck was not on or connected when you entered Capture mode.

3 If the deck/camera still does not appear in the Deck window, choose Deck pop-up menu > Auto-configure. The system will automatically configure the correct deck and display it in the Deck window.

4 If the deck/camera still does not appear in the Deck window, you have to set it up in the Deck Configuration settings. (See the *Input and Output Guide* for your system for more information.

Identifying the Source Tape

To specify the source tape name:

1 Insert a tape into the play deck.

   If the tape deck is in Remote mode, the Select Tape dialog box appears.

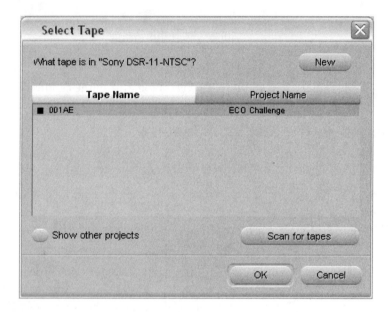

Selecting or adding tape names in the Select Tape dialog box

2 If the name of your tape shows up in the list, move the mouse cursor over the tape icon next to the tape name. Double-click when the cursor becomes a hand. Proceed to step 4.

3 If your tape isn't in the list:

   a Click New, or press Control+N (Windows) or ⌘+N (Macintosh).

      A new tape name line appears at the bottom of the list.

   b Type the tape name and press Enter or Return.

4 Click OK.

Tape Naming Guidelines

Use a unique name for each new tape (and write the same name on the physical tape and on the tape box). The flexibility of the Avid editing system relies in part on the its ability to correctly associate clips with the correct physical tapes. The system cannot distinguish between two tapes with the same name.

Tape naming schemes should reflect the finishing plan for the project. A program that will be finished in an Avid online has considerable tolerance in the length and format of tape names.

Projects that will be finished from an EDL in a linear online session should be assigned tape names of no more than six characters, numbers leading, with no punctuation or spaces, for example, 001ECO. If you plan to create an EDL, check with your online house if you are unsure about how to name your tape.

Selecting Active Tracks

The Capture tool captures information from the active tracks. The Avid system automatically activates the tracks that were active in the previous session.

You can change these settings by clicking tracks to activate or deactivate them.

▸ Select the desired tracks, for example V, A1, A2, and TC.

Avid Xpress Pro with Avid Mojo

 or:

Avid Xpress Pro without Avid Mojo/Avid Xpress DV

Activating tracks in the Capture tool

The number of available audio tracks (two or four) is based on your system configuration. (Tracks A3 and A4 are grayed out in the first illustration; tracks A5 through A8 are grayed out in the second.)

! **Make sure to capture only the tracks you need; capturing unneeded tracks consumes valuable drive space.**

Setting the Video and Audio Input Formats

The Video and Audio pop-up menus in the Capture tool show you the current settings for the video and audio input formats. You can change the Audio settings by selecting the pop-up menu and choosing a different option. The options may vary depending on the Avid system you have.

- Video input:

  - Analog input formats (only with Avid Mojo): Component, Composite, S-Video

  - Digital input formats: DV (with Avid Mojo), OHCI (without Avid Mojo)

- Audio input:

  - Analog input formats: RCA (-10dBU) (with Avid Mojo)

  - Digital input formats: DV (with Avid Mojo), OHCI (without Avid Mojo)

To set the video and audio input formats:

1 Choose an option from the Video Input pop-up menu. Your choice affects the Audio Input options that will be available.

2 Choose an option from the Audio Input pop-up menu.

Choosing the Video Resolution

Before you begin capturing, you must determine the resolution you want to use for both video and audio.

Selecting the OMF or MXF File Format

Note: MXF is not available with the current release of Avid Xpress DV/Pro.

OMF and MXF are industry-standard, platform-independent file formats that let you exchange media and the editing information for your sequence between applications.

- OMF: The OMF Interchange format (OMF or OMFI) is preferred for exchanging files with Pro Tools, animation systems, and other applications that require the transferring of complex metadata.

- MXF: Material Exchange Format (MXF) is a relatively new format. It's a less complex file format than OMF, and its advantage is in improving workflow efficiencies. Its use is expanding in broadcast, post-production, asset management, and archiving applications. Avid|DS and Pro Tools support MXF files.

To select the file format:

▶ Click OMF or MXF, depending on the one used by your facility.

The available resolutions depend on which file format you select.

Identifying the Video Resolutions

The resolution is listed as a ratio, which identifies the level of image resolution for captured video. The lower the ratio, the better the resolution, and the more disk space that will be needed. You can combine single and two-field resolutions, and analog and digital video resolutions, in a single sequence. The only restriction is that you cannot mix interlaced and progressive resolutions.

! **The available resolutions depend on the Video Input option you choose.**

The Avid system offers the following resolutions.

- **Two-field uncompressed resolution:** 1:1 (with Avid Mojo)

- **Single-field interlaced resolution:** 15:1s

- **Two-field interlaced resolutions:** 28:1 (in a 23.976p project)

- **For DV media:** DV-25 4:1:1

  To save storage space when capturing DV media, choose 15:1s draft resolution.

- **Progressive resolution:** DV 24p

  This DV 25 resolution is available only in 23.97p projects.

Interlaced versus Progressive Frames

An interlaced frame consists of two fields, each of which contains one-half the scan lines of the frame. Interlaced frames are standard for NTSC and PAL video media.

Progressive media is composed of single frames, each of which is vertically scanned as one pass. The Avid system creates 24p media by combining (deinterlacing) two video fields into a single full, reconstructed frame.

Choosing the Video Resolution

There are two methods for choosing the video resolution.

Method 1: Using the Capture Tool

In the Capture tool:

Note: MXF is not available with the current release of the Avid system.

1 Select the OMF or MXF file format.

2 Press and hold the shadow box that shows the current video resolution, and choose from the pop-up menu that appears.

The pop-up menu shows a check mark next to the selected video resolution.

Method 2: Using the Media Creation Tool

The Media Creation settings enable you to set compression levels for all media created during capturing, as well as importing, titles, mixdown, and motion effects. It also enables you to assign drives for each type of media.

1 Double-click the Media Creation settings, or choose Tools > Media Creation.

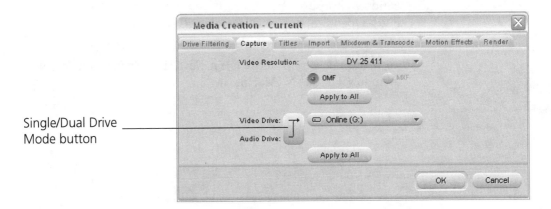

Single/Dual Drive Mode button

Choosing resolutions in the Media Creation tool

2 Select the Capture tab.

Note: MXF is not available with the current release of the Avid system.

3 Select the OMF or MXF file format.

4 Select the resolution from the Video Resolution pop-up menu.

5 To apply that setting to all tabs, click the Apply to All button (under the Video Resolution pop-up menu).

6 Select the drive from the Drive pop-up menu. To select a separate video and audio drive, click the Single/Dual Drive Mode button.

7 To apply that setting to all tabs, click the Apply to All button (under the Drive pop-up menu).

8 Click OK.

Selecting the Target Bin

Any bin that is open can be selected from the Target Bin pop-up menu.

▶ To choose an open bin, click the Target Bin pop-up menu and choose the bin in which you want your captured material to be organized.

If the bin you want to capture to is not in the Target Bin pop-up list do one of the following:

▶ To open a previously created bin, choose the bin from the Project window, choose
File > Open Bin, or press Control+O (Windows) or ⌘+O (Macintosh).

▶ To create a new bin, choose File > New Bin, or press Control+N (Windows) or ⌘+N (Macintosh).

Selecting the Target Drive(s)

The Capture tool displays information about the target drives where your captured video and audio material is to be stored. In addition to the name of the target drives, the tool also displays an estimate of how much time is available on that drive to store new material.

Note: The estimate is based on your resolution settings, the number of tracks to be stored on the drive, and the free space available on the target drive.

You must decide where to store your captured material. To select your target drive(s):

1 If you have not done so, select the desired tracks.

2 Make sure the Single/Dual Drive Mode button shows one drive. If it doesn't, click it once.

Note: If you are capturing complex material, the Time-Remaining display decreases more rapidly than with simple material.

Target Drive pop-up menu

Single/Dual Drive Mode button

3 Choose a drive from the Target Drive pop-up menu.

The drive with the most available free space appears in bold type.

The Time-Remaining display shows an estimate of the amount of storage left on the drive based on your capture settings, number of tracks, and capacity of the target disk.

! **If you choose the Dual-Drives icon, make sure you choose two separate physical drives, not two partitions on the same drive.**

Setting Delay Audio

The Delay Audio option slips the audio in relation to the video and timecode. The delay range is 1 to 5 frames. For most situations, you set the range to its default of 0. However, depending on the camera used, you may need to introduce a delay during capture to compensate for how the camera records.

▸ If you shot footage using the Panasonic AG-DVX 100 camera, set Delay Audio to 1.

Setting Audio Levels

Before capturing, you should choose the audio rate setting and use the Audio tool to prepare audio levels. The process for preparing audio levels involves two steps:

- Step 1: Choose the audio sample rate setting.

- Step 2: Set the audio input levels.

! **Hardware Note: When working with video and digital audio simultaneously, set your digital audio equipment to the same video reference signal as your video equipment.**

Choosing Audio Options

An audio sample rate of 48 kHz has marginally better quality than 44.1 kHz, which has significantly better quality than 32 kHz. CD audio is 44.1 kHz, and DAT audio is 48 kHz.

The higher the sample rate, the more disk space is required to store the audio. However, the difference in disk space used for the various sample rates is not significant and should not influence your choice of sample rates.

To choose the audio sample rate setting:

1 Double-click the Audio Project setting in your Project window.

The setting opens.

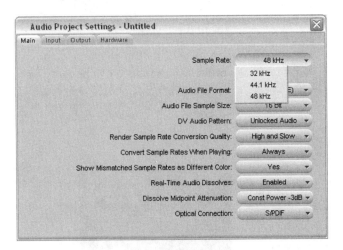

Sample rate options in the Audio Project Settings dialog box

2 Set Sample Rate to 48, 44.1, or 32 kHz. (The default sample rate for Xpress DV/Pro is 48 kHz.)

You can play different audio sample rates within a sequence only if the "Convert Sample Rates When Playing" is set to Always. This will perform a sample rate conversion of your audio on-the-fly to match it to the sample rate chosen in the Audio Project settings. This conversion is useful for offline editing, but may not be suitable for the final version of your sequence.

If you set the "Convert Sample Rates When Playing" option to Never, then audio in your Timeline that does not match the sample rate chosen in the Audio Project setting will play back as silence.

3 If using OMF audio, set the Audio File Format to OMF (WAVE) (Windows default), OMF (AIFF-C) (Macintosh default). An additional option is SDII (Macintosh only).

WAVE and AIFF-C formats can be mixed within a sequence.

4 Set Audio File Sample Size to 24 or 16 Bit.

5 Close the Audio Project settings.

Setting the Audio Input Level

You should always check audio levels before capturing audio media. Use a mixer or output levels on your deck to adjust level.

To set the audio levels:

1 Open the Audio tool by clicking the Audio Tool button in the Capture Tool window, by choosing Tools > Audio Tool, or by pressing Control+1 (Windows) or ⌘+1 (Macintosh).

The Audio tool appears.

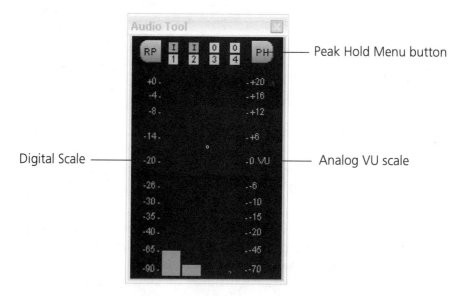

Digital Scale ——— Peak Hold Menu button

Analog VU scale

Audio tool with digital and analog scales

2 Play the tone (this tone should play under color bars at the head of the tape).

If you don't have tone, play a portion of the audio from your source tape, DAT, CD, or other source.

Clipping is indicated when the track numbers at the top turn red. If this happens, your audio will be distorted.

3　To adjust the input level and avoid audio clipping, adjust the output levels on the play deck, if available, or adjust the output on the audio mixer, if one is installed, so that the level of tone is -20 on the digital meter or 0 on the VU meter.

The scale on the right of the Audio tool corresponds to your VU meter. The scale on the left corresponds to digital audio. By default, 0 on the VU meter is set to correspond to -20 on the digital meter.

If you don't have tone, play a portion of the audio; the level should peak around -4.

4　Close the Audio tool, or leave it open to check audio levels while capturing.

Using the Passthrough Mix Tool (with Avid Mojo only)

Use the Passthrough Mix tool if you want to adjust the mix of tracks while monitoring audio input.

In the Capture tool:

1　Click the Passthrough Mix Tool icon.

Adjusting audio mix during capture in the Passthrough Mix tool

2　Keep the tool open while you capture, and you can raise and lower the Volume sliders as you monitor audio.

277

Capturing Footage

Once you have set all your capturing parameters, you can capture your clips. But first, a brief discussion of timecode.

The Importance of Timecode

Timecode helps to keep track of and count individual frames of video. Each video frame is assigned a timecode number in terms of hours, minutes, seconds, and frames. For example, 01:03:45:15 is read as 1 hour, 3 minutes, 45 seconds, and 15 frames.

The Avid system uses the timecode from your video cassette to navigate to various video frames. (Most video cassettes have timecode, including Beta SP, Digi-Beta, and MiniDV; an exception is VHS.) Timecode is also required for the Avid system to perform a batch capture, which we will discuss later in this lesson.

Timecode is recorded onto the video cassette by most consumer and prosumer cameras. In general, after a camera is initially powered on it will start recording at a specific start timecode. For example, most DV cameras start recording at 00:00:00:00.

To save on battery power you might turn off the camera several times over the course of shooting. However, if the camera is powered off in the middle of shooting and then powered back on again, the default recording start timecode might be reset.

When the timecode is reset in the middle of the cassette the result is a discontinuity in timecode, called a timecode break.

Because these timecode breaks can prevent the Avid system from being able to accurately seek video frames and batch capture, you should avoid as many timecode breaks as possible while shooting your footage.

Here are two techniques that might help:

- Pause the camera instead of stopping it. Pausing does not usually create a timecode break.

- If you have stopped the camera, you might prevent broken Timecode by rolling the video back a few seconds before starting to record again.

Capturing from IN to OUT

This method enables you to play the tape and mark an IN and OUT before capturing.

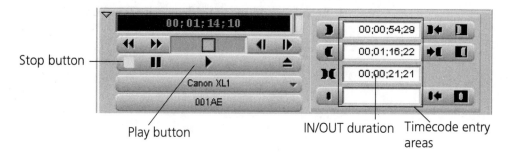

Stop button

Play button

IN/OUT duration   Timecode entry areas

Capture tool's deck control options labelled

To capture from IN to OUT:

1 Check that you did the following:

   a Open the destination bin.

   b Make sure that your camera is on, or that your deck is in Remote mode.

   c Insert a tape and name it in the Tape Name dialog box.

   d Check the Capture Tool settings explained earlier in the lesson.

Tip: Always set your IN and OUT points loose, so you have extra material for trimming and transition effects.

2 Enter the IN and OUT points for the clip you want to capture using either of the following methods.

   • Use the Mark IN and OUT buttons in the Deck Controller tool or the Mark IN/OUT (I, O) keys:

   a. Using the deck controls in the Capture tool, cue your source tape to the point where you want to start the clip.

   b. Click the mark IN icon.

   c. Cue your source tape to the point where you want to end the clip.

   d. Click the mark OUT icon.

   e. Click the Pause button to stop the tape.

or

   • Type the timecodes for the clip's IN and OUT points.

3 Click the large red Record button.

The Capture tool automatically rewinds the tape to a point before the IN point of the clip.

The bar next to the Record button flashes red, indicating that the Avid system is capturing your material.

When the tape reaches the clip's OUT point, capturing stops, and the clip appears in the bin.

4 Type a new name for the clip and press Enter or Return.

Typing a Clip Name and Comments While Capturing

You can type in a clip name and other information while the material is being captured.

! **The information that you type does not appear in the bin until you have completed capturing.**

To type in a name and any comments you want while the clip is being captured:

1 Once capturing has begun, type a name for the clip in the Name entry box.

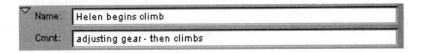

2 Press Tab and type your comments in the Comments entry box.

3 Press Enter or Return.

When capturing stops, the new name and Comments column appear in the bin.

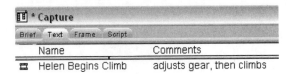

Capturing On-the-Fly

If you do not know the IN or OUT points of your clips, you can capture on-the-fly.

To capture on-the-fly:

1 Check the Capture tool settings explained earlier in the lesson.

2 Clear any marks in the Capture tool's deck controls.

3 Use the deck controls in the Capture tool to get near the material you want to capture, and then click the Play button.

4 To begin capturing, click the red Record button.

The red square adjacent to the Record button flashes on and off.

Stopping Capture

To stop capturing:

1 Click the red Record button again, or press the Escape key.

The clip appears in the bin.

2 Click the Stop button in the Deck Control tool to stop the tape.

3 If you haven't already done so, name the clip by highlighting it in black in the bin and typing a new name.

Generating Subclips/Locators Automatically with DV Scene Extraction

DV Scene Extraction allows you to automatically generate subclips and locators while capturing material in the DV video format. Discontinuities in the DV time-of-day (TOD) data indicate each place where a new take was initiated on a DV camera. Using this feature, you can capture an entire DV tape as a single master clip and have the system automatically locate all the takes for you, eliminating the need to manually log.

! **DVCPro format does not provide TOD metadata; you cannot use DV Scene Extraction with DVCPro format.**

! **DV Scene Extraction will not work on audio-only clips.**

To set up DV Scene Extraction:

Tip: To use DV Scene Extraction after capturing, select the clip(s) for which you want to create subclips or locators, select Bin > DV Scene Extraction, and choose the options you want.

1 Open the Capture settings, and select the DV Options tab.

2 Click DV Scene Extraction.

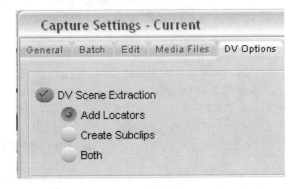

Setting up DV Scene Extraction

3 Select one of the following options:

- **Add Locators**: Creates locator marks where the TOD information breaks occur while capturing.

- **Create Subclips**: Creates subclips where the TOD information breaks occur while capturing.

- **Both**: Creates subclips and locator marks where the TOD information breaks occur while capturing.

4 Click OK.

When capturing has finished, subclips are created with the same source clip name and the extension .sub.01 where TOD information breaks occurred. Locator marks appear in the master clip where TOD information breaks occurred.

DV Capture Offset

If you capture from an analog deck, you need to go from the deck, through a transcoder, and into the Avid system. Routing the signal through the transcoder introduces a time delay. This results in the transport of the DV media lagging behind the timecode, which is travelling from the Avid system to the deck (see the figure below).

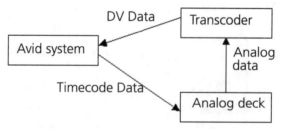

Capturing from an analog deck: A transcoder converts analog data to digital data that is then sent via a FireWire cable to the Avid system. Timecode data is sent via RS-422 controller from the Avid system to the deck.

Configuration of transcoder, analog deck, and Avid system

The DV capture offset allows you to make a corrective offset to correct the problem, adjusting the DV stream coming into the Avid system against the timecode assigned to each frame during capturing.

To use DV capture offset:

1 Perform several captures with the DV capture offset set to 0.

2 Note the first frame of the master clip for each clip.

3 If the first frame of the master clip is not as expected, adjust the DV capture offset to account for this variation.

For example, the first frame of the master clip might be the sixth frame from the IN point on the tape.

4 To adjust for the device behavior in this example, set the DV capture offset to –6 frames.

The result should be a frame-accurate capture. However, the results are dependent on device behavior. If the device behavior for sending streams across a FireWire cable is inconsistent, frame-accurate results on capture will also be inconsistent.

To offset the sequence for capture:

1 Open the Deck Preferences setting.

The Deck Preferences dialog box appears.

Note: The DV Capture Offset option only appears when your hardware configuration includes a transcoder.

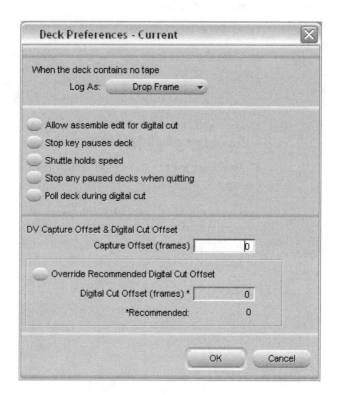

Adding DV Capture Offset in the Deck Preferences setting

2 Determine the approximate offset, and then enter the offset in the Capture Offset (frames) text box.

3 Click OK.

The delay is reflected in the DV Capture Offset box in the Capture tool.

4 Capture your material.

5 Repeat this process until you achieve the appropriate offset.

Logging and Batch Capturing

Many editors prefer to log all their clips (shots) first, and then use the batch capture function to capture their material automatically. This is often considered the most efficient method.

Naming Bins

When you begin mounting a project on an Avid system by logging or capturing footage, you must create a bin(s) in which the system will store the clips. You should also name the bins. Your choice of bin names will affect the editing process. The simplest scheme is to name the initial bins you create by tape name, in other words, a separate "source bin" for each source tape. For example, you would capture all the clips from tape 001 into a bin titled 001.

This strategy will be helpful in two ways:

- The bin becomes a database for a specific tape. A printout of the bin can serve as a useful archiving tool.

- Any scenes that were not logged and captured when the project was initially mounted will be easier to find because of visual associations with the clips in the bin bearing that tape's name.

Logging to a Bin from a Source Tape

You can use the Avid system to control a source deck, log shots (clips) from your source tapes, and record clip data (without associated media) directly into a bin.

To log to a bin from a source tape:

1 Open the bin where you want to store the clips.

2 Choose Tools > Capture.

3 Click the Cap/Log Mode button until you see the Log mode icon.

CAP ——— Capture mode   LOG ——— Log mode

The system switches to Log mode.

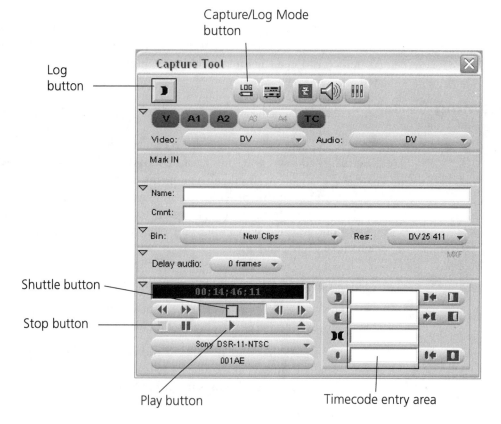

Capture/Log Mode button

Log button

Play button

Timecode entry area

Shuttle button

Stop button

Log mode of the Capture tool with components labelled

4 Play or shuttle to the point where you want to mark an IN for the start of the clip.

5 Mark an IN by doing one of the following:

- Press the IN (I) key on the keyboard or press F4.

- Click the IN mark and Pencil icon in the Log button.

- Type the timecode for the IN point.

The timecode for the IN point is displayed, the icon in the Record button changes to an OUT mark and a pencil, and the bar in the middle of the window displays a message ("Mark OUT"), telling you that the system is waiting for an OUT point to be established.

6 Shuttle or play to the place where you want to mark the OUT point of the clip.

7 Mark an OUT by doing one of the following:

- Press the OUT (O) key on the keyboard or press F4.

- Click the OUT mark and Pencil icon in the Log button.

- Type the timecode for the OUT point.

The Log/Mark OUT button changes to the Log button, and the deck pauses.

8 (Option) Enter a clip name, then press Tab and enter a comment.

9 Click the Pencil icon in the Log button or press F4.

The clip is logged into the bin. The default clip name is the bin name plus a number.

10 The tape pauses for a few seconds, then continues to play.

Tip: You can also click the Pause button (or press the space bar) and rename your clip.

If you have not already named the clip, notice that the default clip name is the bin name followed by a number. You can use this pause to type in a new name (and comments) for the logged clip, and press Enter or Return.

11 Repeat these steps until you have logged all your clips.

12 Stop the tape.

! **If you're using more than one tape, be sure to create a new tape in the Avid system for each physical tape and give each one a unique name.**

Batch Capturing Logged Clips

After you have logged a group of clips, you capture them automatically using the Avid system's batch capture capabilities.

To batch capture your clips:

1 Click the Cap/Log Mode button once in the Capture tool to return to Capture mode.

The red Record button appears.

2 Activate the bin with the clips you want to capture.

3 Select the clips you want to capture.

4 Choose Bin > Batch Capture.

Note: If the bin with the logged clips is not active, Batch Capture is dimmed in the menu.

A dialog box appears.

5 Confirm that the "Offline media only" option is selected. When this option is checked, all selected clips that are offline will be captured.

When this option isn't checked and some of the selected clips have media files, the system deletes the media files and re-captures new media files.

6 Click OK.

Note: You can stop the batch capture process at any time by clicking the Trash icon in the Capture tool.

7 If you have not inserted a tape into the tape deck, a dialog box will prompt you to do so.

a Once the tape is inserted, click Mounted to indicate to the system that the correct tape is loaded and ready for capturing.

A confirmation dialog box opens.

b Click OK to confirm the tape and deck entries.

! **If you insert the wrong tape and the Avid system finds the required timecode, it will capture from this tape.**

The system captures each clip from the tape, in Start Timecode order. If another source tape is needed, the system prompts you for the tape.

At the end of the batch capture process, a dialog box notifies you that the process is complete.

Capturing from a Non-timecode Source

Sometimes you have to capture from a source such as VHS, DAT, or CD that does not have timecode. Or you may choose to capture without timecode simply to acquire video across a timecode break. In these cases, the Avid system will generate timecode based on the time of day. The time-of-day timecode is arbitrary; it does not actually match up to individual frames on the tape and thus cannot be used to batch capture or create an EDL. The flexibility of the Avid system depends on its ability to reference any frame in the clip to its original source tape using timecode.

Capturing from a non-timecode source requires that you capture on-the-fly. When capturing a non-timecode source, you can adjust audio input levels, and enter names and comments as usual.

! **In order to record from a non-DV source you can use a signal transcoder to convert the analog signal to a DV signal.**

! **The timecode generated when capturing from a non-timecode source cannot be used for recapturing or in an EDL because the source never had "real" timecode.**

To capture a non-timecode source:

1 Click the Deck button in the Capture tool.

The system places a red circle with a line through it over the deck icon to indicate that a deck will not be used in the following procedure.

The system removes the Deck Control buttons.

2 Deselect the Timecode (TC) button from the Channel Selection buttons.

TC button

3 Click once in the Tape Name box.

The Select Tape dialog box appears.

4 Do one of the following:

- Choose an existing tape name.

- Click New and enter a new source tape name and press Enter or Return.

5 Click OK to return to the Capture tool.

6 Play the non-timecode source.

7 Click the red Record button to start capturing on-the-fly.

8 Press the Record button again to stop capturing.

Your clip appears in the bin and can immediately be used for editing.

9 Stop playback of your non-timecode source.

10 Click the No Deck icon until it returns to the Deck icon.

 No Deck icon   Deck icon

Using an EDL

If you plan to finish your work using an EDL, make sure to bring a digital cut to the online session so you can manually match the segments in the sequence which do not have timecode.

If you used non-timecode sources for your audio, such as DAT or CD, and you are planning to use your EDL to finish your work, consider using the audio output as your finished audio track. Remember, the Avid system can output CD-quality (44.1 kHz) and DAT- or DVD-quality (48 kHz) audio. This will save you from having to rebuild the audio tracks.

Review Questions

1 Label the following items in the Capture tool:

a The button you click when you are ready to capture a clip

b The button you click to toggle between logging and capturing

c The button to display the Audio tool

d The button you deselect if you are capturing a non-timecode source

e The button you click to set a Mark OUT point for a clip

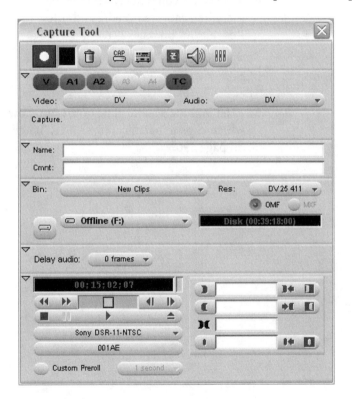

2 What is wrong with naming your tapes: supertape1, supertape2, supertape3, and so on? (See "Identifying the Source Tape" on page 266.)

3 Can you mix single-field and two-field resolutions together in a sequence? (See "Choosing the Video Resolution" on page 269.)

4 Where can you quickly set the video resolution for all media, including captured media and titles? (See "Choosing the Video Resolution" on page 271.)

5 After you log several clips in the bin, how will the system identify which clips to batch capture? (See "Batch Capturing Logged Clips" on page 290.)

Exercise: Capture Video

Note: If you prefer to work more on your own, follow the instructions in the outlined version at the end of the exercise.

Until you actually capture for yourself, it may seem like the most mysterious part of nonlinear editing. The following exercise takes you through the logging and capturing process step-by-step, to help you feel comfortable with all the buttons and tools used in this process. Remember, one of the most important aspects of capturing is being organized.

Set up the Capture tool.

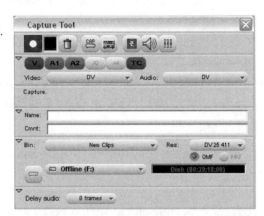

Use Capture tool buttons to log and capture.

To perform this exercise: if you have Avid Mojo, locate a Component tape, such as Beta-SP, or a Composite or digital tape. Without Avid Mojo, use a MiniDV tape.

Goals

- Set up the Capture tool
- Adjust audio levels
- Capture footage
- Log and batch capture footage

Create a New Project and Bin for Capturing

To get started:

1 Do one of the following, based on the status of the Avid system:

- If you have quit the Avid application, launch it now.

- If the Select Project dialog box is displayed, go to step 2.

- If you are in a project, close it to return to the Select Project dialog box.

2 Create a new project by clicking New Project in the Select Project dialog box.

3 In the New Project dialog box, name the new project **Capture**, and choose 30 (or 30i) NTSC or 25 (or 25i) PAL.

4 Click OK.

5 Click OK in the Select Project dialog box.

Now we'll get ready to capture by creating a new bin.

1 Create a new bin which will hold your captured clips, and name it **New Clips**.

2 Choose Toolset > Capture. If the single-monitor Composer monitor is displayed for that Toolset, that should be fine.

The Capture tool is displayed.

3 Insert the tape that you'll capture from into the deck.

"New Tape" appears in the Select Tape dialog box.

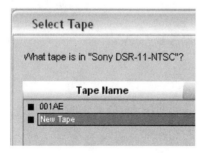

4 Type the name of the tape (the name that's on the tape cassette) and press Enter or Return.

5 Click OK.

Prepare to Capture Material

To prepare to capture material, perform the steps in the following sections, using the Capture tool.

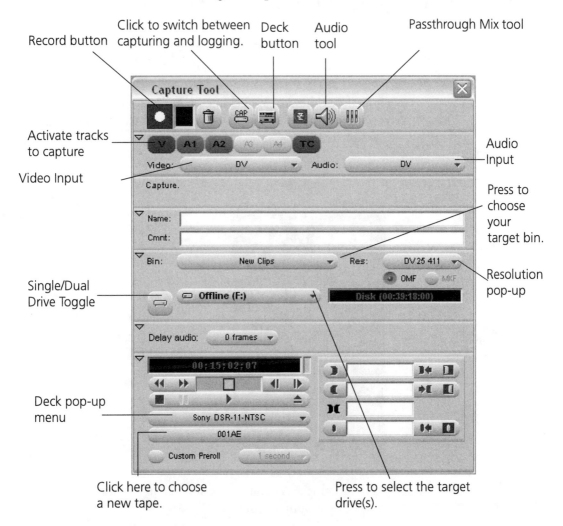

Record button

Click to switch between capturing and logging.

Deck button

Audio tool

Passthrough Mix tool

Activate tracks to capture

Video Input

Audio Input

Press to choose your target bin.

Single/Dual Drive Toggle

Resolution pop-up

Deck pop-up menu

Click here to choose a new tape.

Press to select the target drive(s).

Choose the Video and Audio Input Formats

1 Choose the Video format of your source tape from the Video Input pop-up menu.

2 Choose the Audio format of your source tape from the Audio Input pop-up menu.

Choose the Resolution

▶ Choose 15:1s from the Res (Resolution) pop-up menu.

Setting the Audio Input Level

Use a mixer or output levels on your deck to adjust level.

To set the audio levels:

1 Open the Audio tool by clicking the Audio Tool icon in the Capture Tool window, by choosing Tools > Audio Tool, or by pressing Control+1 (Windows) or ⌘+1 (Macintosh).

The Audio tool appears.

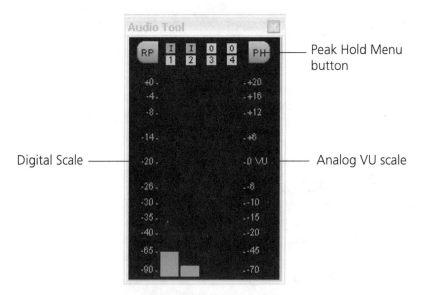

Digital Scale ———

Peak Hold Menu button

Analog VU scale

2 Make sure tracks A1 and A2 are selected in the Track Selection panel of the Capture window.

3 Rewind the tape to the beginning, locating the tone on the tape, and then press Play.

4 Adjust the level on your deck so that audio levels are set to 0 VU on the right side, which is the analog scale, and -20 on the left side, which is the digital scale.

5 Click the Pause button to pause the tape.

6 Keep the Audio tool open so you can monitor levels during capture.

Select Tracks and Target Disks

In this exercise you will capture video and one or two channels of audio.

1 In the top of the Capture tool, click the desired tracks: V, A1, A2. Make sure the TC track is selected. (If only one audio track was recorded on your tape, don't click A2.)

To ensure that captured video and audio material is sent to the same target disk:

2 Click the Single Drive/Dual Drive button until it displays a single drive.

3 Press the Target Drive pop-up and choose your target disk from the menu of available disks.

Capture Footage

To capture footage:

1 Locate the first shot on the tape.

2 Mark an IN by clicking the Mark IN button.

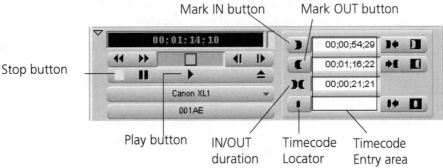

3 Play the tape, and click the Mark OUT button at the end of the shot.

4 Pause the tape by clicking the Pause button.

5 Click the large red Record button to capture the material and simultaneously make a master clip.

Once the system is finished capturing, notice that a master clip icon appears in your bin, and the tape is paused.

6 Name your clip.

Log and Batch Capture

Now you'll log several clips. The Avid system will log the clips' INs and OUTs but will not capture the media until you specify.

To log the clips:

1 Click the Capture/Log Mode button, which is in Capture mode.

The system switches to Log mode.

2 Forward the tape to the next shot.

3 Mark an IN and OUT to select this shot (or a portion of it). (For the sake of time and drive space, limit your clip to a maximum of 5 seconds.)

4 Click the Pencil icon to create a master clip.

A new clip is created, and is ready for naming.

5 Type a new name and press Enter on the numeric keypad.

6 Log two more clips. For each one, mark an IN and OUT, then click the Log pencil and name the clip.

7 When you finish, click the Cap/Log Mode button once in the Capture tool to return to Capture mode.

Batch Capture the Remaining Clips

1 Click in the Bin window that contains the logged clips to make it active.

2 Choose Edit > Select All to highlight all the clips in the bin.

Although you have already captured a clip, you can select all and then choose to capture only those clips for which there is no media. This is very useful when you have a large bin full of captured and uncaptured clips and don't want to have to shift-select only the clips that need to be captured.

3 Choose Bin > Batch Capture. Make sure the option "Offline media only" is selected and click OK.

The clips will now be captured in real-time in the order they appear on the tape.

4 Click OK when the batch capture is complete.

5 Close the Capture tool.

6 Play the clips.

Edit the Clips

Now you will edit all **except one** of the clips you've just captured into a simple sequence of no more than 4-6 edits. You will see why you should leave one clip out of the sequence when you get to the Media Management exercise.

1 Create a new bin and name it **Sequences**.

2 Select a clip for your first edit and load it into the Source monitor.

3 Play the clip to decide where to mark IN and OUT points.

4 Mark an IN and OUT point on the clip.

5 Overwrite the clip into a sequence. If you have more than one bin open, you will have to choose which bin will store the sequence.

6 Name the sequence **Capture**.

7 Splice several additional shots into the sequence.

Note: Your sequence will have clips with different names, but this screen capture is provided for purposes of illustration.

V1	rappel	swim	raft	rappel
A1	rappel	swim	raft	rappel
A2	rappel	swim	raft	rappel
TC1	:00	00;00;35;00		00;00;40;00

Batch Capture a Sequence to a Higher Resolution

Currently, the clips are captured at 15:1s, and therefore the sequence plays at that resolution. As you will see, batch capturing a sequence can be a very efficient way to change your sequence to a higher resolution.

To upgrade the resolution of your sequence:

1 Create a new bin, and name it **Hi Res Sequence**.

2 Duplicate your sequence, drag the duplicate into the new bin, and rename it.

3 If the Capture tool is not displayed choose Toolset > Capture.

4 Change the video compression to a higher resolution (such as 1:1 or DV25 441, depending on your system configuration) in the Resolution pop-up.

What other method could you use to change the video resolution? (Hint: It's a setting.)

5 Highlight the duplicate sequence in the bin and choose Bin > Batch Capture.

6 Turn off the option "Offline media only."

This means that the 15:1s media files will remain on the drive.

7 Leave the handle length set at 60 frames (NTSC) or 50 frames (PAL).

8 Click OK.

The system will recapture the sections of the clips which are part of the sequence at the higher resolution. When finished, your sequence will be linked to the new set of master clips and can be played at the higher resolution.

9 Click OK when batch capturing is done.

You will see new clips in your bin with a .new extension. These represent just the portion of the clips that were used in the sequence, plus 60 or 50 frames of handle length on either side.

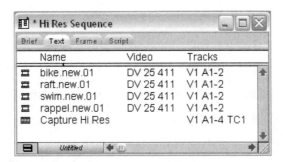

The sequence now contains the clips with the .new extension.

Capture Video (Outlined)

We do not provide you with a tape. Locate a MiniDV tape with footage you can use to go through this exercise.

Get Started

1 Connect the tape deck to the Avid system.

2 Launch the Avid system and create a new project.

3 Create a bin to hold the captured clips, and name it.

4 Open the Capture tool or use the Capture toolset.

5 Insert the tape into the deck and select the correct tape name, if it exists, or create a new one (give it the same name that's on the cassette).

6 Choose the Video and Audio Input for your tape.

7 Choose 15:1s for the resolution.

Calibrate Audio

1 Make sure the audio compression rate is set to 48 kHz on the external audio interface or in the Avid system using the Audio Project settings.

2 Click anywhere in the Capture tool to reselect it.

3 If your tape does not have tone at the head of the tape, use a relatively loud portion of the tape to set levels.

4 Use a mixer or output levels on your deck to adjust level.

Capture Footage

1 In the Capture tool, mark an IN and OUT for the first shot on the tape.

2 Capture and name the clip.

Log and Batch Capture

1 In Log mode of the Capture tool, log each of the next three shots on the tape.

2 Select all the clips in the bin and batch capture them. (What should you do to avoid recapturing any clips already captured in that bin?)

3 Play the clips to make sure they were properly captured.

Batch Capture a Sequence at a Higher Resolution

In this part of the exercise, you capture clips used in a sequence at an online resolution.

To prepare for this part of the exercise:

1 Create a **New Sequences** bin.

2 Edit **all except one of the clips you've just** captured into a simple sequence of no more than 4-6 edits. You will see why you should leave one clip out of the sequence when you get to the Media Management exercise.

3 Name the sequence and make sure it is in the **New Sequences** bin.

The clips were captured at 15:1s, and therefore the sequence plays at that resolution. To upgrade the resolution on your sequence:

1 Create a new bin, and name it **Hi Res Sequence**.

2 Duplicate your sequence and drag the duplicate into the new bin.

3 Open the Capture tool.

4 Choose the target drive and video resolution of 1:1 or DV25 411, depending on the options available.

What other method could you use to change the video resolution? (Hint: It's in a setting.)

5 Highlight the duplicate sequence and choose Bin > Batch Capture.

6 Turn off the option "Offline media only."

7 Leave the handle length set at 60 frames (NTSC) or 50 frames (PAL).

8 Click OK.

The system recaptures the sections of the clips which are part of the sequence at the higher resolution. When done, your sequence will be linked to the new set of master clips and can be played at the higher resolution.

9 Click OK when batch capturing has completed.

You will see new clips in your bin with a .new extension. These represent just the portion of the clips that were used in the sequence, plus 60 or 50 frames of handle length on either side. Batch capturing a sequence can be very efficient.

Lesson 10 **Preparing Your Bin for Editing**

The best time to begin organizing your clips and bins is during the logging process. You can add detailed comments about each clip to identify the shot you need, or create new bins to keep all clips that meet a specific criterion together, for example, all the close-ups in the CU bin.

Objectives

After completing this lesson, you will be able to:

- Show headings in Text view
- Add a custom column to a bin
- Sort and sift clips
- Move clips between bins

Using Text View

Preparing your bin for editing is best done in Text view. A new bin displays only the clip icon and the clip name for new clips.

To add statistical headings to Text view:

1 Choose Bin > Headings.

A window appears displaying all of the available headings, with the ones already displayed in your bin highlighted.

2 To add a heading, click on the heading in the list.

3 To remove a heading that is already selected, click on it in the list.

4 Click OK.

The following table shows some of the statistical column headings available in Text view:

Table 8   Statistical Column Headings

Heading	Description
Name	The name of the clip or sequence (you can rename a clip or sequence after it has been captured)
Audio	The audio sample rate
Audio Format	Audio format
Color	Displays a color that the user associates with a clip
Creation Date	The date and time the clip was logged/captured
Disk	The last known drive on which the media for that master clip existed
Duration	The length of the clip
End	The timecode of the clip's tail frame
FPS	Frames Per Second
IN-OUT	Length of the marked segment, if any
Lock	Displays a Lock icon next to any locked items in the bin

Table 8   Statistical Column Headings (Continued)

Heading	Description
Mark IN	The timecode for the IN, if you have set one for the clip
Mark OUT	The timecode for the OUT, if you have set one for the clip
Offline	Displays the track names for any media files that are offline
Project	Lists the name of the Project in which the clips were created
Start	The timecode of the clip's head frame
Tape	The source tape name
Tracks	All tracks used by this media object
Video	The video resolution under which the media for that clip was captured

Placing the Bin in Custom View

The Custom option of Text view displays only the Clip Name heading. You can customize this view by displaying or hiding statistical column headings, and by creating new columns.

1 Click and hold on the *Untitled* space at the bottom of the bin, also known as the Bin View Name box.

2 Choose Custom.

Adding a Custom Column to a Bin

In addition to the standard headings that can be displayed in Text view, you can add your own custom column headings to describe information about clips and sequences.

Once you create a custom column and enter data for each clip, you can sort and sift the column.

To add a new column:

1 Put the bin into Text view.

2 Click an empty area to the right of all of the headings.

   You can also move any existing column to the right or left (by dragging the column heading) to create an empty area.

3 Type the column heading you want. Column headings must contain fewer than 14 characters, including spaces.

4 Press Enter (Windows) or Return (Macintosh).

   This puts the pointer in the data box, beside the first clip in the bin.

5 Type the information and press Enter/Return to move to the next line.

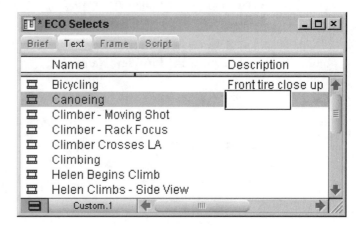

Entering text in a custom column

6 Create any additional columns and enter information.

! **Devise a good naming convention. For example, label all close-ups "CU." Otherwise you will not be able to sort or sift the column in any meaningful way.**

7 Choose Bin Fast menu > Align Columns, or press Control+T (Windows) or ⌘+T (Macintosh) if you need to straighten out the rows.

The following table provides information on adding and modifying column headings and cells in Text view.

Table 9 Operations in Text View

To:	Do This:
Repeat information from another cell in the same column. This modification applies only to custom columns.	Hold down Alt (Windows) or Option (Macintosh) and press on the cell in which you want the text to appear. A pop-up menu of the items already entered in that column appears. Select the correct text from the menu.
Change a column heading after pressing Return. This modification applies only to custom columns.	Hold down Alt (Windows) or Option (Macintosh) and click the heading. The heading text is highlighted. Type the new text for the heading.
Delete a custom column.	Click the column heading and press the Delete key. Note that you can delete only custom columns. You cannot delete statistical columns (but you can hide them).
Hide a column.	Click the column heading and press the Delete key. If you apply this to a custom column, a dialog box appears from which you can choose between deleting or hiding the column.
Show a previously hidden column.	Choose Bin > Headings, and select the previously hidden column.

Suggestions for Custom Column Headings

- Shot Size: Each clip's shot size (wide shot, medium shot, close-up, extreme close-up, and so on)

- Quality: Asterisks for good (*), better (**), and best (***) quality

- Good: Each entry is either Yes or No

- Description: Content of the shot

- Dialog: First few words of each dialog clip

Saving Bin Views

Adding statistical columns to text view or creating columns in custom view creates different bin views that can be saved.

! **If you don't save a bin view with custom columns before you switch views, the columns may be lost.**

To save a bin view:

1 Click and hold the cursor on the Bin View Name box (default is *Untitled*).

Saving a bin view

2 Select Save As.

The following dialog box appears:

3 Type a name and press Enter/Return or select OK. This retains the bin view name.

Suggestions for Bin Views

- Offline: display only the Offline column

- Marks: display Mark IN and Mark OUT columns

- Lock: display only the Lock column, to see which of your clips are locked

- Tape: display only the Tape column (or both the Tape and Start columns)

Sorting and Sifting Clips

You can sort and sift clips to help you organize your footage. You can sort or sift clips in a bin to find a specific clip or to see clips that meet specific criteria.

Sorting and Sifting Defined

- *Sorting clips* arranges clips in alphanumeric order (initial numbers come before initial letters).

  For example, sort the Scene column, in ascending order, and you will create a list of all clips of Scene 1, followed by all clips of Scene 2, and so on. You might sort by Timecode to obtain the order in which the clips appear in your source tapes.

- *Sifting clips* shows only clips that meet specific criteria.

  For example, sift the Name column for the name of a character, or sift a custom column called Shot Size for "CU" to obtain a list of all close-ups.

Sorting Clips in Ascending Order

To sort clips in ascending order:

Tip: You can rearrange columns in Text view any time by dragging the headings to the right or left.

1 In Text view, click the heading of the column that you want to use as the criterion.

The column is highlighted.

Selecting a bin column that you want to sort

2 If you do not see the heading you want, choose Bin > Headings and select desired headings.

Note: If the Sort command is dimmed in the menu, it means that you have not selected a column.

3 Choose Bin > Sort, or press Control+E (Windows) or ⌘+E (Macintosh) or right-click the Column heading and choose Sort on Column, Ascending.

The objects in the bin are sorted.

Tip: To reapply the last sort, choose Bin > Sort Again with no column selected. This is especially useful after new clips are added to a sorted bin.

4 To sort clips in descending order, hold down the Alt (Windows) or Option (Macintosh) key while you choose Bin > Sort Reversed. Or press Alt+Control+E (Windows) or Option+⌘+E (Macintosh), or right-click the Column heading and choose Sort on Column, Descending.

Sorting Multiple Columns

You can sort multiple columns in a bin at once. The left-most column in Text view is the primary criterion for the sorting operation. You can rearrange the columns in the bin, by dragging a column heading to the right or left, in order to establish which column is primary. For example, if you want to arrange your clips according to Start Timecode within Quality, arrange the columns this way:

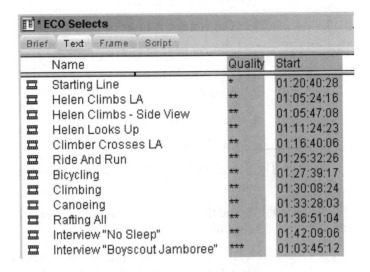

Name	Quality	Start
Starting Line	*	01:20:40:28
Helen Climbs LA	**	01:05:24:16
Helen Climbs - Side View	**	01:05:47:08
Helen Looks Up	**	01:11:24:23
Climber Crosses LA	**	01:16:40:06
Ride And Run	**	01:25:32:26
Bicycling	**	01:27:39:17
Climbing	**	01:30:08:24
Canoeing	**	01:33:28:03
Rafting All	**	01:36:51:04
Interview "No Sleep"	**	01:42:09:06
Interview "Boyscout Jamboree"	***	01:03:45:12

ECO Selects — Brief / Text / Frame / Script

Setting up bin columns for a multiple sort

Useful Application

You can keep your most recent sequence at the top of the bin by giving the name an initial character of "!" (exclamation point). You can keep your old sequences at the bottom of the bin by giving the names an initial character of "z". Then sort the Name column in ascending order.

Sifting Clips

Sifting clips allows you to show only those clips that meet certain criteria. For example, you might want to sift the clips in your bin to show only the clips that contain "CU" in the Name column. You can also use the sift function to perform more complex sifts.

To sift clips:

1 Choose Bin > Custom Sift.

  The Custom Sift dialog box opens.

2 Choose among the following operations in the Criterion pop-up menu:

  - Contains

  - Begins with

  - Matches exactly

3 Click in the Text to Find box, and enter the text that you want the system to find.

4 Choose the column that you want to search from the Column or Range to Search pop-up menu.

  The menu lists the headings in the current bin view. You can also select Any to search all the columns, including those not currently displayed.

5 Repeat the procedure for other search criteria.

6 If you're not sure that you have set up the dialog box correctly, click Apply. The results of the sift appear in the bin, and the Custom Sift dialog box remains open.

7 Revise the search criteria, if necessary.

8 When you are satisfied with your results, click OK.

The clips that meet your criteria appear in the bin, with the word "Sifted" added to the bin name.

Clips sifted for Helen in the Name column

Sifting Multiple Criteria

You can sift more than one criteria, using one of the following methods.

- OR (inclusive) sift: Sifts more than one criterion (in one or more columns), where a clip must meet *only one* criterion to appear in the sifted bin.

  For example, you might want to sift for clips that contain either "CU" or "MS" in the Shot Size column.

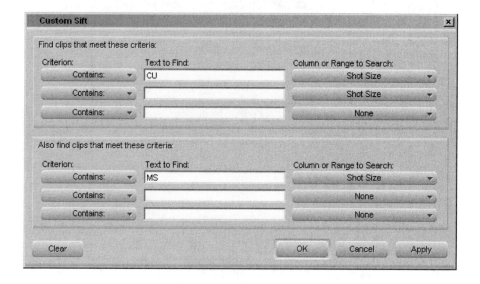

Setting up the Sift dialog box for a multicriterion inclusive sift

Here are the results.

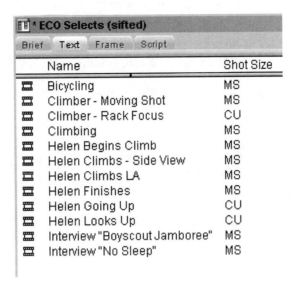

Results of an inclusive sift

- AND (exclusive) sift: Sifts more than one criterion (in one or more columns), where a clip must meet *all* criteria to appear in the sifted bin

For example, you might want to sift for clips that contain both "Helen" in the Name column and "MS" in the Shot Size column.

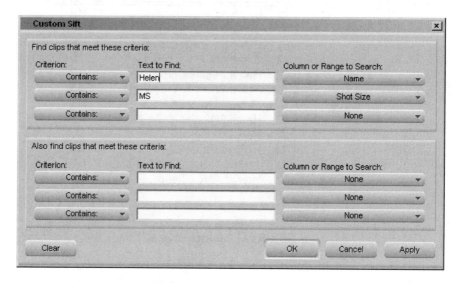

Setting up the Sift dialog box for a multicriterion exclusive sift

Here are the results.

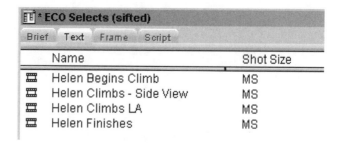

Results of an exclusive sift

Showing Sifted and Unsifted Views of the Bin

After you have sifted the clips in a bin, you can display the bin in a sifted state or in an unsifted state.

Note: The check mark in the menu indicates the current state of the bin.

▶ To view the entire bin, choose Bin > Show Unsifted.

▶ To view the sifted bin, choose Bin > Show Sifted.

Unsifted and sifted are dimmed in the menu if a Sift has not been set up.

Sifting + Storyboard Editing = Great Time Saver

Here is a great time-saver for combing through lots of material:

Let's say you're going to edit a half-hour program on rainforests. When logging and capturing, you can create two large bins, one for plants and one for animals. In the Animal bin, make sure to name each clip to facilitate sifting. For example, the clip name of a parrot shot will include the word "parrot."

Once you've done that, you can sift the Animal bin for all Parrot clips and storyboard edit them into a new sequence. Name this sequence "parrot universe," and keep it in the bin with the clips.

Any time you need a parrot shot, load the sequence in the Source monitor for a quick and easy way to review all of your choices. Then edit directly into the sequence in the Timeline.

This process works best if you storyboard edit the clips just after capturing so that your clips will not yet have IN or OUT marks.

Moving Clips Between Bins

Once you have sifted clips in a bin, you can move or copy them into a new bin. For example, if you sift for all clips with Helen in the Name column, you can move or copy all the clips with Helen into a single bin. Note the distinction between moving and copying clips.

Moving versus Copying Clips

- *Moving* a clip removes it from Bin A and places it in Bin B.
- *Copying* a clip leaves it in Bin A and places a copy of it in Bin B.

To move or copy clips and sequences to a new bin:

1 Create a new bin.

Give the bin a name that describes the clips it will contain. For example, if you move all close-ups to a new bin, name the bin *CU Clips*.

2 Position the bins so that you can see both of them at the same time. You may need to resize the bins to do this.

3 In the original bin, select the clips that you want to move.

4 Do one of the following:

    a Drag the clips to the destination bin to move them.

    b Alt+drag (Windows) or Option+drag (Macintosh) the clips to the destination bin to copy them.

The clips are now contained in the new bin and may or may not reside in the original bin.

Tips for Organizing Your Bins

- You might want to copy sifted clips to a new bin so that you can store and retrieve them easily.

- If you captured clips into a bin based on tape name, you might want to copy clips to new bins based on content. The clips remain in the bin bearing the tape name, and also reside in content bins.

- You can create new bins as the edit progresses. In this way, you can organize the entire body of clips available to the edit in an understandable, project-specific way.

Duplicating versus Alt/Option-Dragging Clips

There is a difference between duplicating (Control+D or ⌘+D) and Alt/Option-dragging clips to a bin.

- Duplicating creates a different clip pointing to the same media.

  For example, if you mark an IN in one clip, the IN mark is not automatically added to the duplicate clip.

- If you Alt/Option+drag a clip, it creates an exact copy of the clip.

  For example, if you mark an IN in one clip, it automatically appears in the other.

Review Questions

1 How can you find the start timecode of your clips? (See "Using Text View" on page 308.)

2 How do you add a custom column to a bin in Text view? (See "Adding a Custom Column to a Bin" on page 310.)

3 Fill in the Custom Sift dialog box to perform the following sift:

Display the clips of Helen (in the Name column) in Disk 2A. (See "Sifting Clips" on page 318.)

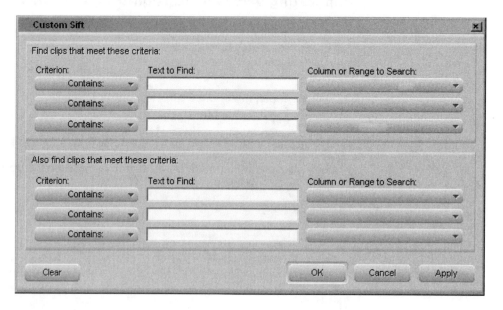

4 You want to list audio clips for tape 002 that were originally captured at 44.1 kHz so you can capture them at 48 kHz. Fill in the Custom Sift dialog box to display only the clips that need to be captured.

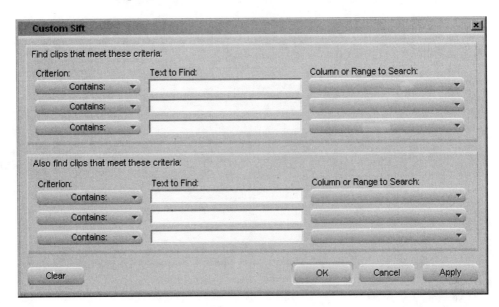

5 Fill in the Custom Sift dialog box to display the clips which contain "Sc1," "Sc2," or "Sc3" in the Name column.

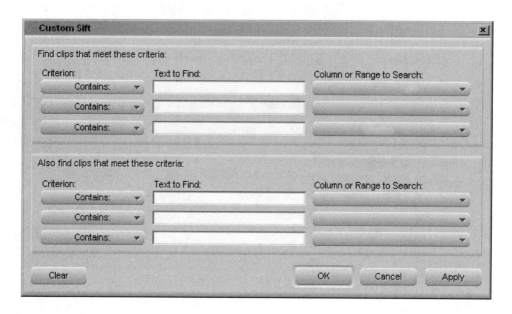

6 What is the difference between duplicating a clip and Alt+dragging (Windows) or Option+dragging (Macintosh) a clip to a new bin? (See "Moving Clips Between Bins" on page 324.)

Exercise: Organize Your Bins

After logging or capturing, it's a good idea to organize clips in different bins so you can easily find what you need during editing. In this exercise, you will organize clips that are in the **ECO Selects** bin in the **ECO Challenge** project.

Clips sifted for Helen in the Name column

Sift results

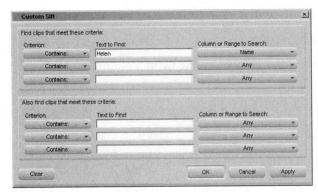

Goals

- Sift bins using content-based criteria
- Create additional bins of sifted clips

Sift the More Activities Bin for All Helen Clips

To sift for all clips of Helen in the **ECO Selects** bin, and copy the clips to a separate bin:

1 Open the **ECO Selects** bin and make sure it is in Text view.

2 Choose Bin > Custom Sift.

The Custom Sift dialog box opens.

3 Choose **Contain** in the top-left shadow box, if it is not selected.

4 Click the Sift Criteria box, and type **Helen**.

5 Press the shadow box before the word "column" and select the **Name** column.

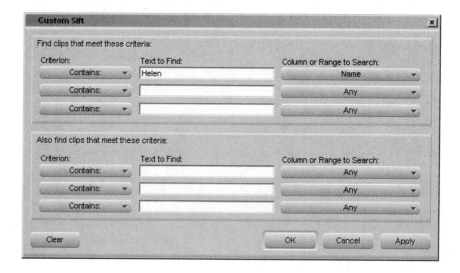

6 Click OK.

Six clips that met your criteria appear in the bin, with the word "sifted" added to the bin name.

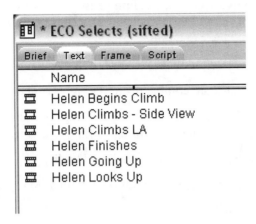

7   Create a new bin and name it **Helen**.

8   Drag the **Helen** and **ECO Selects** bins so they appear next to each other.

9   With the (sifted) Selects bin active, press Control+A (Windows) or ⌘+A (Macintosh) to select all of the clips.

10 While pressing the Alt key (Windows) or Option key (Macintosh), drag one of the clips from the **ECO Selects** bin to the **Helen** bin. The other clips follow. Release the Alt/Option key.

11 Highlight the **ECO Selects** bin and choose Bin > Show Unsifted.

12 Save all bins in the project by activating the Project window and choosing File > Save All.

The ECO Selects bin still contains all the clips, enabling you to continue sifting all of the clips, and perhaps placing a clip in more than one bin. For example, one clip might go in the Helen bin and in a climbing bin.

Add a Quality Column and Sift It

Now you'll create a column based on the quality (*, **, or ***) of the clips in the ECO Selects bin and sift to see all the clips that meet at least the ** level of quality.

1 Place the **ECO Selects** bin in Text view.

2 Click an empty area to the right of all of the headings.

You can also move any existing column to the right or left (by dragging the column heading) to create an empty area.

3 Type the column heading, **Quality**.

4 Press Enter (Windows) or Return (Macintosh).

This puts the pointer in the first clip's data box.

5 Type *, **, or *** to represent good, better, and best. Press Enter/Return to move to the next line.

6 To repeat information from another cell in the column, hold down the Alt (Windows) or Option (Macintosh) key, click and hold the mouse in the empty cell, and choose the desired data from the menu that appears.

7 To see a list of clips that are rated at least "better" quality, sift the bin for all clips that have the quality of either ** or ***:

There are two ways to set up the Custom Sift dialog box to achieve these results. One way uses a single sift; the other uses a multiple sift. You should be able to figure out both ways.

a First set up the Custom Sift dialog box to perform the single sift. Then click Apply to see the results. Notice that the Custom Sift dialog remains open.

b Now set up the Custom Sift dialog box to perform the multiple sift. Then click Apply to see the results. If they are what you expected, click OK. If not, try again.

Additional Exercises

Try the following:

- Add one more custom column to a bin.

Lesson 11 **Creating Titles**

The Title tool is a powerful yet easy-to-use program that is accessed from within the Avid system, and creates high-quality titles and graphics. This lesson introduces the basic concepts of using the Title tool. To learn more about creating titles, see the appropriate Avid system *Effects Reference Guide*.

Objectives

After you complete this lesson, you will be able to:

- Create a title in Title tool
- Create rolling and crawling titles

Getting Started

To get started:

1 In the sequence, place the position indicator within the shot where you want your title to appear. This frame will be visible in the Title tool as a background. This frame is for reference only; it is not part of your title.

2 In Source/Record mode, choose Clip > New Title.

The Title tool opens with the video frame currently displayed in the sequence as a reference. (If there is no sequence in the Timeline, the Title tool opens with a black background.)

Working with the Title Tool

The Title tool creates pages of text and graphics that can be saved over a color background or keyed over video. When titles are created for keying over video, they carry transparency information (in the alpha channel) which makes the pixels around the text or shapes transparent to the underlying video.

Objects created in the Title tool are anti-aliased so that the edges are smooth over any background. You must render titles created in the Title tool to output them.

Each title you create is saved in a bin and can be edited into a sequence using standard editing procedures.

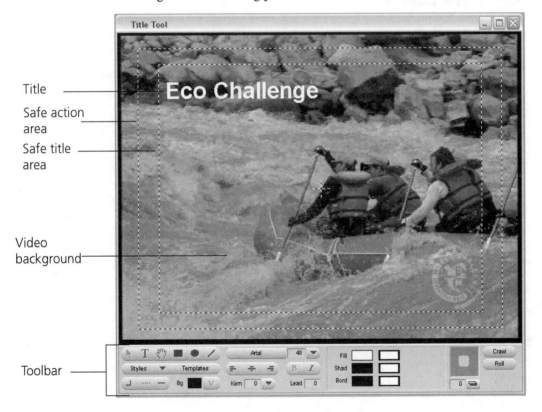

Title tool with components labelled

Using Safe Title and Action Guidelines

By default, the system displays two outlined boxes in the Title tool window to use as guidelines.

- Safe title area is the inner box. All text for television broadcast should remain within this inner box.

- Safe action area is the outer box. This is the area for video display.

These guidelines are self-adjusting for PAL and NTSC projects.

▶ If safe title and safe action area guidelines are not displayed, choose Object > Safe Title Area/Global Grid.

Using Safe Colors

If you plan to use your title for television broadcast, you should make sure Safe Colors is on. This command displays only low saturation colors for use in text, objects, and background. Colors with low saturation look best when combined with video. By default, Safe Colors is turned on.

▶ If Safe Colors is not on, choose Object > Safe Colors.

Understanding the Toolbar

At the bottom of the Title tool window are tools and menus you can use for creating and editing text and objects. They work much like similar tools in other draw and paint programs.

The following illustration identifies the different sections of the toolbar.

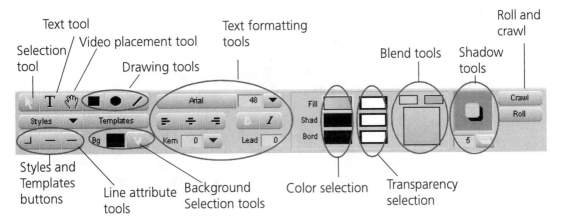

Title tool toolbar with components labelled

After you use a tool, the system reverts to the Selection tool, and the cursor becomes an arrow.

▶ To prevent a tool from automatically reverting to the Selection tool, double-click the tool's icon.

The following table briefly describes each section of the toolbar:

Table 10 Toolbar Options

Tool	Description
Selection tool	Changes the cursor from the text I-beam to an arrow and allows you to select text or objects for operations such as moving and color modification.
Text tool	Changes the cursor to an I-beam and allows you to enter text.
Video placement tool	Changes the cursor to a hand and allows you to scroll the entire video clip in the Title tool window within the frame.
Drawing tools	Allow you to draw boxes, circles, ovals, and lines.
Style sheet	Allows you to set up basic title and drawing parameters that you can use throughout your work.
Display/select styles	Display examples of the styles you defined and allows you to select one.
Line attributes	Allow you to change the corners of boxes, line and border thickness, and arrowhead styles.
Background Selection tools	Allow you to switch between a video and opaque background. Also allows you to change the color of opaque backgrounds.
Text formatting tools	Allow you to set various text formats such as font, font size, kerning, and leading.
Color selection	Allows you to change the color of text and objects.
Transparency selection	Allows you to change the transparency levels of text and objects.
Color and Transparency blend	When a color blend or transparency is associated with a style or object, this area displays the current values.
Shadow tools	Allow you to create drop shadows and depth shadows for text and objects.
Roll and Crawl	Allow you to create rolling and crawling titles.

Creating the Text for a Title

When the Title tool opens, the Text tool is automatically selected, and the cursor becomes an I-beam.

1 If not selected, select the Text tool (T). The cursor becomes an I-beam.

Selection tool   Text tool

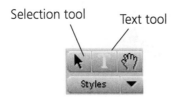

The Text tool remains selected until another tool is selected.

2 Click anywhere in the frame where you want to add text.

A blinking insertion point appears.

3 Type the text.

Repositioning Text

1 Click the Selection tool on the toolbar.

You can Alt+click (Windows) or Option+click (Macintosh) anywhere in the Title tool window to switch between the Selection tool and the Text tool.

2 Click on the text. A box with six handles appears.

Note: If you drag the handles, you readjust the size of the frame.

3 Click and drag inside the text box (but not the handles) to reposition the box.

Formatting Text

You use the Text Formatting section of the toolbar to adjust font, font size, text style, text justification, and kerning and leading.

Text formatting

Selecting a Font

When creating a title, you can use any of the fonts available in your Fonts folder, found in Control Panels (Windows) or the System folder (Macintosh). To select a new font for your text:

1 With the text selected (using the Text or Selection tool), click the Font Selection menu to display the available fonts.

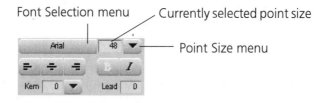

Font Selection menu   Currently selected point size

Point Size menu

2 Choose a font from the menu.

The system displays the name in the Font Selection box and uses the font for text until you change it during the editing session.

Selecting Point Size

The point size controls the size of the selected text. A *point* is a typographical unit of measure. There are 12 points to the pica. As a rule of thumb, there are approximately 72 points/inch (but in fact a 72-point font will rarely be exactly an inch high).

1 With the text selected, click and hold the Point Size Menu button.

2 Choose a standard point size from the menu, or enter a point size between 6 and 500 into the Point Size window and press Enter on the numeric keypad.

You can also select the point size number and use the Up and Down arrow keys to change the value incrementally.

Selecting Text Style

To change the text style:

▶ With the text selected, click the Bold or Italics button.

Bold and Italic buttons

Text Justification

Text justification controls the alignment of all text within a text element.

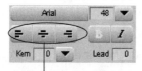

Text Justification buttons

Tip: You can also choose any of the options in the Alignment menu to align the text.

You can use the Text Justification buttons in the Title tool to align the text.

- Click the left Text Justification button to left justify text within the text box.

- Click the center button to center text as you type within the text box.

- Click the right button to right justify the text as you type.

To center the text within the screen, you can also type the text, click the Selection button, drag the handles to the right and left edges of the safe title area, and click the center justification button.

Kerning and Leading

Text Kerning

Kerning

Kerning controls the amount of space between characters. You can expand or condense the character spacing to make text more readable or to create special effects, such as dramatically expanded spacing in a title. The most common way to adjust kerning is to manually kern individual character pairs.

Tip: If you mix italic and plain versions of a font in a title, you might want to adjust the spacing between characters.

To adjust text kerning:

1 Select the Text tool.

Text tool

2 Click between a character pair, or select a group of characters by clicking and dragging the mouse over it.

3 Press the Alt (Windows) or Option (Macintosh) key and use the left or right arrow keys to increase or decrease the spacing.

Leading Adjustment

Leading

Leading adjusts the spacing between lines in a title. Leading is measured in points, from baseline to baseline of the lines of text. It is applied uniformly to all lines in a text box. The Title tool uses the leading that is built into the font as the default.

 Leading text box

Tip: You might want to add leading for sans serif, tall, or boldface fonts, and for fonts with a strong vertical emphasis.

To adjust text leading:

1 Select the lines of text. All of the lines of text should be in one text box.

2 Click in the Leading text box.

3 To increase or decrease the leading values, do one of the following:

- Enter a number for the desired leading value and press Return. Positive leading values add space between lines; negative values decrease space.

- Use the up or down arrow keys.

Leading Between Selected Lines in a Block

By default, leading within the Title tool applies to all lines in a block. However, you often need to add extra leading between certain lines within a block. For example, you might need more leading between one name and title and the next name and title.

Tip: Remember that leading is based on the point size of the text within that line. A leading value of –20 that might be acceptable for text at 64 points is often far too close for text at 24 points.

To add extra leading between two lines, simply add a blank line, select the entire blank line, and change the point size of the text within the line (including the carriage return). You aren't actually modifying leading, but adding an adjustable vertical space between two lines of type.

To add space between two lines in a block:

1 Place the cursor at the end of the line where you want to add space.

2 Press Enter or Return to add a carriage return.

3 Place your cursor at the head of the new line of type and drag downward until the entire new line is highlighted.

4 Change the type size to a smaller or larger amount until you have the desired space.

5 To apply the same space again at a new location, copy the line while it is selected and use paste to insert it where needed.

Accessing Special Characters

Windows

Special characters including language and diacritical marks can be accessed by holding down the Alt key and typing a key code on the numeric keypad. The accessory Character Map provides a map of the additional characters. You can access it by choosing Start Menu > All Programs > Accessories > System Tools > Character Map.

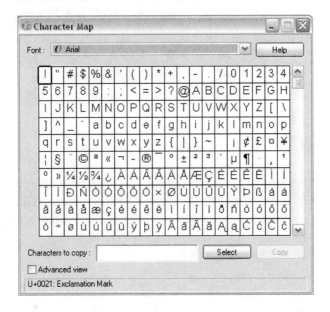

Windows Character Map

Macintosh

Additional characters including language and diacritical marks can be accessed by holding down the Option key and typing a key combination. The desk accessory Key Caps provides a map of the additional characters. You can access it by navigating:
Macintosh internal drive > Applications > Utilities > Key Caps.

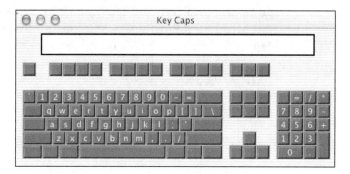

Macintosh Key Caps window

The key codes for common special characters are identical for every roman font on the system. You can also use Character Map or Key Caps to discover the key codes for symbol and dingbat fonts.

Commonly Used Special Characters

Special characters are accessed via the same key codes regardless of the font used. The following table provides the Windows and Macintosh keyboard shortcuts for commonly used special characters:

Table 11   Commonly Used Special Characters

Character	Windows Key Code	Macintosh Key Code
• (Bullet)	Alt+0149	Option+8
' (Proper Apostrophe)	Alt+0146	Option+Shift+]
" (Open Quotes)	Alt+0147	Option+[
" (Close Quotes)	Alt+0148	Option+Shift+]
– (Dash / Endash)	Alt+0150	Option+ - (Hyphen)
— (Long Dash / Emdash)	Alt+0151	Option+Shift+ - (Hyphen)
™ (Trademark)	Alt+0153	Option+2
© (Copyright)	Alt+0169	Option+G
® (Registered)	Alt+0174	Option+R
¼ (One Quarter)	Alt+0188	Not Available
½ (One Half)	Alt+0189	Not Available
é	Alt+0233	Option+e, then e
ñ	Alt+0241	Option+n, then n

Applying Shadows and Borders

This section covers drop and depth shadows, soft shadows and glows, and borders.

Applying Drop or Depth Shadows to Text

Adding a drop shadow to a title gives the perception of depth, as though the title were lying on a different plane than the video beneath. You can apply drop or depth shadows to text, and select their width, direction, and transparency.

Drop shadow
Depth shadow

Drop and depth shadows illustrated

To add a drop or depth shadow:

1 Select the text.

2 Toggle the Drop and Depth Shadow button to select a drop or depth shadow.

- Black for drop shadow

- Green for depth shadow

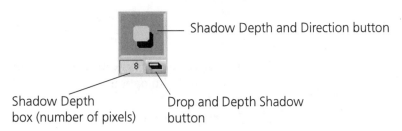

Shadow Depth and Direction button

Shadow Depth
box (number of pixels)

Drop and Depth Shadow
button

3 Choose one of the following methods to create a shadow:

- Click the Shadow Depth and Direction button and drag the cursor around to position the shadow in whatever direction you like.

- Type a value in the Shadow Depth box and press Enter or Return.

- Select the value and use the Up and Down arrow keys to change the value.

Applying Borders to the Text

To apply a border to a text string:

1 Select the text.

2 Click the Solid Line button (in the lower-left corner of the toolbar).

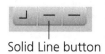

Solid Line button

3 From the menu that appears, choose a standard width selection or the Custom Width option.

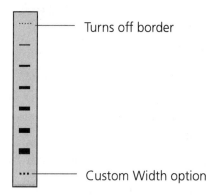

Turns off border

Custom Width option

4 If you choose the Custom Width option, in the dialog box type a whole number in pixels to specify a custom width. The minimum width for a text border is 1; the maximum width is 200.

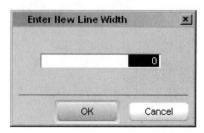

Choosing Colors

You can select the color for text, shadows, and borders.

The following illustration shows the boxes associated with color:

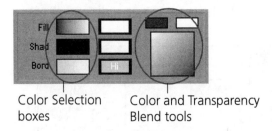

Color Selection
boxes

Color and Transparency
Blend tools

- The Color Selection boxes control the fill (Fill), shadow (Shad), and border (Bord) color selection.

- The Color and Transparency Blend tools appear when you select the Fill or Border Color Selection box.

  The Color and Transparency Blend feature is beyond the scope of this book.

Adjusting the Color

You can select a color from the Title Tool Color Picker, use an eyedropper to select a color from any open application on your computer, or you can use the Windows/Macintosh Color dialog box to select a color. All of these features are available through the Title Tool Color Picker:

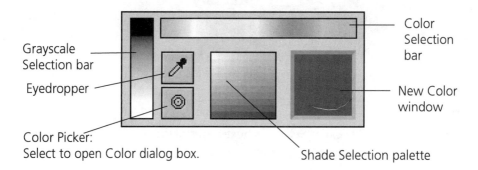

Grayscale Selection bar

Eyedropper

Color Picker: Select to open Color dialog box.

Color Selection bar

New Color window

Shade Selection palette

Title tool color picker with components labelled

Selecting a Color from the Title Tool Color Picker

1 Select the text.

2 Click and hold one of the Color Selection boxes on the Title toolbar: fill (the text itself), shadow, or border (text outline). Keep holding, and drag the Title Tool Color Picker to the side, so that the window stays open.

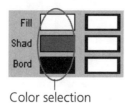

Color selection

Tip: To choose a grayscale value, choose a value from the Grayscale Selection bar.

3 To choose a color:

   a Click or drag the cursor along the Color Selection bar to the color you want.

   b Click or drag the cursor in the Shade Selection palette to choose a shade. The New Color window displays the shade.

   c Change the color and shade until you achieve the results you want.

4 Close the Title Tool Color Picker.

The color is applied to the selected object.

To use the Eyedropper

1 Select the text.

2 Click and hold one of the Color Selection buttons on the Title toolbar.

3 Drag the mouse to the eyedropper, and release the mouse button.

The cursor becomes an eyedropper.

4 Click the eyedropper on the color you want to pick up from the window or from any open application on your screen. The tip of the eyedropper should be on the color you want.

The color is applied to the selected object.

Saving, Fading, and Revising Titles

In this section, we cover how to save, fade, and revise titles.

Saving the Title

When creating a new title, you should save the title soon after you begin working on it, for safety.

To save a title:

1 (Option) Create a bin for your titles and open it.

2 Choose File > Save.

The Save Title dialog box appears.

Saving the title

3 In the dialog box:

- Name the title.

- Select a destination bin.

- Choose a target drive for the associated media files.

4 Select a resolution.

5 Click Save, or click Fast Save if you don't want to render the title yet.

6 You are returned to the title page and can continue working on this title, or you can quit the Title tool by choosing File > Close.

When you quit the Title tool, a two-minute title is placed into your target bin, and the media is stored on the drive you specified.

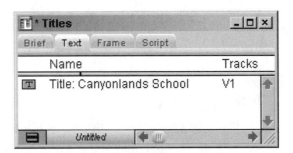

Editing the Title into the Sequence

To key the title over video:

1 If necessary, edit your background video onto track V1.

2 To add a V2 track to your sequence, choose Clip > New Video Track, or press Control+Y (Windows) or ⌘+Y (Macintosh).

3 Mark IN and OUT points in the Timeline to set the duration of the title.

4 Mark an IN or OUT in the Source monitor.

5 In the Timeline, patch the title from source V1 to record V2.

Tip: Click the empty area to the right of V1 Record Track button to display the V1 Monitor icon if you want to view only track V1.

When you patch one track to another, the system automatically monitors the selected record track, so the system is now monitoring V2. Since the sequence plays all tracks below and including the monitored track, make sure to monitor V2 to view V1 and V2.

6 Overwrite the title onto track V2.

7 If you need to render the title:

   a Park the blue position indicator on the Title Effect icon in the Timeline.

   b Click the Render Effect button in the Tool Palette.

   c Click Okay in the dialog box.

Fading a Title

To fade the title:

1 Place the position indicator in the title segment.

To fade multiple titles in a sequence, click either Segment Mode button, press the Shift key, and click the desired title segments in the Timeline.

2 Make sure the appropriate Track button is on.

3 Make sure the Timeline window is active.

4 Click the Fade Effect button from the Tool Palette Fast menu.

5 In the dialog box, enter the number of frames for the Fade Up and Fade Down.

6 Click OK.

Revising the Title

If you need to revise a title that is edited into your sequence:

1 In the sequence, place the position indicator within the shot where you want your title to appear so that this frame will be visible in the Title tool as a background.

2 Make sure the video track for the title is highlighted in the track panel.

3 Control (Windows) or ⌘ (Macintosh) + double-click the title clip in the bin where you saved it.

4 Revise the title.

5 Choose File > Close to close the Title tool.

6 Choose Save when prompted.

7 Play your title.

Rolling and Crawling Titles

A rolling title scrolls the title vertically, and a crawling title scrolls the title horizontally.

To create a rolling or crawling title:

1 Choose Clip > New Title.

The Title tool appears.

2 Click the T button to enter Text mode.

3 Click the Roll or Crawl button in the lower-right corner of the Title tool.

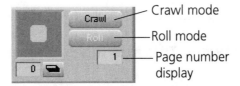

Roll and crawl section of the Title tool toolbar

These options allow you to create multipage titles.

4 Type your title text.

You can let the text wrap automatically (by continuing to type), manually (by pressing Return), or you can create separate text blocks and lead it by eye using the Selection tool.

As you type a rolling title, text wraps within the safe action area and the title scrolls down.

5 If necessary, resize your text box so that the title is within the title safe area.

6 Adjust the text formattings (font, size, color, and so on).

7 If you are creating a crawl, choose Object > Make Crawl to convert the text into a single-line crawl. Use the scroll bar at the bottom of the frame if you want to scroll along the title.

Since crawling titles do not scroll as you type, you might want to type in a small point size and then increase the size when you like the results.

8 Adjust kerning and leading.

9 Save your title by choosing File > Save Title.

A dialog box appears.

10 Enter a name for the title in the text box; select the bin, target disk, and resolution from the pop-up menus; and click OK.

11 The title is loaded into the Source monitor, placed into your target bin, and the media is stored on the drive you specified.

12 Render a rolling and crawling title:

    a In the Timeline park the position indicator on the Title Effect icon.

     b Click the Render Effect button in the Tool palette.

    c When the dialog box appears, click OK.

Editing a Rolling or Crawling Title into the Sequence

Use a three-point edit to add a rolling or crawling title to the sequence. Just as you edit any clip, you can use a combination of IN and OUT points, with the following consequences:

1 Mark IN and/or OUT points in the Source monitor to change the start and finish points of the rolling or crawling title.

By default, a rolling or crawling title clip begins and ends with the title just off screen. You might prefer the title to begin with the screen full of text rather than start off screen.

If you don't set an IN mark, the system uses the position indicator as the IN point.

2 To set the duration of the roll, mark the IN and OUT points in the Timeline before editing the title into the sequence.

This affects the speed as well as the duration of the roll or crawl, because the entire roll or crawl shrinks to fit within the marked segment in the sequence.

3 To adjust the speed of the roll, trim the end of the title clip in the sequence to shorten or lengthen its duration. Shortening the title clip increases the speed; lengthening the title clip decreases the speed.

Trimming a rolling or crawling title does not remove any part of the title contents.

Review Questions

1 If a font does not appear in the Font Selection menu, what would be the reason? (See "Selecting a Font" on page 340.)

2 What is the difference between kerning and leading? (See "Kerning and Leading" on page 343.)

3 How do you edit a title so it is keyed over video? (See "Editing the Title into the Sequence" on page 355.)

4 How do you speed up a title's roll? (See "Editing a Rolling or Crawling Title into the Sequence" on page 358.)

5 For the Title tool, answer the following questions:

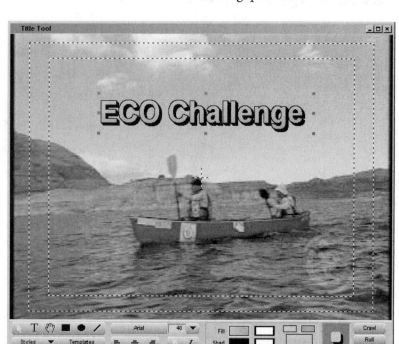

a Which area is safe for titles?

b How can you toggle between Selection and Text modes without clicking those buttons?

c If you want the text 'ECO Challenge' to match the color of the helmet, what would you do?

d What button do you select to toggle between drop and depth shadows?

Exercise: Create Titles

Note: If you prefer to work more on your own, follow the instructions in the outlined version at the end of the exercise.

In this exercise, you will finish the ECO Challenge advertising spot by adding an opening title, "Canyonlands Outdoor Adventure School."

Goals

- Create a title
- Adjust the title's font and point size
- Add color and shadow to the title
- Save the title
- Edit the title into the sequence
- Modify the title
- Fade the title in and out

Create Titles

In this exercise, you will add an opening title, "Canyonlands Outdoor Adventure School," to your sequence.

Get Started

To get started:

1 Create a new bin for storing your title. Keep it open.

2 Duplicate the sequence you worked on in the previous exercise, and name the duplicate.

3 Load the duplicated sequence into the Timeline.

Create a New Title

To create the "Canyonlands Outdoor Adventure School" title for your sequence:

1 Mark an IN and OUT in your Timeline where you want your title to begin and end.

2 Place the position indicator within the scene where you want your title to appear. This frame will be visible in the Title tool as background.

3 Choose Clip > New Title.

Use the Title Tool

The Title tool opens and displays the frame from the Timeline in the background.

1 Click in the image where you want the "Canyonlands Outdoor Adventure School" title to start.

2 Type "Canyonlands Outdoor Adventure School."

Modify the Title

1 Click the Selection tool.

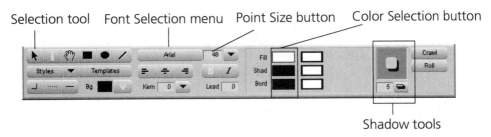

Selection tool   Font Selection menu   Point Size button   Color Selection button

Shadow tools

2 Select the text box by clicking on the text.

3 Choose a new font from the Font Selection menu.

4 Click the Point Size button to choose a new point size.

5 Drag the text box and reposition it.

To change the text's color:

1 Click and hold the Fill Color Selection box. Drag the box to the side so the Title Tool Color Picker stays open.

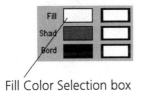

Fill Color Selection box

The Title Tool Color Picker:

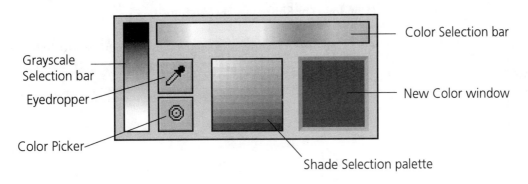

Grayscale
Selection bar

Eyedropper

Color Picker

Color Selection bar

New Color window

Shade Selection palette

2 To choose a color:

   a Click or drag the cursor along the Color Selection bar to the color you want.

   b Click or drag the cursor in the Shade Selection palette to choose a shade. The New Color window displays the shade.

   c Change the color and shade until you achieve the results you want.

3 Close the Title Tool Color Picker.

To add a drop or depth shadow:

1 Click the Shadow Depth and Direction button and drag the cursor around and out to position the shadow in whatever direction and to whatever depth you desire.

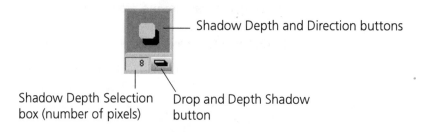

Shadow Depth and Direction buttons

Shadow Depth Selection box (number of pixels)

Drop and Depth Shadow button

2 Toggle the Drop and Depth Shadow button to select a drop or depth shadow.

To soften the edge of the shadow:

1 Choose Object > Soften Shadow or press Shift+Control+H (Windows) or Shift+⌘+H (Macintosh).

Tip: To create a glow effect, set Shadow Softness to a non-zero value and Shadow Depth to zero.

2 Enter the desired softness level. (Values range from 4 to 40.)

3 To preview the softness, click Apply.

4 Click OK when you are satisfied with the look.

Save the Title

1 Choose File > Save Title.

The Save dialog box appears.

2 In the dialog box:

    a Name the title "Canyonlands School."

    b Select the bin for storing your title.

    c Choose a target drive for the associated media files.

Tip: Select a high resolution, such as 1:1 or DV 25, which you can use in your finished sequence.

3 Select a resolution.

4 Click Save.

The title renders.

5 Quit the Title tool by choosing File > Close.

The two-minute title is automatically loaded into the Source monitor and into the target bin.

Edit the Title into the Sequence

To edit the title into the sequence:

1 Mark an IN a few seconds into the title clip, so you have material for trimming and transition effects.

2 If your sequence doesn't have a V2 track, add a second video track by choosing Clip > New Video Track.

3 Patch the title from source track V1 to record track V2. Turn off any audio tracks.

4 Click Overwrite.

5 Play your title to see the results.

Reposition the Title

After you create a title, you may need to go back and reposition the title in the frame.

1 In the sequence, make sure the position indicator is parked on the frame you want to be visible in the Title tool as a background.

2 Make sure V2 is highlighted in the track panel.

3 Control (Windows) or ⌘ (Macintosh) + double-click the title clip in the bin where you saved it.

4 Activate the Selection tool, click on the text box, and reposition the title within the safe title area.

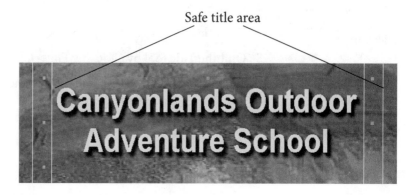

Safe title area

5 Choose File > Close to close the Title tool.

6 Choose Save when prompted.

7 Play the result.

Fade a Title

1 Place the position indicator over the title icon in your sequence.

2 Make sure V2 is highlighted in the track panel.

3 Click the Fade Effect button from the Tool Palette Fast menu.

4 In the dialog box, enter the duration for the Fade Up and Fade Down and click OK.

5 Play the result.

Additional Exercises

Try any of the following:

- Open the title you just created and modify it by adjusting additional parameters.

- Create credits in the Title tool and apply rolling to them. Add the credits to V2 over black or video.

- Create any other titles and add them to the sequence.

Create Titles (Outlined)

In this part of the exercise, you create an opening title for your ECO Challenge sequence, and edit it into the beginning of the sequence.

The title should provide at minimum the name of the event, "ECO Challenge." It should also draw people into the show and stylistically fit the program's content.

1 Open your sequence into the Record monitor.

2 Create a new bin for your titles.

3 Mark the portion of the sequence where you would like to place the opening title, and place the position indicator within the marks.

4 Open a new title on your monitor.

5 Type one or more lines of text. If you want to create multiple lines of text, do one of the following:

- To create a second line of text that will have the same properties as the first line, press Return/Enter and type the second line of text.

- If you want to position and color each line in the title differently, you will need to create another separate text element. Click the Text cursor in another part of the frame. Type the text.

6 Modify any the following characteristics of your title, for one or more lines of text:

- Font type and point size

- Kerning and/or leading

- Color

- Drop or depth shadow

7 Save the title in the Title bin.

8 Overwrite the title to the beginning of your sequence on track V2. (You may have to add the track to your sequence.)

9 Play the result.

Revise the Title

In this part of the exercise, you reposition at least one line of the title within the frame.

1 Open up the title you created within the Title tool. (Hint: Go to the Title clip in the bin.)

2 Reposition at least one line of the title, making sure to stay within the safe title area.

3 Make any other changes you like.

4 Save the title and close the Title tool.

5 Fade the title up and down.

If you have more time, see "Additional Exercises" on page 367.

Lesson 12 **Media Management**

An important component of editing on an Avid system is managing media and available storage space in the system. Avid systems provide many functions and tools to aid with the process. In this lesson, we cover some of them.

Objectives

After you complete this lesson, you will be able to:

- Lock items in a bin
- Delete media files
- Use the Media tool

Locking Items in the Bin

You can lock any item in the bin — including source clips, master clips, subclips, and sequences — to prevent deletion. Locked items can still be edited and modified.

To lock items:

1 Display the Lock heading in the bin by choosing Bin > Headings, clicking the Lock heading, and clicking OK.

2 Click a clip, subclip, or sequence to select it.

3 Select additional items if necessary.

4 Choose Clip > Lock Bin Selection.

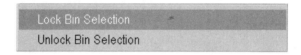

A Lock icon appears for each locked clip in the Lock column of the default Statistics Bin view.

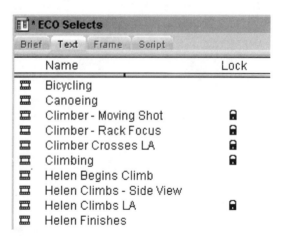

Locked clips in a bin

To unlock previously locked items:

1 Select the items in the bin.

2 Choose Clip > Unlock Bin Selection.

Deleting Clips and Media Files

Let's revisit some of the information learned in Lesson 1; it's particularly relevant now. Master clips, subclips, and sequences consist of statistical data that occupies very little drive space on the internal disk, while the media files associated with them take up substantial room on the external media drives. If you need to free up a lot of drive space to work on a new project, you can delete the media used in an old project *as long as you save the master clips, subclips, and sequences*. Deleting media files will not harm the related master clips, subclips, and sequences.

As long as you have the master clips, subclips, and sequences, you can always batch capture and re-edit the program again, if necessary. You can recapture media as long as it has timecode and you keep the clip information.

Tip: If you are unsure if the audio is silent or offline, choose Bin Fast menu > Show Offline Clips.

After deleting audio and video media files, the associated clips and sections of sequences play silence and display the Media Offline frame. Offline audio-only clips will display a black frame and play without sound. They will not display the Media Offline message.

Two Ways to Delete Clips and Media Files

There are two ways to delete clips and media files; you can delete from the bin or from the Media tool. In this section, we discuss the first method; in the next section we discuss Media tool.

You can use either method to delete clips and/or the media files linked to the clips. Using the Media tool gives you more options, as you shall see.

Deleting from a Bin

When deleting clips from a bin you have the option to delete the master clip, its associated media files, or both.

- "Delete associated media files" is used for clearing space on the drives without losing any information about the clip. This will enable you to recapture all the offline clips in the future based on their text information and timecode.

- Deleting both the master clip and its associated media files is done when a clip will not be needed anymore for a project.

! **If you delete the clips and sequences of the deleted media files and have no backups, you will not be able to recapture the material later, unless you log everything again. You should always make a backup copy of the project and bins, just in case you need them some time in the future.**

To delete media files associated with master clips, sequences, and effects from a media drive:

1 Click to activate the bin, and select the clips whose media files you want to delete.

2 Choose Edit > Delete, or press the Delete key, to open the bin's Delete dialog box.

3 Select the media objects that you want to delete, as shown in the following figure.

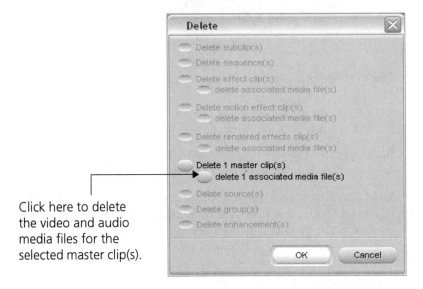

Click here to delete the video and audio media files for the selected master clip(s).

Options in the Delete dialog box

- Selecting only "Delete 1 master clip(s)" will delete only the clip, which contains the text instructions such as its start and end timecode. The clip will disappear from the bin but the media is still stored on the external drives. You should avoid doing this.

- Selecting only "Delete 2 associated media file(s)" will delete the actual captured picture and sound associated with the clip. The clip will remain in your bin with all its text information; however, Frame view will display the message Media Offline.

That means that the Avid system cannot currently find a media file on the external drives which correspond to the timecode information of the clip.

Offline clips in a bin

- Selecting both options will delete both the text information of the clip and all its associated media files.

! **Remember not to delete the selected master clips and/or sequences if you will need to recapture them later.**

! **You cannot undo the deletion of media files. Make sure no one else needs the media files you are planning to delete, and make sure no other project is using these media files.**

4 Click OK.

A confirmation dialog box appears.

5 Click Delete.

The Media Tool

The Media tool allows you to see the media files on all hard drives online in a display that is similar to your bin formats. You can use the Media tool to view or delete the available media files or specific tracks contained in the media file. The Media tool also allows you to track down all media files used in a particular project or sequence.

Setting the Media Tool Display

You can set the Media tool to display different types of files from the current or other existing projects. To set the Media tool display:

1 Choose Tools > Media Tool.

   The Media Tool Display dialog box appears.

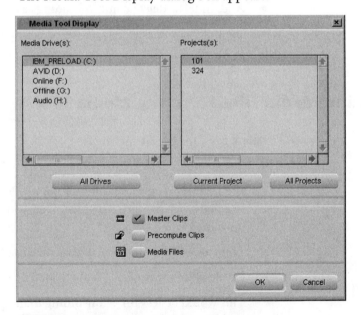

Options in the Media Tool Display dialog box

Note: To deselect All Drives, click in an empty area of the pane.

2 Select one or more media disks. To include all disks, select All Drives.

3 Select one or more projects. To include all projects, select All Projects.

Note: You will rarely need to display media files.

4   Select one or more file types you want to view (Master Clips, Precompute Clips, and Media Files).

- A master clip can have many associated media files: one or more video and up to eight audio media files.

- Precompute master clips are rendered effects.

Sorting, Sifting, and Managing Data in the Media Tool

The Media tool provides the same database functionality as a bin. You can:

- Sort single or multiple columns in ascending or descending order as you would in a bin

- Perform a custom sift as you would in a bin

- Add, hide, or delete column headings as you would in a bin

- View clips in Frame, Text, Brief, or Script view

- Click and drag master clips from the Media tool into bins

Deleting Media Files From the Media Tool

Delete from the Media tool to:

- Delete media files for specific tracks associated with a master clip.

  For example, you might unintentionally leave the video track selected when capturing a voice-over. You could delete the unwanted video track and leave the audio online.

  This capability is not available by deleting from a bin.

- Delete all of the media files for a specific project or sequence.

  This would be less time consuming than opening every bin for a project and deleting the associated media files.

!   **You cannot undo deletion of media files. Make sure no one else needs the media files you are planning to delete, and make sure no other project is using these media files.**

To delete media files from the Media tool:

1 Display the master clips and/or precompute master clips from your project, depending on what you want to delete.

2 In the Media tool, select the item(s) whose media files you want to delete.

3 Press the Delete key to open the Media tool's Delete Media dialog box.

4 Select the media objects that you want to delete.

Options in the Delete Media dialog box

! **Notice that the Delete Media dialog box allows you to select media files by media type. This capability makes it possible to delete all of the video and batch capture at a new resolution without affecting mixed audio tracks.**

5 Click OK.

A confirmation dialog box appears.

6 Click Delete. The media files are deleted from the drive. The master clips remain stored in their bins.

Identifying Media Relatives

With the Avid system, you can identify the media objects (master clips, subclips, precomputes, sequences) that share the same media files, regardless of whether the media files are present on the system. Media objects that share the same media files are called *media relatives*.

Useful Applications

Identifying media relatives can be useful if you want to know:

- Which master clip a subclip was drawn from
- Which subclips and media are "related" to a specific master clip
- All of the master clips, subclips, and precomputes associated with a sequence or project
- Which media files to delete from a project without taking offline any of the media used in a sequence

Identifying Media Relatives

To identify the media relatives of a clip or sequence:

1 Open the bins that contains the master clips, subclips, and sequences of the media files that you want to find, making sure that all items are deselected. (You can open them in the SuperBin or in individual bins.)

2 Select the master clip(s), subclip(s), or sequence(s) for which you want to identify the media relatives.

! **All items must be in the same bin.**

3 Choose Bin > Select Media Relatives.

The media relatives of the selected items are highlighted in all open bins.

Deleting Unused Media from a Project

You can use Select Media Relatives to select and delete media files that were not used in a project. This is useful if you want to delete any media files that were not used in order to open drive space. In this procedure, you use a bin and the Media tool together to identify media relatives in both places.

To identify and delete unused media files associated with a particular sequence:

1 Open the bins that contain the master clips, subclips, and the sequence of the media files that you want to find, making sure that all items are deselected.

2 Open the Media tool and select Current Project and Master Clips in the Media Tool Display dialog box.

3 Resize and position the bin(s) and the Media Tool window so that you can see both of them.

4 Select the sequence for which you want to identify the media relatives.

5 Choose Bin > Select Media Relatives.

The media relatives of the selected items are highlighted in the Media tool and in all open bins.

6 Choose Media Tool Fast menu > Reverse Selection.

This reverses the current selection, highlighting all the media files in the Media tool that are unrelated to your clips and sequences.

7 Press the Delete key.

! **If you are using master clips in your sequence that come from tapes associated with another project, the Current Project selection in the Media Tool Display dialog box will not show those clips.**

Review Questions

1 Explain the different consequences of deleting a clip and deleting a media file. (See "Deleting Clips and Media Files" on page 373.)

2 When would you want to delete only a clip's media file, and when would you want to delete both the media file and the clip? (See "Deleting Clips and Media Files" on page 373.)

3 Why might you want to display Media Files (along with Master Clips) in the Media Tool dialog box? (See "Setting the Media Tool Display" on page 377.)

4 How do you identify unused media files? (See "Deleting Unused Media from a Project" on page 381.)

Exercise: Media Management

In the Capture exercise, you created a small sequence of 4-6 shots. That sequence is finished and now you want to delete the media not used in the sequence to free up drive space. (Imagine, of course, that you are dealing with a much larger sequence, and many unused clips!)

Prepare to display the Media tool.

Display the project's clips in the Media tool.

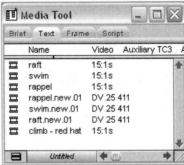

Highlight the sequence's media relatives.

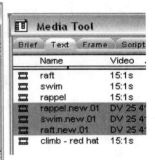

Reverse the selection, to display the unused media.

Delete the unused media.

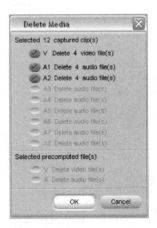

Goals

- Identify clips not used in your sequence
- Delete media not used in your sequence

Delete Unused Media

Remember that you left one captured clip out of the sequence? This procedure will delete the media file associated with that clip.

Delete Unused Media from the Capture Sequence

To identify and delete unused media files associated with the Capture sequence:

1 Open the **Capture** project.

2 Open the **New Clips** bin and the bin that contains the **Capture hi res** sequence. Make sure no objects in either bin are selected.

3 Choose Tools > Media Tool.

4 In the Media Tool Display dialog box:

   a   Select Current Project and Master Clips.

   b   Click the Media Drive that holds your media; if you're not sure click the All Drives button.

   c   Click OK.

   The Media tool is displayed.

Note: Your Media tool will have clips with different names, but this screen capture and subsequent ones are provided for purposes of illustration.

Clips captured at 15:1s

Clips captured at DV 25 411

Clip not used in sequence

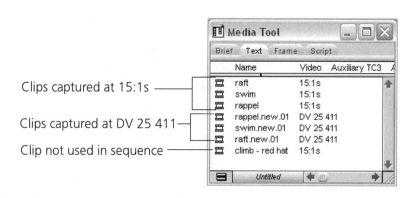

5 Resize and position the open bins and the Media Tool window so that you can see them.

6 Select the **Capture hi res** sequence.

7 Choose Bin > Select Media Relatives.

The media relatives of the sequence are highlighted in the Media tool and in all open bins.

8 Choose Media Tool Fast menu > Reverse Selection.

This reverses the current selection in the Media tool, and the one clip not used in your sequence should be highlighted, along with the 15:1s clips you previously captured.

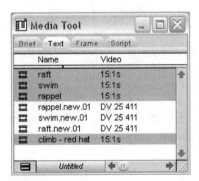

9 Delete the media files from the Media tool.

Delete Unused Media from the ECO Challenge Sequence

You have finished working on your ECO Challenge sequence. Now that you have a final sequence, you want to save all the media used in the sequence, but you'd like to delete media not used in the sequence to free up drive space.

To preserve media for the sequence, you'll copy or move the final sequence (and anything else you might want to save that's not in any of the final sequences!) into a single bin.

To prepare:

1 Open the ECO Challenge project.

2 Create a new bin and call it Final Sequence.

3 Copy or move your final ECO Challenge sequence into this new bin.

4 If you want to save anything not in this final sequence, also copy or move those objects into the bin.

5 Keep this bin open, and make sure all objects are deselected.

To identify the media relatives of these sequences:

1 Open all of the bins that contain the master clips and subclips for your ECO Challenge sequence, and make sure that all items are deselected.

2 Select your final sequence in the new bin.

3 Choose Bin > Select Media Relatives.

The media relatives of the sequence are highlighted in all open bins.

Now it's time to delete the media not used in the ECO Challenge sequence. (You will stop just short of actually deleting media!)

To identify and delete unused media files associated with the sequence:

1 Choose Media Tool Fast menu > Reverse Selection.

This reverses the current selection, and the media files not used in your sequence should be highlighted.

2 **Do not perform this step:** Now you would delete the selected media files from the Media tool.

Lesson 13 **Recording a Digital Cut**

The Avid system offers different methods for outputting your completed sequence. You can create an Edit Decision List (EDL) for a linear online edit; create a QuickTime file for a web site, DVD-ROM, or CD-ROM; or output to videotape, which is also called recording or creating a digital cut. The method or combination of methods you choose depends on your situation. If you are working with film originated material and need to generate a cut list, you can use Avid Matchback to generate negative cut lists for 16mm and 35mm film projects from your sequence.

This book covers creating a digital cut.

Objectives

After you complete this lesson, you will be able to:

- Record a digital cut

Preparing to Record a Digital Cut

When you record a digital cut, the Avid system plays the digital video and audio for the sequence from the storage disks and records the information onto a master tape.

You can record your digital cut by creating an insert edit, assemble edit, or manual edit.

When performing a digital cut to an IEEE 1394 format camera or deck, the digital cut is frame accurate. If you have a transcoder that can convert the IEEE 1394 digital signal into analog video and audio signals, you can perform a non-frame accurate digital cut to an analog Betacam or VHS deck.

Preparing Effects and Audio

Note: For more information about rendering effects, see the *Avid Effects Guide*.

You must render all effects and make sure all audio is the same sample rate before creating a digital cut.

To prepare effects with Avid Mojo:

1   Mark an IN at the beginning of the sequence, and mark an OUT at the end of the sequence.

2   Select Clip > Expert Render.

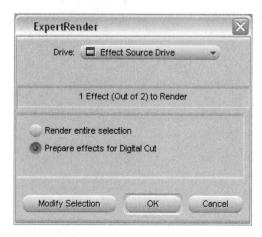

Setting up the ExpertRender dialog box

3 Click Prepare effects for Digital Cut, and click OK.

The system will render the effects it needs to in order for you to record a digital cut.

To prepare effects without Avid Mojo:

1 Select Special > Enable Digital Video Cut.

The Digital Video Out button turns blue.

2 Mark an IN at the beginning of the sequence, and mark an OUT at the end of the sequence.

3 Select Clip > Expert Render.

4 Click OK.

The system will render the effects it needs to in order for you to record a digital cut.

To prepare audio:

The audio should all be at the same sample rate.

1 Show the Audio heading in the bin to see if the audio has the same sample rate.

If the audio has different sample rates, resample the sequence to the desired sample rate.

2 Select the sequence in the bin.

3 Right-click the sequence and choose Change Sample Rate.

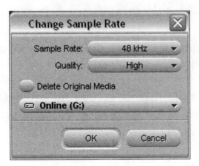

Changing the audio sample rate

4 Choose the desired sample rate from the Sample Rate pop-up menu.

5 Choose High for the quality.

6 Click OK.

New master clips will be created for each converted clip. Those clips already at the correct sample rate will be unaffected.

Changing to Drop-Frame or Non-Drop-Frame (NTSC Only)

If your sequence needs to be changed to drop-frame or non-drop-frame before recording your digital cut, follow this procedure:

1 With your sequence in the Timeline, click in the **Record** monitor.

2 Choose File > Get Sequence Info or press Control+I (Windows) or ⌘+I (Macintosh).

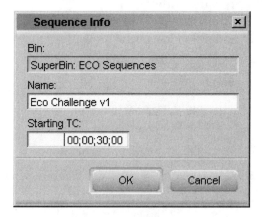

Changing between a drop-frame and a non-drop-frame sequence

3 Click in the Starting TC box and press ; (semi-colon) on the keyboard to change to drop-frame, or press : (colon) to change to non-drop-frame.

Creating Insert, Assemble, and Manual Edits

You can record three types of digital cuts:

- Insert edit—This method requires an entire pre-blacked tape. This is the preferred method.

- Assemble edit—This method requires that you pre-black only a portion of the tape.

- Manual edit—Use this method if you are recording to a deck that does not support timecode.

Creating an Insert Edit

Note: The procedure to record black and stripe timecode to a MiniDV cassette before performing the digital cut may be as simple as recording on your camera with the lens cap still in place. However, every deck and camera varies slightly in the procedure to engage the timecode. For more information on recording timecode on your videocassette consult your deck's or camera's operating manual.

The insert edit is the preferred method of digital cut. It requires a pre-blacked tape, which is a tape with control track and timecode for at least the duration of your digital cut. Control track can be laid down on your videotape by recording a black video signal to it. As you "black" your videotape, your record deck or camera can also record proper timecode to it.

To prepare to create an insert edit:

1 Load a sequence into the Record monitor.

2 If you want to record only a portion of the sequence, mark an IN and OUT around the desired part of the sequence.

3 Load a blacked tape striped with timecode into the record deck or camera.

4 Turn on the Remote switch on the record deck. If recording to a camera, make sure the camera is in the proper recording mode. Consult your camera's operating manual for more information.

5 To set the parameters for an insert edit, choose Clip > Digital Cut.

Tracks in
sequence to
be recorded

Record Start-
Time
Options pop-
up menu

Deck/Camera
controls

Deck/Camera
Selection

Logging
controls
for
marking
IN and
OUT
points

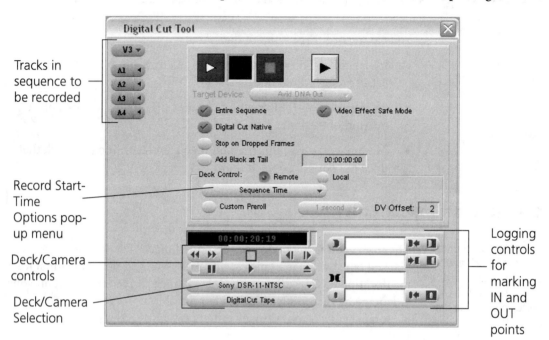

Digital Cut tool with components labelled

(Avid Mojo only) If you are recording to a non-DV device, the Digital Cut tool displays the channels that you will record to on tape, in addition to the tracks in the sequence to be recorded.

Tracks in
sequence to be
recorded

Channels
recording to on
tape

To set up the Digital Cut tool and record the digital cut:

1 Make sure Deck Control Remote is selected.

2 Make sure your deck (or camera) is recognized in the Deck Selection pop-up menu.

If the Digital Cut tool displays "No Deck" in the Timecode window, choose Autoconfigure from the Deck Selection pop-up menu.

3 Select Entire Sequence if you want to record the entire sequence from start to finish.

The system ignores any marks found on the sequence. (If this option is deselected, the system records from IN to OUT, or if there are no marks, from the position indicator to the end.)

4 (Avid Mojo only) Select Digital Cut Native if you are outputting a DV 25 sequence.

5 (Avid Mojo only) Select Stop on Dropped Frames. If the digital cut recording stops, render the effect it stopped on and continue.

6 (Option) Select Add Black at Tail and type the duration for the black you want to add at the end of the digital cut.

7 Choose an option from the Record Start-Time Options pop-up menu:

- Sequence Time: Recording starts at the sequence's start timecode. (Generally choose this option.)

- Record Deck Time: Recording starts at the timecode on the master tape on which the record deck is parked.

- Mark IN Time: Recording starts at a master tape timecode you select.

When you choose Mark In Time, you can use the Deck controls within the Digital Cut tool to cue the tape and log IN and OUT points for frame-accurate recording.

! **If you are doing a digital cut of a portion of the sequence (defined by an IN and OUT) and deselect Entire Sequence, the system inserts a black slug in the middle of the tape.**

8 (Option) Select Custom Preroll and choose the number of seconds from the pop-up menu to indicate how many seconds the tape rolls before the digital cut starts.

9 If you already recorded a digital cut in which the video and audio are out of sync, you can fix the problem using the DV Offset option. Change the DV Offset (the default is 2) and rerecord. Repeat until you achieve sync.

10   Select the tracks in the sequence you want to record from the left-most row of track buttons in the Digital Cut window.

Tip: For more information about rendering effects, see the *Avid Effects Guide* or the book, *Avid Xpress Pro Effects and Color Correction.*

11   (Avid Mojo only) Select Video Effect Safe Mode (on by default) so that the system will notify you if any effects need to be rendered.

During a digital cut, real-time effects can drop frames. The Effect Safe Mode option identifies real-time effects that might cause dropped frames during the digital cut and allows you to render them.

If your sequence has effects that need to be rendered, it's best to render them before this stage in the process.

!   **(Without Avid Mojo) You must render all effects before creating a digital cut. (See the *Effects Guide* for your Avid system for more information on rendering effects.)**

12   (Recording to a non-DV device only) Select the Record Track Selection buttons to the right of the Source Track Selection buttons which specify the channels you will record to on tape. (Choose the highest video track in the sequence, and the appropriate audio tracks.)

If you are recording to a DV device, this option does not appear because the channels are fixed at one video channel and two audio channels.

Note: To stop the digital cut recording at any point, select the blue Halt Digital Cut button or press the space bar.

13   Click the Play button.

If you have not yet loaded a tape into the record deck, the system asks you to load a tape and name it.

The system records the digital cut and plays it on the Edit monitor.

Creating an Assemble Edit

This option gives you the same precise control over your start time as an insert edit, by only having to black a short portion of the master tape.

An assemble edit begins your digital cut at a specific timecode and commands the record deck to generate control track and timecode on-the-fly as the digital cut progresses. When the digital cut is complete, timecode and control track end. The result is that the end of your digital cut will not be a clean edit. Instead it will be a distorted visual edit that transitions to "snow" (or whatever else is present on the tape). (You may have encountered this situation if you ever accidentally recorded over a previously used tape on a tape deck.)

When you realize your mistake and stop recording, the tape deck stops recording control track. When you play back the tape to survey the damage, you notice that there is a period of distortion and "snow" before your previously recorded material reveals itself.

! **Many deck-specific issues arise with the use of assemble edit. If you are not familiar with deck issues, avoid using assemble edit.**

To record an assemble edit:

1 Load a sequence into the Record monitor.

2 If you want to record only a portion of the sequence, mark an IN and OUT around the desired part of the sequence, preferably on a cut.

3 Load a blacked tape striped with timecode into the record deck. You only need to black a short portion the tape (pre-roll plus 10 seconds) for this option to work.

4 Select "Allow assemble edit for digital cut" in the Deck Preferences settings. **You will not be able to record an assemble edit without enabling the setting.**

5 To set the parameters for an assemble edit, choose Clip > Digital Cut.

The Digital Cut tool appears.

6 Make sure Deck Control Remote is selected.

7 Make sure the correct deck is displayed in the Deck Selection pop-up menu.

8 Choose Assemble Edit from the pop-up menu.

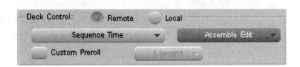

This option is only available if you enable it in the Deck Preferences settings.

9 Follow the rest of the procedure from Step 8 in the section, "Creating an Insert Edit" on page 393.

! **After assemble-edit recording, a freeze frame is usually added after the OUT point for 1 second or more. This provides several frames of overlap for the next IN point before the control track and timecode break up.**

Creating a Manual Edit

If you are recording to a video deck that does not support timecode, you will not have deck control. Instead, you must perform a manual, or "crash record" edit. To do this:

1 Load a sequence into the Record monitor.

2 If you only want to record a portion of the sequence, mark an IN and OUT around the desired part of the sequence.

3 Load a tape into the record deck.

4 Choose Digital Cut.

The Digital Cut tool appears.

5 Select Deck Control Local.

6 Make sure the correct deck is displayed in the Deck Selection pop-up menu.

7 Select Entire Sequence if you want to record the entire sequence from start to finish.

The system ignores any marks found on the sequence. (If this option is deselected, the system records from IN to OUT, or if there are no marks, from the position indicator to the end.)

8 (Option) Select Add Black at Tail and type the duration for the black you want to add at the end of the digital cut.

9 Select the Sequence Track Selection buttons from the row of track buttons in the Digital Cut tool to specify the tracks you will record to on tape. The display of tracks varies depending on the tracks existing in the sequence.

Note: To stop the digital cut recording at any point, select the blue Halt Digital Cut button or press the space bar.

10 Manually press the Record button on the deck.

11 Click the Play button in the Digital Cut window.

The system records plays the digital cut and plays it on the Edit monitor.

Review Questions

1 Where does recording start for each of the three settings in the Record to Tape option in the Digital Cut tool? (See "Preparing to Record a Digital Cut" on page 390.)

   a Sequence Time

   b Record Deck Time

   c Mark In Time

2 What is the difference between preparing tape for an insert edit compared to an assemble edit? (See "Preparing to Record a Digital Cut" on page 390.)

3 Under what circumstance might it be preferable to record an assemble edit as opposed to an insert edit? What risk, if any, is involved? (See "Creating an Insert Edit" on page 393.)

4 If you need frame-accurate recording, should you crash record? (See "Creating a Manual Edit" on page 398.)

Index

A

activating a bin 14
Add Black at Tail 395
Add Dissolve
    Duration options 106
    in Effect Mode 108
    Position options 106
Add Dissolve button 110, 120, 121
Add Keyframe button 240
Add Locator button 200
adding
    a border, Title tool 350
    dissolves in Trim mode 108
    keyframes 240
    locators 200
    next audio track 203
adjusting
    keyframes 241
    speaker volume 83
AG-DVX 100 camera (Panasonic) 273
Align to Grid command 23
anti-alias 335
Apply to All Transitions checkbox 110, 121
assemble edit 396
Attic 168
    recovering bins from 170
audio
    clipping 276
    crossfading 107
    fading 107
    input formats 268
    input level
        adjusting for Pro Tools 277
        monitoring 82
        rubberbanding 239
        sample plot 240
    tracks
        adding next 203
    waveform 85
Audio Editing toolset 234
Audio Gain Automation 239
    filter 247
    recording 245
    tool 246
Audio Mix
    command 233
    tool 235
Audio Project settings 107, 275
Audio Tool command 276, 298
Auto Save 166
Avid Mojo DNA 2
Avid Unity 2
Avid Xpress Pro Help 26

B

backing up 170, 174
backing up a project
    Macintosh 171
    Windows 170
basic editing steps 2
Batch Capture command 290
batch capturing 290

bin
  activating 14
  Brief view 21
  closing 12
  creating new 13, 33
  defined 4, 20
  deleting 16
  display statistical headings 308
  Fast menu 25
  Frame view 22, 35
    changing frame size 23
    changing representative frame 24
  locking items in 372
  opening 12
  opening from another project 25, 36
  opening from Project window 11
  saving 167
  Script view 22
  SuperBin 128
  Text view 21
    adding column headings 310
    custom 309
  to select media relatives 380
  view, saving 313
Bin Fast menu 25
bold type, for listing drives 273
buttons
  Add Dissolve 110, 120, 121
  Add Keyframe 240
  Add Locator 200
  Digital Video Out 104
  Edit 60
  Extend 183
  Extract 60
  Extract/Splice-in 211
  Fade Effect 356
  Fast Forward and Rewind 131
  Go to Previous and Next Edit 131
  Lift 60
  Lift/Overwrite 211
  Make Subclip 146
  Mark Clip 59
  Mark IN 50
  Mark OUT 50
  Marking 51
  Master Volume 83
  Match Frame 136
  Motion Control 49
  Overwrite 57
  Splice 55
  Text tool 339
  Trim 100

C

Capture tool
  Time Remaining indicator 273
capturing
  batch 290
  Delay Audio option 273
  non-timecode source 291
  on-the-fly 278
    with known IN and OUT points 280
    without known IN and OUT points 282
  source tape, identifying 266
  tracks, selecting 267
Clip Comments command 207
Clip Frame command 207
Clip Name menu 131
Clip Text command 207
clip/media file relationship 4
clipping audio 276
clips
  clearing from monitors 44
  copying 324
  defined 4
  loading into the Source monitor 43
  locking 372
  moving 324
  playing 42, 47
  rearranging in bins 24
  relation to media files 4
  sifting in bins 315, 318
  sorting in bins 315

subclipping 145
closing
    a bin 12
    a folder 15
color
    setting for text 352
Color Picker 352
Color Selection boxes
    using to set text color 352
column headings
    statistical 308
    Text view, adding in bins 310
commands
    Align to Grid 23
    Audio Mix 233
    Audio Tool 276, 298
    Batch Capture 290
    Clip Comments 207
    Clip Frame 207
    Clip Text 207
    Custom Sift 318, 330
    Dupe Detection 207
    Fill Window 23
    Filter Audio Gain Automation 247
    Get Sequence Info 392
    Headings 312
    Lock Bin Selection 372
    Media File Names 207
    New Audio Track 203
    New Bin 272
    New Title 334
    Open Bin 272
    Point Size 341
    Redo 62
    Safe Colors 336
    Save All 167
    Save Bin 167
    Select All 20, 208
    Select Media Relatives 380, 385, 387
    Show Sifted 323
    Show Unsifted 323
    Sort 316

Sort Again 316
Sort Reversed 316
Style 341
Undo 62
Unlock Bin Selection 373
Composer monitor 40
Composer window
    Record monitor 59
    Source monitor 59
        loading clipsinto 43
        viewing clips in 47
compression
    impact on storage 269
Compression tool, opening 275
copying clips 324
crawling titles 357
Create User Profile 10
creating
    a folder 14
    a new bin 13
    a new project 9
    a new sequence 52
crossfading audio 107
Custom Preroll 395
Custom Sift command 318, 330

D

Default Snap-To Edit 212
Delay Audio option 273
deleting
    all keyframes 247
    bin 16
    clips from a bin 375
    folder 16
    keyframes 242
    media files 373
        from a bin 375
        from the Media tool 379
depth shadows 348
digital audio scrub 84
    while trimming 104

digital cut
Add Black at Tail 395
assemble edit 396
Custom Preroll 395
DV Offset 395
insert edit 393
manual edit 398
Record Start-Time options 395
Stop on Dropped Frames 395
Video Effect Safe Mode 396
Digital Video Out button 104
disks
freeing space 373
target, selecting for capturing 273
displaying
customized Timeline view 210
more or less detail in the Timeline 63
sifted views in bins 323
sync breaks 189
unsifted views in bins 323
dissolve
handle 106
in Trim mode 105
drives, listed in bold type 273
drop shadows 348
drop-frame to non-drop-frame 392
dropped frames 396
dual-roller trimming 99
procedure 100
Dupe Detection command 207
duplicating a clip versus Option+dragging 325
duration and speed of title 358
DV Capture Offset
described 285
procedure for 286
DV Offset 395
DV Scene Extraction
explained 283
setting up 283

E

Edit buttons 60
edit points
marking 50
editing
basic steps 2
Extend 183
in Timeline 199
displaying customized Timeline view 210
saving customized Timeline view 209
interface 40
segments in Timeline 211
extracting and splicing-in 211
lifting and overwriting 213
storyboard 147
titles into a sequence 355
effects
real-time 104
rendering 106
emptying the Trash 17
Extend
button 183
edit 183
Extract button 60
Extract/Splice-in button 211
extracting 59
extracting and splicing in 211
eyedropper, Color Picker 352

F

Fade Effect button 356
fading
a title 356
audio 107
in Trim mode 110
Fast Forward button 131
file formats
MXF 269
OMF 269

files
     viewing in Media tool 378
Fill Window command 23
Filter Audio Gain Automation command 247
folder
     closing 15
     creating 14
     deleting 16
     opening 15
font
     selecting for text in Title tool 340
formats
     video and audio 268
frame
     finding 134
     typing an offset 135

G

Get Sequence Info command 392
global level and pan 237
Go to Next Edit button 131
Go to Previous Edit button 131

H

handle
     defined 90
     for dissolve 106
hardware components 2
Headings command 312
headings, column, adding in bins 310

I

input level
     audio, adjusting for Pro Tools 277
insert edit 393

J

J-K-L
     shuttling 86
     trimming 179

K

kerning
     of title text 343
Keyboard settings 140
keyframes
     adjusting 241
     deleting 242
     deleting all 247
keying titles in a sequence 355

L

leading
     between selected lines 344
     of title text 344
level and pan
     setting 232
     using marks 238
Lift button 60
Lift/Overwrite button 211
lifting 59
lifting and overwriting 213
link a toolset to a setting 143
locators
     adding to source material 200
     creating automatically with DV 283
     moving to 202
     removing 202
Lock Bin Selection command 372
locking
     bin items 372

logging
    and capturing on-the-fly
        with known IN and OUT points 280
    automatically with DV 283
    before batch capturing 287
    directly to bin from source tape 287
    from known IN 288
    from known OUT 289

M

Macintosh special characters 345
Make Subclip button 146
manual edit 398
mapping
    menu commands 140
    user-selectable buttons 139
Mark Clip button 59
marking edit points 50
master clips
    locking 372
Master Volume button 83
Match frame 136
Media File Names command 207
media file/clip relationship 4
media files
    defined 4
    deleting 379
    managing for maximum storage 373
    viewing in Media tool 378
media objects
    selecting media relatives of 380
Media Offline message 373
media offline, defined 5
media relatives
    selecting using Media tool 380
Media tool
    setting display 377
    using for deleting media files 379
menu commands
    mapping 140

monitor
    Timecode display in 133
monitoring
    audio tracks 82
    video tracks 355
Motion Control buttons 49
moving clips 324
multi-level sorting 317
multiple versions of a setting 127
MXF file format 269

N

New Audio Track command 203
New Bin command 272
New Title command 334
non-drop-frame to drop-frame 392
NTSC frame rate
    safe title/action guidelines and 336

O

object color menu
    selecting colors for text 352
Offset, DV Capture 286
OMF file format 269
online Help 26
Open Bin command 272
opening
    a bin 12
    a folder 15
    a project 8
    and closing windows 63
output
    digital cut, playing 390
    digital cut, recording 390
Overwrite button 57
overwriting 56

P

PAL frame rate
    safe title/action guidelines and 336
Panasonic AG-DVX 100 camera 273
Passthrough Mix tool 277
playing
    clips 42
    digital cut 390
point size
    selecting for text in Title tool 341
Point Size command 341
project
    defined 4
    new 9
Project window
    closing 19
    identifying 11
    locating 11, 19
    opening bin from 11
    settings 18

R

real-time effects playback 104
Record Start-Time options 395
recording
    Audio Gain Automation 245
    digital cut 390
red oval
    in Timeline 200
redo/undo 62
redoing an edit 62
removing
    locators 202
rendering effects 106
rendering effects before creating a digital cut 396
representative frame in clip, changing 24
resolutions 270
Rewind button 131
rolling titles 357

S

Safe Action area 336
Safe Colors command 336
Safe Title area 336
sample plot 85, 240
saturation of color, and Safe Color options 336
Save All command 167
Save Bin command 167
saving
    a bin 167
    a bin view 313
    automatically 166
    customized Timeline view 209
    titles 354
scrubbing audio 84
segment editing 211
    versus sliding 220
Select All command 20, 208
Select Media Relatives command 380, 385, 387
selecting
    text point size in Title tool 341
sequence
    creating 52
    defined 4
    fine tuning 115, 123
    sifting in bins 318
    sorting in bins 315
setting
    global level and pan 237
    level and pan
        using marks 238
    text color with the color palette 352
setting media display 377
settings
    Audio Project 107, 275
    introducing 18
    Keyboard 140
    multiple versions 127
    viewing and changing 126

shadow
    depth 348
    drop 348
Shadow Attributes menu 348
Show Sifted command 323
Show Unsifted command 323
showing
    customized Timeline view 210
    sifted views in bins 323
    unsifted views in bins 323
sifted views
    displaying in bins 323
    showing in bins 323
sifting
    clips in bins 315, 318
    defined 315
    sequences in bins 315
single-roller trimming
    explained 90
    procedure 96
    to edit dialog 178
sliding 218
    versus segment editing 220
slipping 216
snapping to an edit point 62
Sort Again command 316
Sort command 316
Sort Reversed command 316
sorting
    defined 315
    in bins 315
    multi-level 317
speaker volume
    adjusting 83
Splice button 55
splicing 54
split edits 182
starting the system 6, 31, 38
statistical column headings in bins 308
Stop on Dropped Frames (digital cut) 395
storyboard editing 147

style
    selecting for text in Title tool 341
Style command 341
subclips
    creating 145
    creating automatically with DV 283
SuperBin 128
sync breaks
    displaying 189
    fixing 189
sync lock 186
system hardware 2

T

target disk, selecting for capturing 273
text (in titles)
    changing attributes 340
    color, setting with color palette 352
    kerning 343
    leading 344
    leading between selected lines 344
    repositioning of 339
    selecting font 340
    selecting style 341
Text tool
    using to create text in Title tool 339
Text tool button 339
Text view
    adding column headings 310
    statistical column headings 308
Time Remaining indicator (Capture tool) 273
Timecode display 133
Timeline
    adding keyframes 240
    configuring 206
    configuring tracks
        enlarging and reducing specific tracks 208
    defined 40

displaying
    clip frames 207
    clip names 207
    position bar 207
editing 199
editing in
    displaying customized Timeline view 210
    saving customized Timeline view 209
editing segments 211
    extracting and splicing-in 211
    lifting and overwriting 213
Fast menu 207
hiding
    clip names 207
    position bar 207
    waveforms 207
    snapping to transitions 62
Timeline view
    displaying customized 210
    saving customized 209
Timeline window
    closing 63
    opening 63
Time-of-Day Information, using to log 283
title
    duration 358
    editing into a sequence 355
    keying in a sequence 355
    saving 354
    speed of play 358
Title tool
    adding a border 350
    Color Picker 352
    Color Selection boxes 352
    crawls 357
    drop and depth shadows 348
    fading a title 356
    kerning 343
    leading 344
    leading between selected lines 344
    revising a title 356
    rolls 357

    saving titles 354
    selecting text style 341
    special characters 345
    using 335
    using Text tool in 339
Title tool bar 337
Tool palette 61
tools
    Audio Gain Automation 246
    Audio Mix 235
    closing and opening 63
    Media tool
        deleting media files with 379
        setting display 377
    Passthrough Mix 277
    Title 335
Toolset
    Audio Editing 142, 234
    Basic 142
    customizing 142
    Effects Editing 142
    linking to a setting 143
    Source/Record Editing 142
    using 142
Track Selector panel 43
tracks
    active, selecting for capturing 267
    configuring in Timeline
        enlarging and reducing specific tracks 208
    monitoring 355
Transition effect
    insufficient source 109
transitions, dragging
    in Trim mode 103
Trash
    emptying 17
    viewing contents of 16
Trim buttons 100
Trim mode
    adding dissolves 105, 108
    adding fades 110
    dragging transitions 103

trimming
    adding and removing frames 102
    creating split edits 182
    defined 88
    dialog 178
    dual-roller 99
    J-K-L 179
    on-the-fly 179
    single-roller 90
    sliding 218
    slipping 216
    Trim boxes 103
    while audio scrubbing 104
    with sync lock 186
two-field resolutions 270

U

undo/redo 62
Unlock Bin Selection command 373
unsifted views, displaying in bins 323
User profile 10
user-selectable buttons
    mapping 139

V

video
    input formats 268
    resolutions 270
Video Effect Safe Mode 396
viewing
    files in the Media tool 378
volume
    adjusting on speaker 83

    , sample plot 85

    characters 345

windows
    closing and opening 63

Z

Zoom slider 63
zooming in/out 63